Get the eBook FREE!

(PDF, ePub, Kindle, and liveBook all included)

We believe that once you buy a book from us, you should be able to read it in any format we have available. To get electronic versions of this book at no additional cost to you, purchase and then register this book at the Manning website.

Go to https://www.manning.com/freebook and follow the instructions to complete your pBook registration.

That's it!
Thanks from Manning!

Contract Testing in Action

Contract Testing in Action

With Pact, PactFlow, and GitHub Actions

Marie Cruz, Lewis Prescott

Foreword by Mark Winteringham

MANNING
Shelter Island

For online information and ordering of this and other Manning books, please visit www.manning.com. The publisher offers discounts on this book when ordered in quantity. For more information, please contact

Special Sales Department
Manning Publications Co.
20 Baldwin Road
PO Box 761
Shelter Island, NY 11964
Email: orders@manning.com

Manning Publications Co.
20 Baldwin Road
PO Box 761
Shelter Island, NY 11964

Development editor: Marina Michaels
Technical editor: Laura M. Castro
Review editor: Angelina Lazukić
Production editor: Deirdre Blanchfield-Hiam
Copy editor: Julie McNamee
Proofreader: Jason Everett
Technical proofreader: Karsten Strøbaek
Typesetter: Dennis Dalinnik
Cover designer: Marija Tudor

ISBN: 9781633437241
Printed in the United States of America

brief contents

contents

PART 2 CONSUMER-DRIVEN CONTRACT TESTING 63

foreword

Contract testing, as I stated in *Testing Web APIs*, is a technical solution to a people problem. Ideally, if teams communicate regularly with one another, the risk of failing integrated systems would be mitigated. But ideals aren't always the same as reality. We have seen a shift from monolithic products to distributed platforms that see us responsible for potentially hundreds of integrated services. We work in organizations that have embraced remote working or global workforces, creating more disconnected workforces that face new challenges in communication. A testing strategy has to be sensitive to these context changes, and that is why contract testing has become necessary.

I see contract testing as a tool to aid teams: to help facilitate conversation and increase a team's confidence in developing products in an agile way. Whether you are the consumer of a service or the provider, having contract testing in place eases the fears of making risky changes. Integrations between services change—they have to in order to grow and develop a platform's features. But with robust contract testing in place, those changes can be rigorously tested early enough in a pipeline to not only catch potential bugs but also enable teams to have the necessary conversations to bring both consumers and providers in line with one another.

Contract testing also helps us appreciate the technical complexity involved in developing and maintaining integrations between services, which sets Marie and Lewis's book apart from other material on contract testing. They have demonstrated the value of contract testing with a deep exploration of the many ways in which it can be applied across different contexts and technologies, enabling us to establish contract testing as a testing activity as well as understanding the technical intricacies of using contract testing in different tech stacks. They demonstrate not just the "how" of contract testing, but the "why." From showing us how contract testing is part of a holistic testing strategy to enabling teams to test, document, and share the inner workings of their integrated systems, *Contract Testing in Action* will help you, the reader, establish a framework that will make you more confident in developing distributed systems safely and to a higher degree of quality.

— MARK WINTERINGHAM,
author of *Testing Web APIs* and *Software Testing with Generative AI*

preface

The first time I came across contract testing was at a healthcare startup by the CTO Eike Dawid and then later at a large, more established online retailer with the backing from Neil Syrett, did I explore it in more detail. But it wasn't until I read one of Marie's blog posts on how to implement contract testing in a really simple, easy to follow way that I fully understood contract testing. Therefore, when Marie approached me to collaborate on a book about contract testing, I jumped at the chance. I knew that Marie would not only bring a great writing style that readers love but also bring her extensive experience in her testing career to deliver a book with great real-life examples.

We've been working with contract testing for five years. We constantly hear the same questions and same challenges from people we meet at testing conferences or in the testing community. The advice we often give people is that you can't truly see the benefits until you start implementing contract testing, which is why this book had to happen.

As contract testing champions, we've always had so much support and developed great friendships with the team at Pact and PactFlow. Now that we've managed to write and have this book published, which is the first book dedicated to contract testing, we truly hope you can learn from our learnings and experience with contract testing with Pact and PactFlow.

While writing this book, between us we've had one promotion, a house move, two job changes (both Lewis), and two new babies. It's been a huge effort to deliver this book alongside day-to-day commitments.

acknowledgments

This book has been in the making for a long time. We must have been discussing the idea for at least six months before we even started writing anything! But we're so happy that we've delivered a high-quality book.

First, I (Lewis) want to thank my wife, Charlie. You've been very patient throughout the year of writing the book, always offering to take our lovely girls Alicia and Julia out for a couple of hours.

I (Marie) want to thank my partner, Stuart, for being patient and supportive during this time. There were a lot of late nights, and you've always been understanding and curious about the book. I would also like to thank my coach, Jenna Sinclair, for giving me the tools and support I needed to make sure I delivered the book chapters on time.

Next, we'd like to acknowledge our editors at Manning, Marina Michaels and Laura Castro. Laura Castro is a professor at the University of a Coruña (UDC) in Spain, where she coordinates two undergraduate courses for CS students: Software Architecture and Software Testing and Validation. Always active in maintaining an active connection with the software development industry, she is part of the BEAM (Erlang/Elixir) community, where she is a member of the Erlang Ecosystem Foundation and its Education Working Group, and also a member of the ACM SIGPLAN Erlang Workshop Steering Committee. Thank you for all your patience and for raising the quality of our book; we couldn't have delivered such a high standard without you both.

Thanks as well to all the other folks at Manning who worked with us on the production and promotion of the book: our production editor Deirdre Blanchfield-Hiam, our copyeditor Julie McNamee, and our proofreader Jason Everett. It has been a pleasure working with you all.

We'd also like to thank the reviewers who took the time to read our manuscript at various stages during its development and who provided invaluable feedback: Yousaf Nabi, Matt Fellows, and Bas Dijkstra. Special thanks to Karsten Strøbæk, technical proofreader, for his careful review of the code, saving the "works on my machine" moment. To all of the other reviewers: Alessandro Campeis, Amol Gote, Andres Sacco, Andy Wiesendanger, Conor Redmond, David Cabrero Souto, Dileep Pandiya, Dylan Scott, Eric Jones, Ethien Daniel Salinas Domínguez, Francesco Basile, Goetz Heller, Hugo Sousa, Jasmeet Singh, Joel Luukka, Jorge Bo, Laud Bentil, Laura Castro, Mandar Kulkarni, Matt Fellows, Nicolas Fantoni, Patrick Wanjau, Piergiorgio Faraglia, Raj Agrawal, Richard Meinsen, Ryan Kienstra, Siddharth Parakh, Simeon Leyzerzon, Timothy Jones, Yousaf Nabi, and Zorodzayi Mukuya, your suggestions helped make this a better book.

Finally, thank you to the entire Pact community and PactFlow team. You've created something that's so powerful for developers and testers around the world.

about this book

Contract Testing in Action was written to help teams adopt contract testing. It begins by focusing on the concepts and theory behind how contract testing fits into the software life cycle. The book then walks through how to implement the different parts of contract testing in different environments and infrastructures.

Who should read this book

Contract Testing in Action is for developers, quality engineers, architects, and software development managers who are looking to understand contract testing in more detail. Both beginner and experienced engineers will be able to learn how to use their skills within the Pact framework. While plenty of blogs and example repositories exist online, this book brings together all the different components in a structured, easy-to-follow way that will benefit anyone wanting to implement contract testing.

How this book is organized: A roadmap

The book has 3 parts and 12 chapters. Part 1 introduces a technical overview of contract testing and how it fits into wider testing concepts:

- Chapter 1 introduces contract testing and what problems it solves. It also gives a high-level overview of contract testing end to end and why you should care about it.
- Chapter 2 goes into the benefits of contract testing fits within a test automation strategy. It also describes how to introduce contract testing to a software project.

- Chapter 3 describes the contract testing life cycle, core concepts, and key approaches. It also describes the tools available and different communication types supported.

Part 2 covers implementing consumer-driven contract testing (CDCT):

- Chapter 4 explains how to implement consumer-driven consumer contract tests for web applications with Pact in JavaScript.
- Chapter 5 explains how to implement consumer-driven consumer contract tests for Android mobile apps with Pact in Kotlin.
- Chapter 6 explains how to implement consumer-driven provider contract tests with Pact in JavaScript.
- Chapter 7 explains how to implement consumer-driven consumer contract tests for GraphQL clients with Pact in JavaScript.
- Chapter 8 explains how to implement CDCT for event-driven architecture with Pact in JavaScript.
- Chapter 9 describes Pact Broker and its options. It goes into detail about how to host an open source broker and set up a broker with software as a service (SaaS) provider PactFlow.
- Chapter 10 explains how to set up contract testing in a continuous integration/continuous deployment (CI/CD) pipeline with GitHub actions. It also goes into the advanced features available within Pact Broker such as webhooks.

Part 3 covers implementing provider-driven contact testing (CDCT) and migrate integration tests to contract tests:

- Chapter 11 explains how to implement provider-driven contract tests with PactFlow using the Cypress, WireMock, Dredd, and Postman tools.
- Chapter 12 provides guidance on finding suitable integration or end-to-end tests that can be migrated to contract tests and how to refactor them.

We recommend that you start by reading the first three chapters so that you have a strong understanding of the core concepts. From there, choose whichever consumer test chapter is relevant for the tech stack, followed by chapter 6 for provider tests. Then, pick up from chapter 9 to set up Pact Broker. Those working on greenfield projects can skip chapter 12, as there shouldn't be any legacy test code to refactor (very lucky people).

About the code

Source code for the examples in this book is available for download from GitHub at https://github.com/mdcruz/pact-js-example. The main tools used in this book—Pact, PactFlow, and GitHub Actions—have active communities and support. For community support on the open source Pact framework, check out their documentation or join their slack channel (https://pact.io). For PactFlow, contact their sales or support team (https://pactflow.io). For support on GitHub Actions, checkout their documentation (https://docs.github.com/en/actions) or ask the GitHub community (https://github.com/orgs/community/discussions).

This book contains many examples of source code both in numbered listings and in line with normal text. In both cases, source code is formatted in a `fixed-width font like this` to separate it from ordinary text. Sometimes code is also **`in bold`** to highlight code that has changed from previous steps in the chapter, such as when a new feature adds to an existing line of code.

In many cases, the original source code has been reformatted; we've added line breaks and reworked indentation to accommodate the available page space in the book. Additionally, comments in the source code have often been removed from the listings when the code is described in the text. Code annotations accompany many of the listings, highlighting important concepts.

The main tools used in this book—Pact, PactFlow, and GitHub Actions—have active communities and support. For community support on the open source Pact framework, check out their documentation or join their slack channel (https://pact.io). For PactFlow, contact their sales or support team (https://pactflow.io). For support on GitHub Actions, checkout their documentation (https://docs.github.com/en/actions) or ask the GitHub community (https://github.com/orgs/community/discussions).

You can get executable snippets of code from the liveBook (online) version of this book at https://livebook.manning.com/book/contract-testing-in-action. The complete code for the examples in the book is available for download from the Manning website at https://www.manning.com/books/contract-testing-in-action and from GitHub at https://github.com/mdcruz/pact-js-example.

liveBook discussion forum

Purchase of *Contract Testing in Action* includes free access to liveBook, Manning's online reading platform. Using liveBook's exclusive discussion features, you can attach comments to the book globally or to specific sections or paragraphs. It's a snap to make notes for yourself, ask and answer technical questions, and receive help from the author and other users. To access the forum, go to https://livebook.manning.com/book/contract-testing-in-action/discussion. You can also learn more about Manning's forums and the rules of conduct at https://livebook.manning.com/discussion.

Manning's commitment to our readers is to provide a venue where a meaningful dialogue between individual readers and between readers and the authors can take place. It is not a commitment to any specific amount of participation on the part of the authors, whose contribution to the forum remains voluntary (and unpaid). We suggest you try asking the authors some challenging questions lest their interest stray! The forum and the archives of previous discussions will be accessible from the publisher's website as long as the book is in print.

Other online resources

- https://testautomationu.applitools.com/pact-contract-tests/
- https://smartbear.com/academy/pactflow/introduction-to-contract-testing/
- https://www.ontestautomation.com/an-introduction-to-contract-testing-part-1-meet-the-players/
- https://youtu.be/U05q0zJsKsU?si=4mM_uVTdJuT_3DZ5

about the authors

MARIE CRUZ is a Software Tester with almost 10 years of experience in various industries. Currently, she works as a Senior Developer Advocate for Grafana Labs, where she is focused on helping developers and testers from an observability and performance testing perspective. In the past, she has been an Engineering Manager responsible for driving continuous testing and quality improvements within the organization. She has also been a Principal Engineer focused on introducing recommended practices for testing and test automation frameworks.

LEWIS PRESCOTT is a QA advocate with 9 years of experience working with various industries. Currently, he is a QA Lead at IBM. He is focused on building quality across the whole engineering team and scaling a holistic, agile testing approach. In the past, he has been a Test Automation Lead, where he was responsible for building testing architecture and teaching automation best practices within the organization. He has also been an ASOS QA Engineer, scaling microservices across distributed teams in scenarios such as Black Friday events.

about the cover illustration

The figure on the cover of *Contract Testing in Action*, "Femme Dalmate" or "A Dalmatian woman" is taken from a nineteenth-century collection by Frane Carrara, the first director of the Museum of Antiquity in Split, Croatia.

In those days, it was easy to identify where people lived and what their trade or station in life was just by their dress. Manning celebrates the inventiveness and initiative of the computer business with book covers based on the rich diversity of regional culture centuries ago, brought back to life by pictures from collections such as this one.

Part 1

Introduction to contract testing

In software testing, various testing types provide different values to ensure that when your application is deployed to your users, it meets their expectations, and risks are diminished as much as possible. You're likely familiar with testing types such as unit testing, integration testing, functional testing, and end-to-end testing, so you might wonder why we're introducing contract testing with all of these other testing types out there.

As more teams adopt a microservices architecture, where software projects are broken down into smaller modules or components and developed independently by different teams, the need to test and deploy the changes independently will increase. The microservices architecture poses new challenges to how teams traditionally approach testing activities. Multiple teams need to deploy their service to a dedicated test environment. Imagine if you have a lot of them! How will you test the services efficiently? This is where contract testing shines through.

This part of the book delves further into the concept of contract testing. Chapter 1 provides a high-level overview of contract testing. Chapter 2 discusses how contract testing fits into wider testing concepts and whether it replaces other testing activities. You learn about the numerous benefits and challenges of contract testing. You also learn how to introduce contract testing to your teams. Chapter 3 discusses the technical side of contract testing. You learn what is meant by *consumer*, *provider*, *contract*, and *broker* in this context, as well as get an overview of the contract testing life cycle. You gain an understanding of the various contract testing tools available, the difference between consumer-driven contract testing (CDCT) and provider-driven contract testing (PDCT), and the different communication types that contract testing supports. By the end of this part of the book, you'll be equipped with the core knowledge needed to start implementing contract testing into your projects.

1 Introduction to contract testing

> ***This chapter covers***
> - What this book is about and why it's important
> - A high-level overview of contract testing
> - Why you should care about contract testing
> - When contract testing is appropriate to use and not use
> - How contract testing works on a high level
> - Contract testing in action

Imagine this scenario. It's 4 p.m. on a Friday, and you decided to deploy a small change of updating one of your API's data responses. All the automated tests from your pipeline are returning green, which gives you the confidence that you haven't broken anything. You hit deploy, and a few minutes after the deployment, you get a message from another team that something is broken in production. It couldn't be the change you recently deployed because it was a small change, and all the tests are passing . . . right? As it turns out, this other team using your API has certain expectations. During the incident, you've learned that these expectations are different from yours. Rather than enjoying your Friday afternoon, you're left with a production bug you must deal with.

During the incident postmortem, you identify that there are API integration tests written by this other team that would have caught this problem. Still, your change didn't trigger those tests because it's in a separate project repository and pipeline. On top of that, these API integration tests are notorious for being flaky and slow. One of the action items from the postmortem is to find alternatives to better catch these changes, and one of the suggestions was to look into contract testing. You've heard this term before, but you're not sure how this will help with your problem.

Well, you've come to the right resource! This book covers all the important things you need to know about contract testing, such as what it is, how it works, how it's different from other testing types, and why you should care about it. We'll cover the technical implementation and show you from the ground up how to use relevant tools and integrate contract testing as part of your continuous integration (CI) pipelines. Our main goal is to convince you that contract testing is an essential part of your testing strategies, especially when you work within a microservices architecture.

As teams move from a monolithic application to a microservices architecture, they face new challenges when it comes to testing because the integration points between different services can increase exponentially. There is also the challenge of testing all the different microservices together in a dedicated test environment. Different teams can deploy changes at different times or at the same time, which can result in unexpected changes that can break an environment. Relying on traditional testing techniques won't scale up well when applied to complex systems, so it's now important for teams to know how contract testing can help ensure that every change you make doesn't affect other teams negatively.

1.1 An overview of contract testing

In its simplest definition, *contract testing* is used to test that two systems have a shared understanding of expectations. For example, when a web application sends a `GET` request to a data service, the web application has expectations regarding how the data service should respond. Contract testing captures the interactions between these two systems, which are then stored in a contract that both systems must adhere to.

It's similar to when you sign a contract in the real world. A great example is when we signed our contract with Manning. The contract details the expectations from our side, which is to deliver this book, and at the same time, it includes what is also expected from Manning. If changes need to be made to the contract, both parties will need to be notified, and changes will only be made once everyone approves. Contract testing is similar in this sense. If a data service suddenly responds with a set of data that is different from what a web application expects, this change will be flagged and reviewed by both systems before the change is deployed to production.

To further explain contract testing, it's helpful to have an overview of how traditional API integration testing works. Let's take an example of a web application that displays user details, which you can see in figure 1.1.

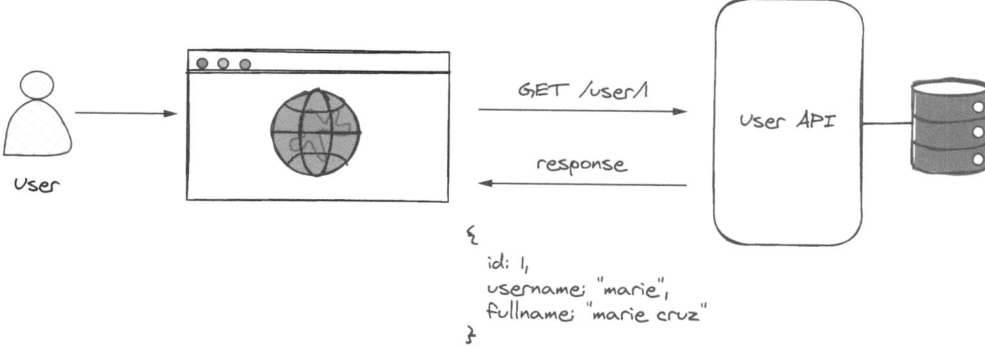

Figure 1.1 An example web application communicating with the User API. When a user sends a request to get their details, the User API sends the expected response.

A simple API integration test, as shown in figure 1.1, would send a `GET` request to the real User API and assert that it has the correct ID, username, and full name.

Contract testing, similar to API integration testing, will also assert that when the web application makes a `GET` request to the User API, their expectations should be true. The main difference here is that the web application and the User API don't need to interact directly. Instead, they interact via a shared contract, as shown in figure 1.2.

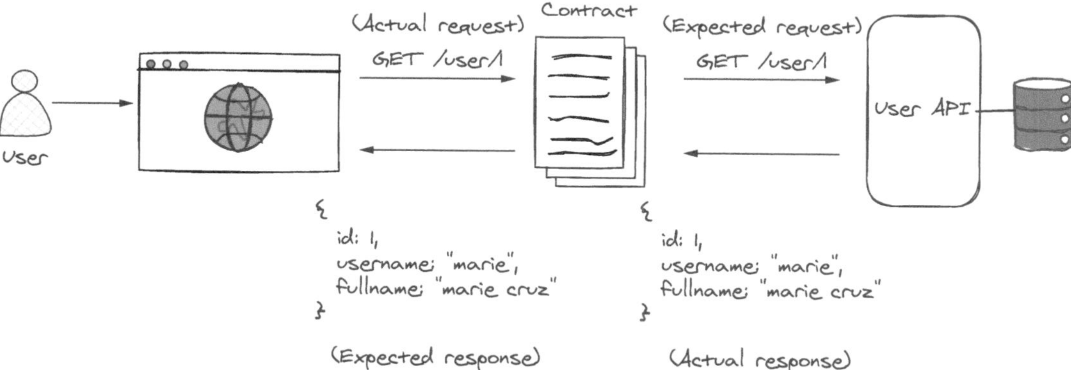

Figure 1.2 A web application and User API communicating via a contract, instead of directly with each other

The contract is in a JSON file containing the names of the two interacting systems: in this case, the web application and the User API. The contract also lists all interactions between these two systems, which we'll discuss further in chapter 3. The web application records the actual request and the response expected from the User API in the shared contract, which is uploaded to a shared broker that the User API can access directly. The User API pulls down the contract from the shared broker and replays the expected request from the web application. The contract testing tool will compare the User API's actual response to the expected response the web application requires.

1.2 Why contract testing matters

In an ideal world, there should be no breaking changes between two systems. However, we know that these scenarios can happen unfortunately. For example, suppose the User API changes the field from `fullName` to `name` and deploys this change to production. In that case, the two systems are now incompatible because the web application is expecting `fullName`, as shown in figure 1.3.

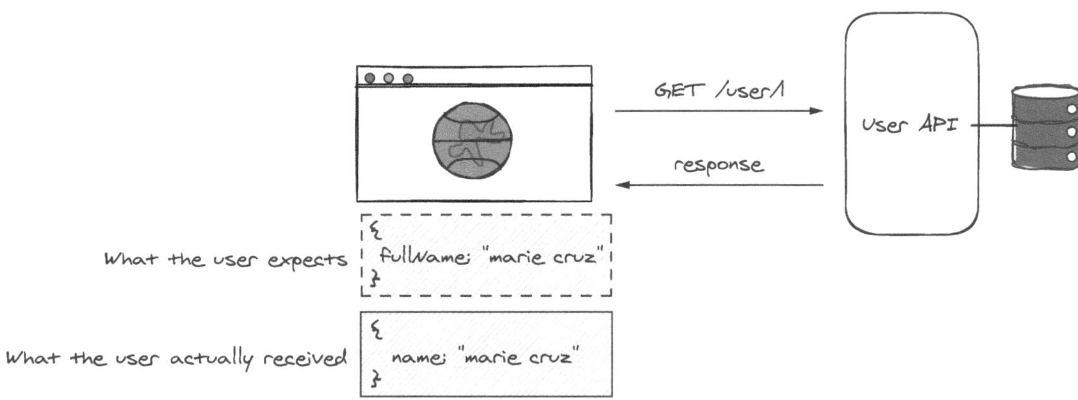

Figure 1.3 A web application communicating with the User API but with different expectations when it comes to the name key

At this point, the user accessing the web application won't be able to see their name, and there have been several complaints already. The worst-case scenario that could happen is that the production environment is broken until the team responsible for the User API either reverts the change or the team responsible for the web application updates their code, so they use the `name` key instead.

If both teams had contract testing, this breaking change would have been caught earlier, allowing the User API team to ask the web application team if the contract could be modified. If the web application team doesn't agree, then the breaking change needs to be reverted.

Another great reason why contract testing matters is that it gives data providers the confidence to introduce new requirements independently and safely. For example, let's imagine that apart from the web application team, the User API team also has another consumer. This other consumer, a mobile application, wants to display additional information about the user, such as the user's favorite items. The mobile application consumer creates a different contract detailing their expectations from the

User API. The User API can use this contract as a guide to introduce the changes safely with the mobile team, which isn't dependent on the web application team's contract, as shown in figure 1.4.

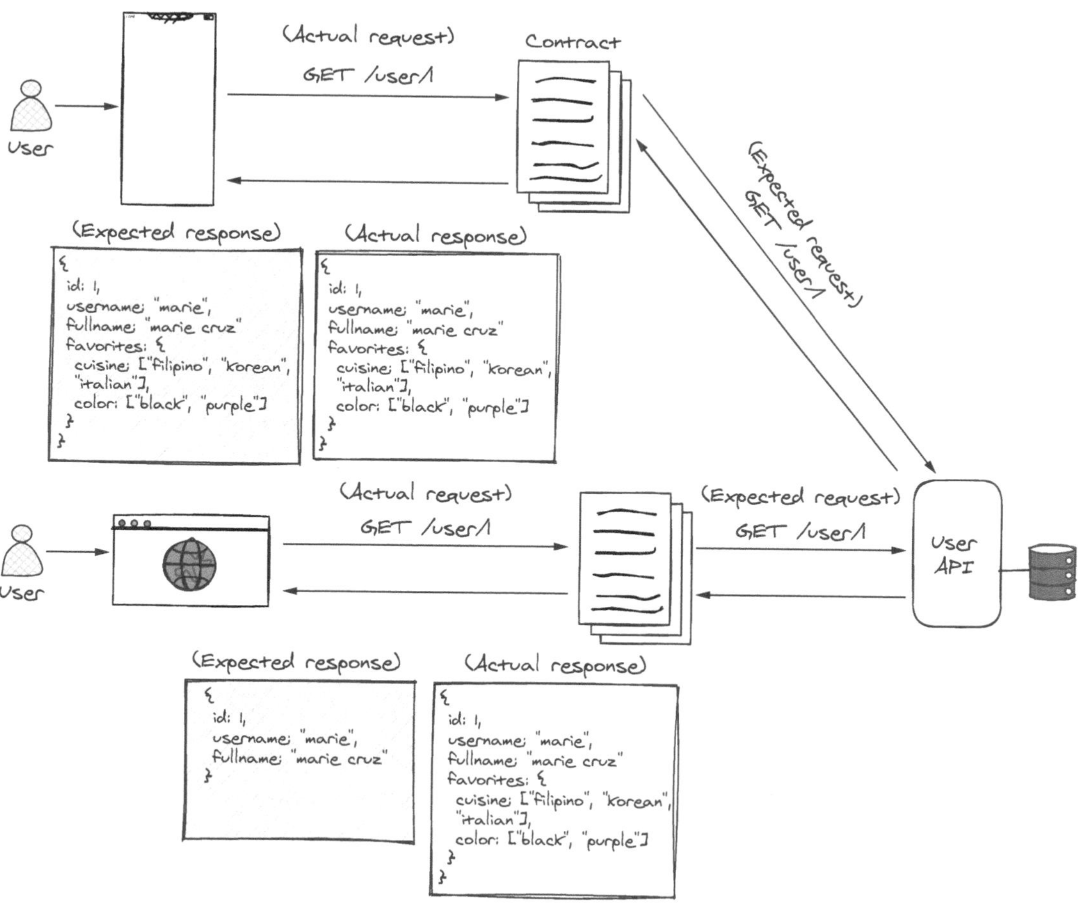

Figure 1.4 A User API with two consumers and two independent contracts

When the mobile application makes a `GET` request to the `/user/1` endpoint, they will see the additional field `favorites`, but this shouldn't introduce any unexpected problems to the web application because the contract defined with the User API still stands true. From the User API perspective, they are still meeting the requirements of both the web and mobile applications and sending the same set of responses, but only the mobile application is using the additional `favorites` field.

The contracts generated by web and mobile application consumers are also uploaded to a shared broker, meaning multiple teams can see the different contracts easily. It also makes it easier for the team responsible for the User API to track who their consumers are. Having a shared broker for all the contracts makes it easier to visualize which teams have dependencies among each other so that any contract changes can be spotted more easily.

Another reason contract testing matters is that the cost of a bug gets exponentially more expensive when it's not found early, which Rafaela Azevedo explained in detail in her blog post (https://mng.bz/Dpa0). Contract testing combines the best qualities of an API integration test and a unit test. It combines the high confidence that an API integration test provides with the speed, low maintenance, and cheaper cost of running a unit test. Contract testing can also help minimize the number of integration or end-to-end (E2E) tests, which are also proven to be slow, flaky, and prone to errors.

> **TIP** If your team already has a substantial number of integration tests, many of these tests can also be shifted earlier in the development process to the contract level. However, this doesn't entirely replace the need for integration or E2E testing because contract testing doesn't verify any environmental problems caused by configuration problems or unexpected behaviors caused by system side effects. We cover this in more detail as part of chapter 2.

Apart from detecting bugs missed by proper communication among teams, there are also other reasons why contract testing matters (not an exhaustive list):

- Speeds up the development process and provides a fast feedback loop because contract tests don't need to communicate to one or more systems
- Enables teams to deploy changes independently and safely
- Makes problems easier to debug because the scope of a contract test is much smaller
- Enables developers to run contract tests and update them locally when needed, creating a shared responsibility when it comes to writing tests
- Promotes better code quality because it removes the need to introduce requirements that won't be used
- Ensures that any breaking changes are communicated to teams because the contract will always be up-to-date with these changes, especially with contract testing tools that generate a contract from the development codebase

1.3 When is contract testing appropriate to use?

Contract testing is appropriate to use whenever you need to test an integration point between two systems for which you want to catch problems early. This could be between a web (or mobile) application and an API or between two data services, communicating via different protocols, with HTTP being the most common one.

Although you can use contract testing when working with just two different systems that communicate with each other, it shines the most within a microservices architecture, especially if it involves a large number of microservices. Relying on API integration tests or E2E tests alone will be difficult to manage and scale up. Contract testing provides a great alternative.

> **TIP** Contract testing can be used between two connected systems. However, the same principles will apply when you write a contract between a web application communicating to multiple microservices.

In some scenarios, contract testing might not be appropriate to use, such as the following:

- Testing all the business logic of the provider and side effects of a particular functionality (should be covered by a functional test instead from the provider)
- Testing the UI's components such as its visual look or accessibility requirements
- Testing other requirements such as performance or security
- Using third-party APIs where you don't have much control over how contract tests can be added to their pipelines
- Using public APIs where you don't know who is consuming your data

We'll explain in chapter 11, however, how you can still use contract testing if you're working with third-party or public APIs via an approach called bi-directional contract testing.

1.4 How contract testing works on a high level

There are a few approaches to adopting contract testing, all of which we'll discuss in more detail in later chapters. However, as part of this introduction, we've only described how contract testing works at a high level, which covers the original consumer-driven contract testing approach in which the consumer (see chapter 3, section 3.1, for more details on consumers) creates the contract and shares with the data providers.

Earlier in the chapter, we described how traditional API integration testing works. We highly recommend understanding the fundamentals of API testing before learning how contract testing works. If you haven't already, we suggest reading about RESTful APIs and API testing, especially, Mark Winteringham's book, *Testing Web APIs* (www.manning.com/books/testing-web-apis). Contract testing can be seen as a form of integration testing but with some differences, such as an asynchronous unit test.

Imagine you're buying a house (in the UK). When someone makes an offer on a property in the UK, the buyer and seller must communicate to iron out the details of the contract; however, both sides have their own copies until later in the process. Think of this in software terms as distributed development teams when teams are developing the backend or frontend in different programming languages. API documentation is often created in different forms, either as a wiki page, OpenAPI spec (www.openapis.org/), or another format. Let's explore OpenAPI and compare how it's different from the contract generated by contract testing.

OpenAPI, formerly called the Swagger specification (https://swagger.io/docs/specification/about/), is a standard that defines an API's details and makes it human-readable for other people to use the API. Let's have a look at an example OpenAPI specification:

```
openapi: 3.0.3
info:
  title: Contract Testing - OpenAPI 3.0
  version: 1.0.0
tags:
  - name: user
    description: Operations about user
paths:
  /user/{id}:
    get:
      summary: Get an existing user
      operationId: getUser
      parameters:
        - name: id
          in: path
          description: Id of user to return
          required: true
          schema:
            type: integer
      responses:
        '200':
          description: successful operation
          content:
            application/json:
              schema:
                $ref: '#/components/schemas/User'
components:
  schemas:
    User:
      type: object
      properties:
        id:
          type: integer
          format: int64
          example: 10
        firstName:
          type: string
          example: Marie
        lastName:
          type: string
          example: Cruz
```

An Open API specification details what the API structure looks like. It defines the available endpoints and the properties they can provide. An Open API specification can be used by teams to author integration tests. However, relying on an Open API specification doesn't enforce the prevention of integration bugs automatically because teams can deploy multiple changes to test environments. The contract generated through contract testing can prevent integration bugs because it informs consumers and providers when changes are detected, especially when integrated into a CI pipeline, even before deploying the changes to a test environment.

Integration tests are also often authored by just one team. This could be the team maintaining an API or the team using the API. This can cause challenges when it comes to sharing resources and knowledge across different services or applications. Meanwhile, in consumer-driven contract testing, the tests are authored by the team using the actual API service (messages are also supported, which we'll discuss in chapter 8), and the same set of tests are also verified by the team maintaining the API service.

1.4.1 Contract testing from the consumer side

When working with consumer-driven contract testing, most of the test writing will happen on the consumer side because they will define the contract. Let's consider an example. Imagine a frontend engineer working on the web application is working on a new user page. The frontend engineer writes a contract test using a contract testing tool called Pact (https://pact.io/) to ensure that the user page doesn't have any unexpected problems related to the data it's supposed to display. The process of writing the contract test from the consumer side can be visualized in figure 1.5.

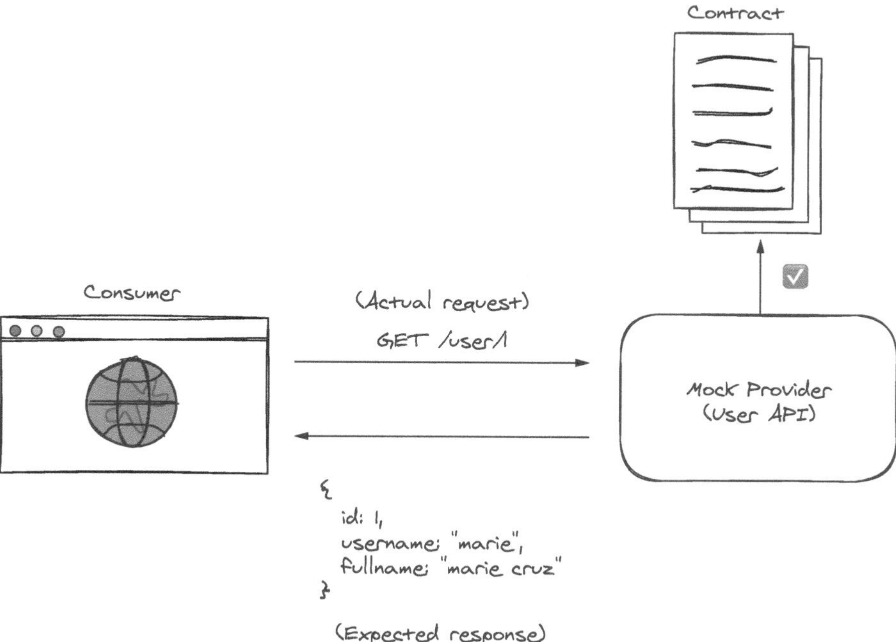

Figure 1.5 A contract test between a consumer and a mock data provider

A consumer contract test, illustrated in figure 1.5, can be explained on a high level in a few steps:

1. The frontend engineer, or the consumer in general, defines the interaction with a mock provider. An *interaction* is the request and response that will be registered to the mock provider. The *request* describes what the consumer will send to the provider, while the *response* describes what the provider needs to return.
2. The frontend engineer runs a test against the mock provider at unit test time, and the mock provider checks if the actual request from the consumer is registered as an interaction. If so, the mock provider returns the expected response, and the consumer confirms that the expected response is understood.
3. If all tests of this type are successful, a contract will be generated automatically, which includes the defined interaction. The contract will then be uploaded to a shared broker that the actual data provider can access. There are different ways to store the contract, which we'll cover as part of chapter 9.

We'll further explain the process of writing a consumer contract test in chapter 4.

1.4.2 Contract testing from the provider side

On the provider side, which will typically be found in a separate project repository, one of the backend engineers has been notified that a new contract was generated by the consumer. As part of the contract testing on the provider side, the provider verifies the contract. Similar to the consumer test, the provider doesn't communicate with the actual consumer but with a mock consumer instead. A provider contract test, illustrated in figure 1.6, can be explained on a high level in a few steps:

1. The provider downloads the contract generated by the consumer from the shared broker.
2. Using the contract testing tool, the expected request is replayed, and the provider sends the actual response to the expected request.
3. The contract testing tool compares the actual response and the expected response defined by the consumer in the contract. If the results match, the verification is successful.

Once the contract verification is successful, the consumer can deploy the new user page to an environment suitable for a product demo with more confidence that the demo will go smoothly.

This is a simple example to demonstrate how contract testing works. However, in the real world, things can get much more complicated. Imagine having multiple applications using the User API service with legacy fields and multiple versions knocking about, or a web application communicating to different data services, not just the User API.

For now, the core fundamental to understanding contract testing is that engineers can safely deploy their changes without requiring dedicated test environments. The predefined contract designed before development is now part of the test suite created

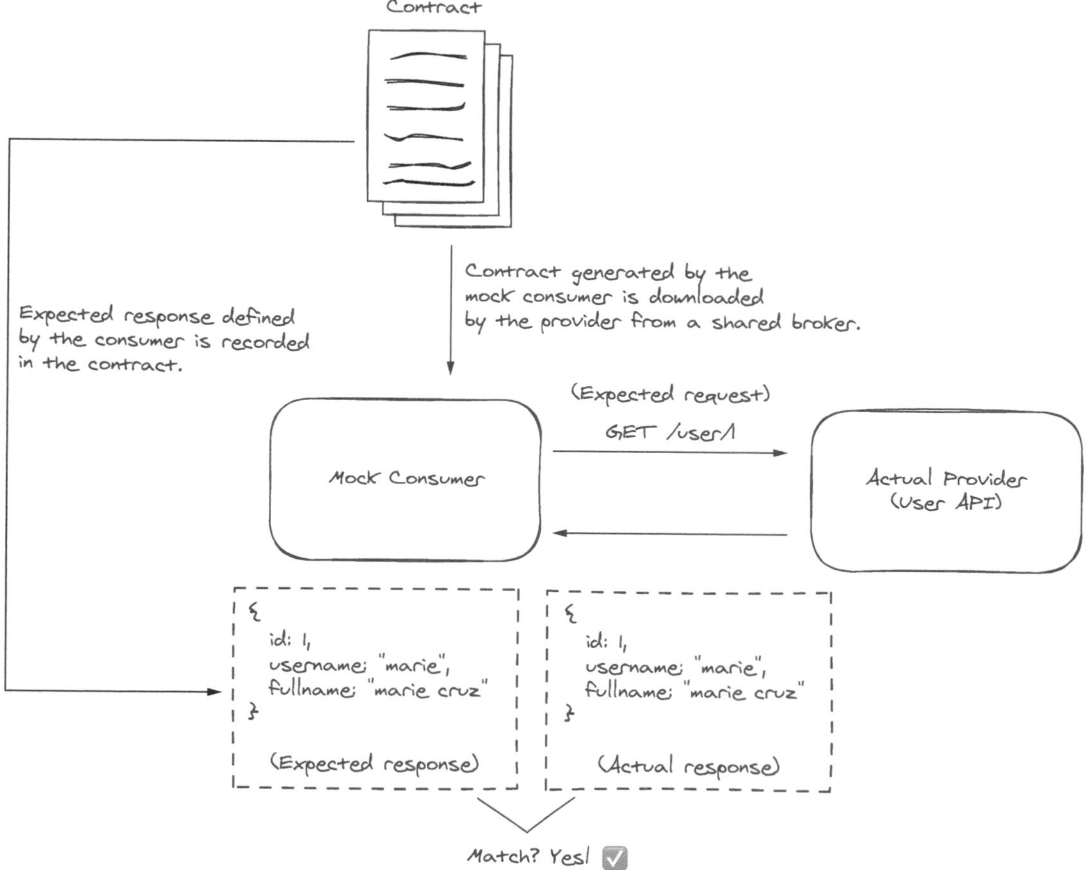

Figure 1.6 A contract test between the provider and mock consumer

by the consumer teams. As the contract test is directly connected to the request within the consumer implementation, any changes to the request itself will automatically update the contract. The provider teams will automatically verify the new contract if it's compatible with the existing implementation of their service. Conversely, any changes to the implementation from the provider will check that any change is still compatible with the existing applications using the service.

1.5 Contract testing in action

To guide you with hands-on material, we created an example GitHub project, found at https://github.com/mdcruz/pact-js-example, which contains a comprehensive contract testing suite for web applications, mobile, GraphQL, and events, ready to be run as part of a workflow using GitHub actions. This GitHub project will be referred to from chapter 4 onward in much more detail, but let's look at the coding perspective to see how it all works.

1.5.1 Example of a consumer contract test

Looking at the consumer-web/consumer-contract.spec.js file of the example GitHub project, one of the example tests is getting a list of movies. A contract test from a consumer perspective looks like the following:

```
const provider = new PactV3({
  consumer: 'WebConsumer',
  provider: 'MoviesAPI',
})

const EXPECTED_BODY = {
  id: 1,
  name: "My movie",
  year: 1999
}

...

provider
  .uponReceiving('a request to all movies')
  .withRequest({
    method: 'GET',
    path: '/movies',
  })
  .willRespondWith({
    status: 200,
    body: eachLike(EXPECTED_BODY)
  })
})

await provider.executeTest(async mockProvider) => {
  const movies = await fetchMovies(mockProvider.url)
  expect(movies[0]).toEqual(EXPECTED_BODY);
})
```

Set up the mock provider.

Set up expectations from the provider.

Run the consumer test against the mock provider. The mock provider validates the test, and, if successful, the contract is generated.

The key thing to note here is that the consumer doesn't interact with the real provider but with a mock provider instead, which is provided by the contract testing tool. We'll further explain the process of writing a consumer contract test in chapter 4. Once the test is run, a contract, similar to the one shown here, is generated by the contract testing tool, which contains the expectations the consumer has from the provider:

```
{
    "description": "a request to all movies",
    "request": {
      "method": "GET",
      "path": "/movies"
    },
```

The request from the consumer

```
    "response": {
      "body": [
        {
          "id": 1,
          "name": "My movie",
          "year": 1999
        }
      ],
      "headers": {
        "Content-Type": "application/json"
      },
      "matchingRules": {
        "body": {
          "$": {
            "combine": "AND",
            "matchers": [
              {
                "match": "type",
                "min": 1
              }
            ]
          }
        }
      },
      "status": 200
    }
  }
```

The response the consumer expects from the provider when the request is made

The matching rules applied. In this example, the matching rule is that the data type of the data should match the consumer expectation. For example, the movie name should be of type string, whereas the ID and year should be of type integer.

The status code the consumer expects from the provider

After the contract is generated, the consumer uploads the contract with a version to a shared broker that the provider can access. At this stage, if the test is running as part of a CI pipeline, the consumer waits for the provider to verify the contract before deploying the changes to production. This is made possible with the use of the can-i-deploy tool, which we'll talk about in more detail in chapter 10.

1.5.2 Example of a provider contract test

To verify the expectations from the consumer, a provider contract test needs to be set up. Looking at the provider/provider-contract.spec.js file of the example GitHub project, you can see the provider contract test, which is similar to the following:

```
const options = {
  provider: 'my-provider',
  providerBaseUrl: 'http://localhost:4000',
  pactBrokerUrl: PACT_BROKER_BASE_URL,
  pactBrokerToken: PACT_BROKER_TOKEN,
  publishVerificationResult: true,
};

const verifier = new Verifier(options);

describe('Pact Verification', () => {
  test('should validate the expectations of movie-consumer', () => {
    return verifier
```

Sets up the provider and where to pull the contract that the consumer uploaded

```
        .verifyProvider()                          <-- Verifies the contract
        .then(output => {
          console.log('Pact Verification Complete!');
          console.log('Result:', output);
          app.close();
        })
    });
});
```

Before running the provider contract test, the provider needs to be running in the background because the expectations from the consumer will be run against the real provider. As part of the test, the provider validates the request from the consumer and sends the actual response to that request. The contract testing tool compares the actual response with the expected response from the consumer and then sends the results back to the shared broker. We'll further explain the process of writing a provider contract test in chapter 6.

Once the provider verification result is recorded to the shared broker, the contract testing tool notifies the consumer that their changes have been verified. If the test passes, both the consumer and provider are safe to deploy their changes to production.

The high-level example shows how consumer and provider contract tests work together. When we first started learning about contract testing, the high-level description of contract testing went completely over our heads. It wasn't until we started implementing it and created a proof of concept that we fully understood the true value of contract testing. After reading the first chapter, we hope you don't have the same experience, but if you do at this point, don't worry. We're sure everything will make sense once we start writing some test code and walking through each step in detail.

Summary

- Contract testing is a form of integration testing that verifies two connected systems have a shared understanding of expectations.
- In contract testing, interactions between two systems are presented in a contract, normally in a JSON file.
- Contract testing offers high confidence from an API integration test with a unit test's speed and low cost.
- Contract testing can help teams find defects early without needing integrated environments.
- Contract testing is a great alternative to traditional API testing, which is difficult to manage and doesn't scale up well, especially when working with a microservices architecture.
- Contract testing is unsuitable to verify a system's other requirements, such as the business logic, UI, accessibility, security, or performance.

- When writing contract tests, the tests are authored by the team consuming a data service, especially in consumer-driven contract testing. The team maintaining the data service also verifies the same set of tests.
- Contract testing tools, such as Pact, help communicate changes to the contract by automatically informing the affected teams.

2 How contract testing fits into wider testing concepts

This chapter covers

- Contract testing and other testing types
- Whether contract testing can replace other types of tests
- Benefits of contract testing
- Introducing contract testing to your teams
- Challenges with contract testing
- Practical guidance on introducing contract testing to projects

Contract testing is unique when compared to other testing types because it requires developing two sets of tests to fully reap the benefits. A consumer test can exist without a provider test, but it won't be useful. You can initiate the contract testing process by writing either a consumer test or a provider test individually, but it's important to note that these individual tests alone don't give you real benefits. To unlock the full potential of contract testing, you must implement and execute both consumer and provider tests in tandem, in a continuous integration (CI) pipeline ideally.

Let's consider an example to highlight the problem of only writing either consumer or provider tests. In a previous project undertaken by one of the authors, there was a web application communicating to a GraphQL service. This GraphQL layer was responsible for communicating with various data services, both legacy and brand new. In this scenario, contract testing was introduced between the GraphQL layer and the data services. The GraphQL layer played the role of the consumer, while the different data services served as the providers. During the initial implementation of contract testing, only the consumer tests were developed within the GraphQL codebase, as illustrated in figure 2.1. The consumer is generating the contract, but it's not being verified.

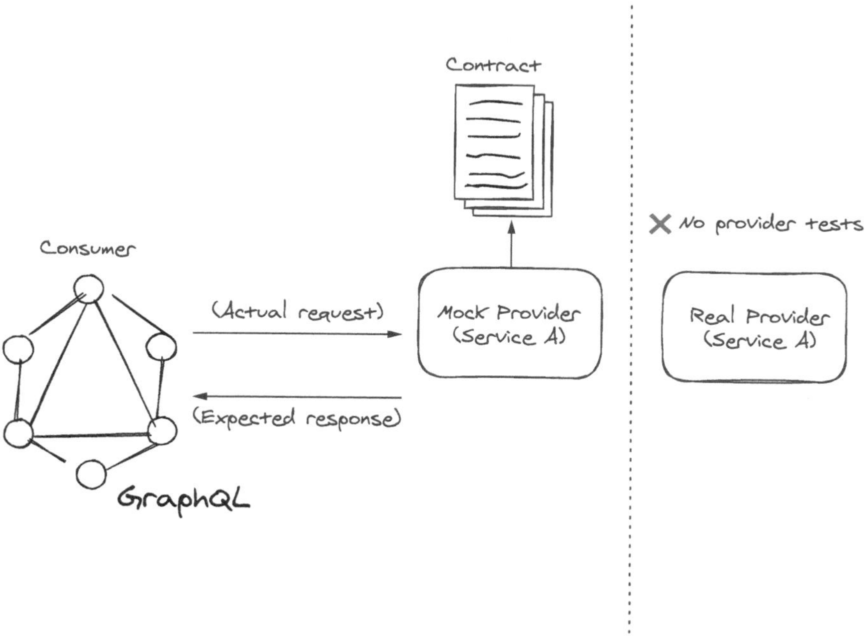

Figure 2.1 Contract testing setup for a GraphQL consumer communicating to a data service. The consumer has generated the contract, but it's not verified by the real provider because there are no provider tests.

None of the data providers had corresponding provider contract tests in place. Despite the presence of consumer contract tests within the GraphQL layer, the data providers lacked the means to verify the established contract, which means that breaking changes could be introduced and then slip into testing and/or production environments. This is especially true if the end-to-end (E2E) tests, which assess the functionality of an application from start to finish, have also missed covering this change. Let's visualize this in an example build pipeline, as illustrated in figure 2.2.

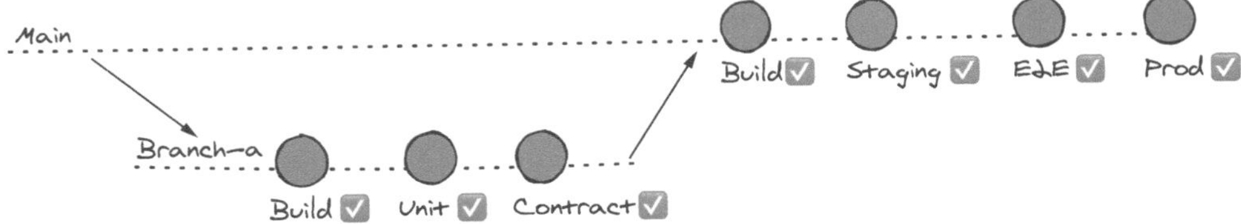

Figure 2.2 Build pipeline with consumer contract tests added, but no provider verification. This can lead to silent errors being deployed to production.

The build pipeline didn't throw any errors because no additional contract verification had been added. The absence of contract tests for the data providers led to a gap in knowledge, preventing teams from grasping the complete functionality and significance of contract testing. This situation also highlighted a lack of comprehensive understanding among the teams regarding the concept of contract testing and its role within the broader testing processes. Developers working on the GraphQL codebase wrote consumer contract tests just because it was being done on the other features.

If provider tests were in place in this project, breaking changes or contract errors, such as differences in status codes, data structure, or data types, could be detected and stop the build pipeline from progressing, as illustrated in figure 2.3, leading to errors being caught at an earlier stage. For example, if the data provider changed to rename some of the fields they expose to the GraphQL consumer, then this change would be caught by the contract verification process. Even if there is a schema in place in verifying the GraphQL structure, a schema can't tell you how consumers use it and what fields aren't used, which we explain further in chapter 3.

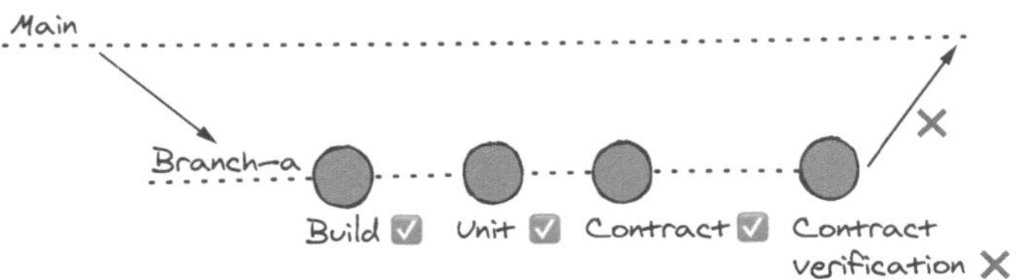

Figure 2.3 Consumer build pipeline with contract verification from the provider service. If there are breaking changes, the build pipeline won't continue.

Contract testing is a process that works best when there is open communication and agreement between teams. Following the same agreements between teams enhances the contract testing process. To avoid situations where the value of contract testing isn't properly used, we'll guide you step-by-step to understand how contract testing integrates into the broader testing strategy as part of this chapter. We'll clarify whether contract testing is a replacement for other forms of testing such as integration or E2E, and provide more additional benefits that it can offer when implemented correctly. Furthermore, we'll provide some guidance for persuading multiple teams to collaborate in contract testing, as well as address the challenges that may arise during the introduction and implementation of contract testing. Finally, we'll look into providing you a practical guide of introducing contract testing to your teams.

2.1 Contract testing and other testing types

Many engineers, specifically software developers or software development engineers in test (SDET), rely on the test automation pyramid, a popular guideline for implementing automated tests. The test automation pyramid has gained significant attention across the industry, offering a structured approach to test automation. While various versions of the test automation pyramid exist, we'll only focus on the original version proposed by Mike Cohn, as we've illustrated in figure 2.4.

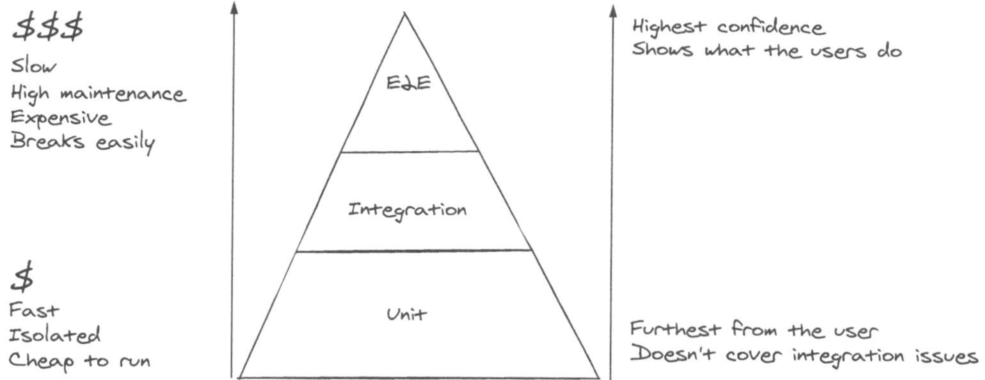

Figure 2.4 The original test automation pyramid comprising three horizontal sections: unit tests, integration tests, and E2E tests

In the original test automation pyramid, there are three primary layers: unit tests at the base level, followed by integrations tests in the middle, and E2E tests at the top level. The test automation pyramid suggests that most automated tests should be predominantly unit tests, complemented by a smaller number of integration tests, and a further reduced number of E2E tests because the higher you go up the pyramid, the slower and more expensive the tests are, even though the higher-level tests are the closest to verifying the user's experience.

The test automation pyramid also provides a visual representation of the ideal test automation distribution and highlights the need for a balanced approach. With the balanced approach, teams can use the speed and isolation of unit tests, the integration validation of integration tests, and the full user coverage of E2E tests. Let's take a look at these different types of testing briefly.

2.1.1 Unit testing

Unit testing is a software testing technique by which individual units are tested to determine that a software component does what it's supposed to do. Tests that are written at the unit level are known for their fast execution because they run in isolation and don't require integrated environments. However, it's important to note that these unit tests only focus on individual methods or components, so they don't verify any integration points. Any dependencies are mocked so the full code and testing coverage are contained within a specific code. Consequently, they also stand the furthest apart from the end-user experience and may not provide a complete validation of system behavior.

2.1.2 Integration testing

To address the limitations of unit testing, it's essential to develop integration tests to assess the interaction between one or two components to other components or services. By validating the integration points between components or services, teams can identify and address any potential problems or inconsistencies that may arise when different parts of the system interact.

2.1.3 End-to-end testing

At the top of the test automation pyramid, we find the E2E tests. E2E tests offer the highest level of confidence because they closely mimic user interactions and replicate real-world scenarios. E2E tests provide comprehensive coverage by testing the entire system, validating the flow and behavior across various components and services. An E2E test is commonly driven from a user interface (UI) and requires all connected services to be deployed to a dedicated environment.

While E2E tests offer the greatest level of confidence, it's important to consider the tradeoffs associated with E2E tests. E2E tests tend to be slower to execute, cost more to develop because they require a dedicated test environment that is similar to production, and involve a higher level of maintenance. E2E tests can also be difficult to debug because the problems can arise from any of the interconnected systems.

2.1.4 The ice cream cone of test automation

A phenomenon that can occur when there are a lot of E2E or UI tests, fewer integration tests, and even fewer unit tests, is the ice cream cone of test automation, which is a known anti-pattern first mentioned by Alister Scott (https://alisterscott.github.io/TestingPyramids.html)—and it's not the good ice cream cone that you're thinking about! The ice cream cone is simply the inverse of the test automation pyramid that also includes executing a huge amount of tests manually, which you can see in figure 2.5.

We see the ice cream cone anti-pattern a lot in organizations where the responsibility of testing falls only on testers. When we were starting our journey to writing automated tests, they began by writing automated tests from a UI perspective and

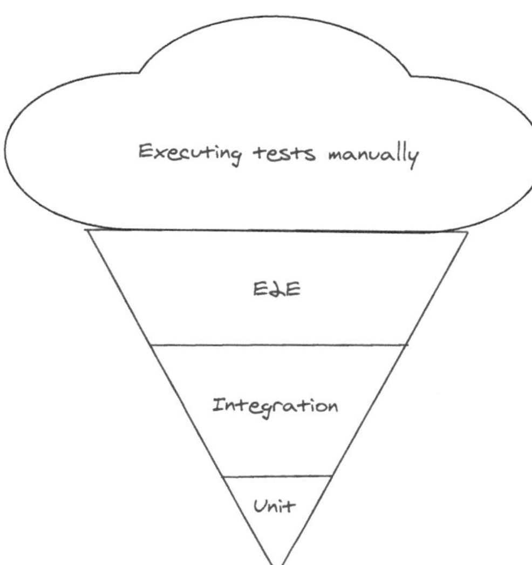

Figure 2.5 The ice cream cone of test automation

driving all test automation efforts to write them on the E2E level because writing tests involving a UI or a web browser is closer to what our users do. However, it's difficult to convince developers to write tests on the E2E level, not because they don't like to do it, but because tests on the E2E level are more prone to brittleness and are more difficult to maintain. A test is considered flaky when it produces inconsistent results without introducing any changes to the code or environment. To avoid the ice cream cone anti-pattern, there needs to be a good balance of automated tests closer to the code, and contract testing can provide this balance because it's closer to the bottom of the test automation pyramid, as you'll see next.

2.1.5 Contract testing in the test automation pyramid

As mentioned in chapter 1, contract testing brings together the best qualities of both unit and integration tests. To restructure the test automation pyramid slightly, contract tests are found between unit and integration tests, which you can see in figure 2.6.

Contract testing provides higher confidence of API implementation than unit testing because it verifies the expectations between two systems, without the requirement of integrated environments. When adopting contract testing to evaluate APIs or microservices, teams can gain early feedback so that any potential misunderstandings or discrepancies between interconnected systems are identified and addressed before deploying them to a specific environment and running integration tests.

Because contract testing can be run earlier on, it prevents communication breakdowns between the consumer and provider services. This proactive approach mitigates the chances of encountering compatibility problems during integration or E2E tests.

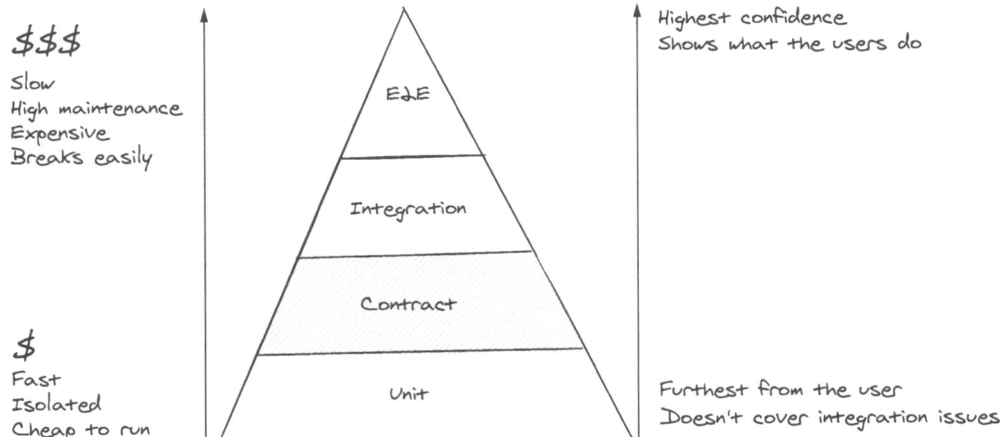

Figure 2.6 Test automation pyramid with contract testing

2.2 Does contract testing replace other types of tests?

You may wonder whether having contract testing in place eliminates other types of tests. Hopefully, by now, you get the idea that this isn't the case, especially with the introduction of the revised test automation pyramid. Contract testing doesn't replace these tests but rather complements them.

To prove this point, let's consider a simple scenario. Imagine that your team is working on a new login feature. During the development process, you and your team collectively identify the following 10 potential failures for this feature:

1. The username is null.
2. The username is empty.
3. The password is null.
4. The password is empty.
5. The username exceeds the limit of 20 alphanumeric characters.
6. An unauthorized user tries to log in.
7. A user tries to log in but with an incorrect password.
8. A user tries to log in but with an incorrect username.
9. The login service is responding slow due to a bottleneck of incoming requests.
10. A user clears their browser cookies and their session hasn't been cleared.

If we reference the revised test automation pyramid in figure 2.6, let's assume that scenarios 1 to 5 can be captured at the unit level, while scenarios 6 to 10 require some form of verification involving other systems. From scenarios 6 to 10, scenarios 6 to 8 can be identified through contract testing, scenario 9 through integration testing, and scenario 10 through E2E testing. Now, without contract testing in place, as illustrated on the left side of figure 2.7, scenarios 6 to 9 are potentially caught on the integration level. This complicates the debugging process and introduces a slower feedback loop because integration tests are positioned higher in the test automation pyramid. By the time these problems are discovered, they have already been deployed to an integrated environment, making them more challenging to rectify. This may also block other teams especially if they are also using the shared integrated environment for other testing purposes.

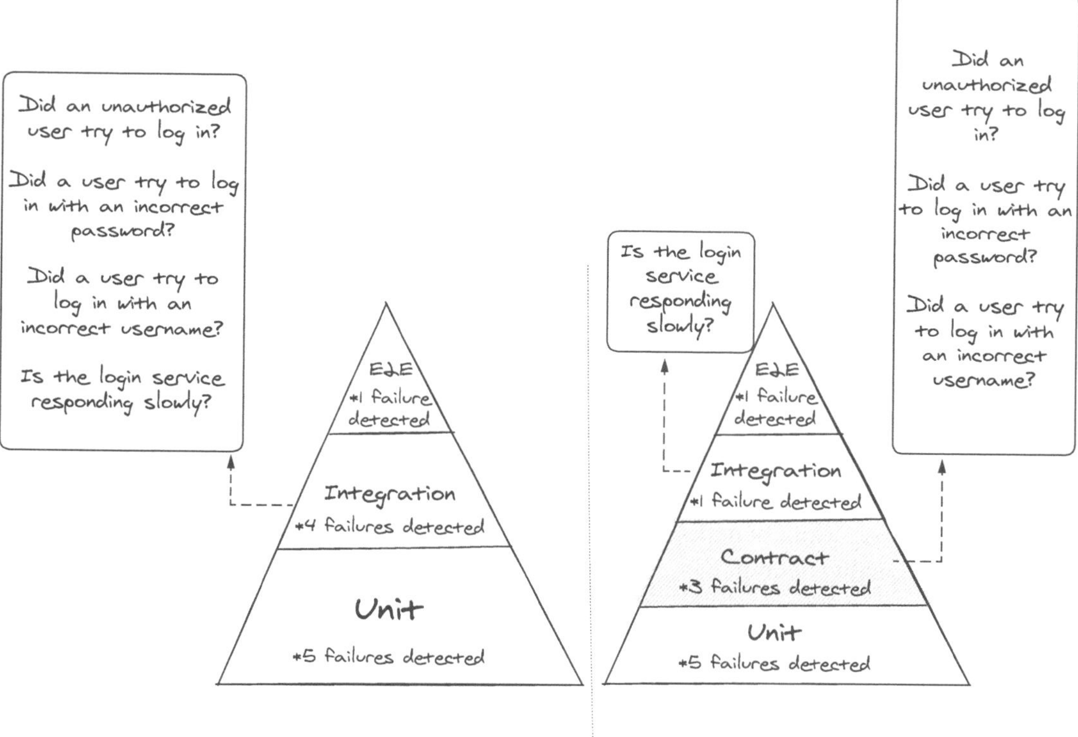

Figure 2.7 Side-by-side flow of a testing process with and without contract testing. Debugging a problem takes longer when it's detected further up the test automation pyramid.

On the other hand, when contract testing is implemented, as shown on the right side of figure 2.7, there is a better understanding of which specific reasons could cause an integration test to fail. By having contract testing in place, it proactively identifies and addresses these compatibility problems earlier in the development cycle. Consequently, the integration test only encounters problems not caught by contract testing, streamlining the debugging process and enabling a faster feedback loop. By detecting these problems earlier, organizations can prevent them from propagating to integrated environments.

If your team already has a substantial number of integration tests, many of these tests can also be shifted earlier in the development process to the contract level. However, this doesn't entirely replace the need for integration or E2E testing because contract testing doesn't verify the following:

- Environment problems caused by configuration problems
- Network problems such as timeouts or dropped requests
- Data integrity relating to how the data is stored
- The end-user workflow journey and any consequences to other parts of the system
- Misunderstandings in the business requirements

If you do want to move some of your integration or E2E tests with contract tests, a good rule of thumb is to make sure that you're only moving the tests that can be duplicated. If the test can be covered already on the contract level, this gives you increased confidence that you don't need to have the same test on the integration or E2E level. We'll explore how you can move integration and E2E tests in more detail as part of chapter 12. Specifically, section 12.3 looks at converting an integration test to a contract test, while section 12.4 looks at converting an E2E test to a contract test.

2.3 Benefits of contract testing

In chapter 1, we explained a few benefits of contract testing. However, if you're still not convinced to consider contract testing, here are additional benefits that contract testing can provide to you and your teams:

- Cost saving benefits
- Quality benefits
- Team benefits

2.3.1 Cost saving benefits

Because contract testing sits above unit testing, as represented in our revised test automation pyramid, it offers quicker execution times compared to integration and E2E tests. This means that it can provide additional cost-saving benefits in finding bugs earlier in the software development life cycle. By catching bugs at an early stage, organizations can significantly reduce the time and resources spent on subsequent debugging and fixing. Contract testing takes time, however, because of its higher complexity in the initial setup, which we'll cover as part of section 2.5.1.

An additional cost-saving aspect of contract testing lies in its close integration with the application codebase. Typically, contract tests are co-located within the same codebase as the application itself. This proximity allows developers to easily execute and validate the contract tests locally on their machines before pushing their changes to an environment. By identifying and addressing problems early on, developers can prevent bugs from propagating to production environments. This localized bug fixing not only saves time but also minimizes the effect on the overall build pipelines. The developer experience is also better because they don't need to check out a different project repository or use an unfamiliar tool because there are contract testing tools that allow them to write the tests in their programming language of choice, which is also similar to the codebase language.

We've mentioned that the cost of fixing a bug increases exponentially when it's detected later in the development process. Early bug detection through contract testing helps mitigate costs by identifying problems earlier. By catching bugs before they spread to integrated environments or production systems, organizations can minimize the ripple effects and avoid costly ramifications that may arise.

2.3.2 Quality benefits

Contract testing plays a vital role in catching misunderstandings between interconnected systems at an early stage, where the testing process is shifted earlier in the development life cycle rather than doing it on a later stage.

By identifying and addressing contract problems before they affect end users, contract testing enables a proactive and preventive testing strategy. This approach significantly reduces the likelihood of contract-related problems reaching users, resulting in enhanced software quality.

One of the notable advantages of using contract testing, particularly consumer-driven contract testing, is the ability to enforce requirements from the consumer's perspective. By defining clear contracts, the consumer sets expectations for the data providers. This approach ensures that data providers only develop and deliver functionalities that align with consumers' needs. This approach improves efficiency and reduces the risk of developing unnecessary or redundant features.

Contract testing offers benefits similar to those of test-driven development (TDD), a software development technique aimed at improving code quality. The *red-green-refactor* life cycle, illustrated in figure 2.8, outlines the process of TDD. In a nutshell, TDD starts with writing a failing test, guiding the implementation of a feature (red stage). The code is then developed to pass the test (green stage), followed by continuous refactoring to improve code quality (refactor stage).

In consumer-driven contract testing, when a consumer writes a contract test against a data service that is yet to be developed, it acts as a failing test. This failing test signals the team responsible for the data service to write the necessary code to make the contract test pass. This iterative process aligns with the principles of TDD, driving the development of the data provider service based on the requirements defined by the consumer.

Furthermore, contract testing provides a fast feedback loop, enabling continuous refactoring and improvement of the codebase. With contract testing serving as a reliable and efficient validation mechanism, the team responsible for the data service can confidently refactor their codebase while ensuring compliance with the defined contracts. This fast feedback loop enhances code quality, promotes maintainability, and allows for effective evolution of the system.

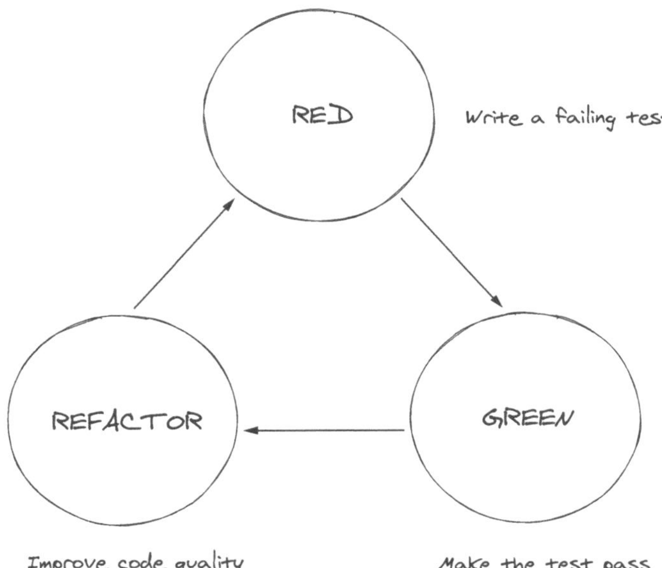

Figure 2.8 The red-green-refactor cycle of test-driven development

2.3.3 Team benefits

Contract testing enforces various teams to communicate with each other, leading to improved project delivery and ensuring a shared understanding of requirements. By enforcing communication between consumer and provider teams, contract testing mitigates the risk of misinterpretations and misunderstandings that can arise during the development process. Contract testing enables teams to work more independently and autonomously.

One of the key aspects of contract testing is the creation of contracts in a clear and unambiguous manner. These contracts outline the expected interactions and outcomes between the consumer and provider services. They are typically written in plain English, using a standardized format such as the Given-When-Then (GWT) structure, known as the Gherkin syntax, which is popularized by the introduction of behavior-driven development (BDD). By having contracts written in a clear and accessible language, contract testing can serve as a source of truth and documentation for the entire team. The contract can also help with onboarding new team members, as well as ensuring continuity and consistency in development and testing practices.

2.4 Introducing contract testing to your teams

At this point, we hope you're now convinced that contract testing is an important testing activity, especially when working with microservices architectures. Before introducing contract testing and a new tool to your team, there are a few things to consider because—let's face it—this is an additional investment. As mentioned, contract testing takes time and requires changing your team's mindset. However, if you want to take your team into the contract testing journey, it will require everyone's buy-in, which may be difficult, especially if you face initial reluctance from different teams. Here are a few things to keep in mind when introducing contract testing:

- Start with "Why"
- Start small and incrementally
- Communicate benefits and progress visibly
- Find allies or champions

2.4.1 Start with Why

Simon Sinek's book, *Start with Why* (Portfolio, 2011; https://simonsinek.com/books/start-with-why/) is a valuable resource that explores the Golden Circle model, as depicted in figure 2.9. The model emphasizes the importance of starting with the "Why" rather than the "What" when communicating the purpose and value of a business or initiative. According to Sinek, successful businesses begin by explaining why they do what they do, as opposed to solely focusing on what they offer customers. He highlights the idea that people are more compelled to engage with a business or idea when they understand the underlying motivation behind it. This principle can also be applied when introducing new testing activities, particularly contract testing.

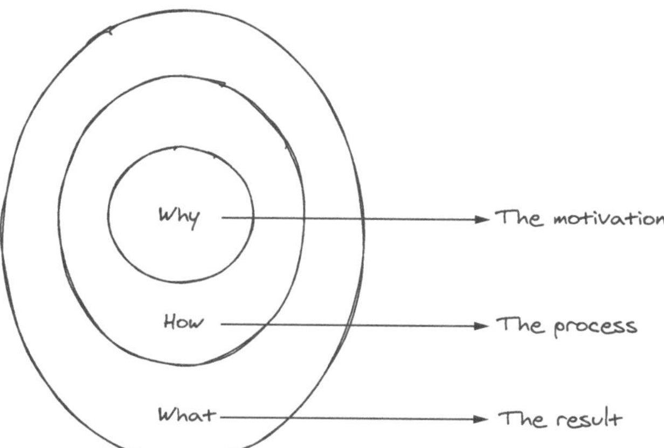

Figure 2.9 The Golden Circle model by Simon Sinek

When introducing contract testing to your teams, it's crucial to start by explaining the Why behind the initiative. Consider your motivations for adopting contract testing. Is it to replace flaky integration tests and gain confidence earlier in the development process? Is it to improve communication and collaboration with other teams? Is it to identify and address problems before they affect your users? Is it to safely deploy breaking changes to production environments? Clearly articulating your reasons for introducing contract testing will enable you to influence your teams more effectively and obtain buy-in more quickly than simply explaining the technical aspects of contract testing and the tools involved.

By focusing on the Why, you connect with your teams on a deeper level, appealing to their intrinsic motivations and shared goals. When team members understand the purpose and benefits of contract testing, they are more likely to be engaged and actively support its adoption. Starting with the Why helps create a sense of purpose, aligns the team's efforts, and fosters a shared understanding of the value that contract testing brings.

2.4.2 Start small and incrementally

Once you've secured buy-in from at least two teams, it's advisable to begin implementing contract testing gradually. A good starting point is to add one new test or convert an existing integration test to a contract test. In chapter 4 and onward, we'll provide detailed explanations of the technical implementation process, guiding you on how to write contract tests, both on the consumer and provider perspective, and integrate them into your CI pipelines.

When introducing contract testing, it's essential to consider the complexity and nature of the APIs or data services you're working with. In work projects, it's very common to work with more than one API or data service. If you're dealing with numerous data services, it may be more straightforward to begin by introducing contract testing to a brand-new API rather than starting with a legacy API that may pose more significant testing challenges. Starting with a simpler, less complex scenario allows you to familiarize yourself with the process and gain confidence before tackling more complex systems.

Chapter 10 will delve into the setup required to establish a fully automated contract testing process within your CI pipelines. It's important to note that this setup may involve various configurations and integrations that could take some time. To ensure a smooth transition and avoid overwhelming the team, we advise starting incrementally, even if it means triggering the contract testing job manually in the initial stages from both the consumer and provider pipelines.

Taking an incremental approach allows you to gradually build up your contract testing infrastructure, gain experience, learn from any mistakes, and address any challenges that could arise. It gives you the opportunity to validate the effectiveness of contract testing in your specific context and make necessary adjustments along the way.

2.4.3 Communicate benefits and progress visibly

To increase buy-in and support for contract testing, it's crucial to communicate the benefits clearly to stakeholders and decision-makers. When presenting the case for contract testing, it's valuable to highlight how contract testing complements existing quality and testing strategies. Emphasize how contract testing can enhance the overall effectiveness of testing efforts and contribute to improved software quality.

Documenting the process and learnings of your contract testing journey is highly recommended. By documenting your experiences, challenges, and successes, you create a valuable resource that can be shared with other teams who are considering or are interested in contract testing. This documentation serves as a knowledge base, enabling teams to learn from your experiences, understand the benefits, and navigate potential pitfalls more effectively.

In one of the author's previous projects, incorporating contract testing progress updates into regular team communication, such as during show-and-tells or project updates, was highly effective. Contract testing started as an initiative from one team, but it later expanded to cover multiple teams, with teams from other business domains also getting interested. By visibly demonstrating the improvements and outcomes achieved through contract testing, it also attracted the attention of the leadership team and other stakeholders. Sharing success stories, showcasing measurable improvements, and highlighting the value brought by contract testing can help garner support and position it as a standard practice for testing APIs.

2.4.4 *Find allies or champions*

When introducing contract testing or any new testing activity, having allies or champions who are willing to embark on the contract testing journey with you is crucial. Finding individuals within your team who are open to collaboration and eager to explore new approaches to testing sets a solid foundation for successful adoption. These allies or champions will help drive the implementation of contract testing and inspire others to join the cause.

Starting the process of collaboration begins by identifying team members who are willing to try contract testing. Seek out individuals who are open-minded, enthusiastic about improving testing practices, and willing to embrace change. These team members can become your core group of advocates and collaborators in championing the adoption of contract testing.

To gain support from the wider team, it's essential to effectively communicate the reasons behind the decision to introduce contract testing. Clearly articulate the benefits of contract testing and demonstrate how contract testing addresses existing pain points and resolves common integration challenges. When team members understand the purpose and advantages of contract testing, they are more likely to join the cause and become allies or champions themselves.

In addition to communicating the benefits, create a safe environment that encourages open dialogue and fosters a culture of collaboration. Provide opportunities for team members to share their thoughts, concerns, and ideas about contract testing. Encourage discussion and actively listen to their perspectives. By engaging in meaningful conversations and considering their viewpoints, you can gain more allies and champions for the contract testing journey.

Finally, you can also seek the support of the wider community. The more you engage with the community, the more you also improve your knowledge about contract testing in general. Communities such as the Ministry of Testing (www.ministryoftesting.com/) and Pact (https://docs.pact.io/help) have resources related to contract testing. There are also tons of online or in-person talks, tutorials, blog posts, or videos shared by other professionals about contract testing. Here are some examples:

- Bas Dijkstra's series of article about contract testing: https://mng.bz/86gP
- Marie Cruz's article on contract testing: https://mng.bz/EO6J
- Lewis Prescott's podcast on contract testing: www.pactman.co.uk/contract-testing-podcast

2.5 Challenges with contract testing

While contract testing offers numerous benefits to software development teams, it's important to acknowledge that it also presents challenges. Understanding and addressing these challenges is crucial for a successful implementation and for reaping the full advantages of contract testing. In this section, we'll discuss some of the common challenges associated with contract testing. Contract testing

- takes time.
- requires a mindset shift.
- requires a lot of buy-in.
- is more technical than other testing activities.
- is difficult to do when there are external teams involved.

2.5.1 Contract testing takes time

From our experience working as software testers, implementing contract testing takes longer than integration or E2E testing. There is a higher bar for adoption to put contract testing into place because of its complexity in the initial setup, which involves setting up the necessary build pipelines, developing contract tests from both the consumer and provider, and integrating them into the development and testing processes. It's crucial to factor in this investment and plan accordingly to ensure a smooth transition.

If we compare the time and effort required for contract tests and E2E tests, as shown in figure 2.10, you can see that while contract tests require more effort, you might not see the benefits immediately. However, contract tests are easier to maintain once this is in place, and the effort over time will decrease. In contrast, E2E tests might be easier to set up initially, but as time progresses and the number of E2E tests increase, it becomes increasingly difficult to maintain and therefore requires a high level of effort the longer you rely on these tests.

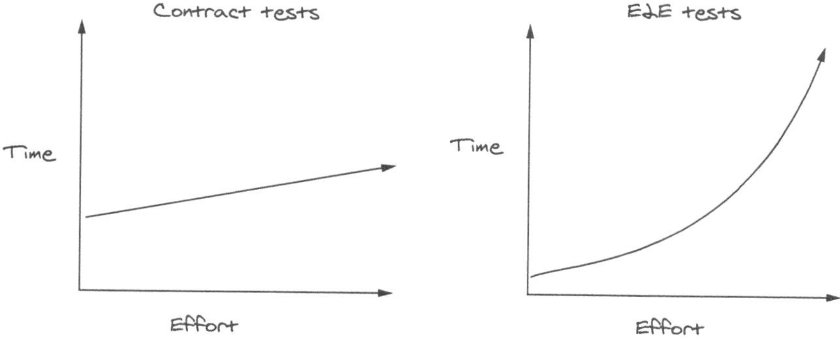

Figure 2.10 The time and effort required for contract tests vs. E2E tests. More time and effort are required for contract tests, but, over time, the effort is minimal compared to E2E tests.

2.5.2 Contract testing requires a mindset shift

Contract testing requires a shift in the team's mindset, encouraging a more collaborative and communicative approach. Contract testing promotes a shared responsibility for ensuring system compatibility, and developers are highly encouraged to write or update any contract tests. If only software testers are writing the contract tests and playing catch-up with the feature that is already implemented, this won't scale over time. Contract testing should be factored in at the same time the code is being developed.

Contract testing also challenges traditional thinking of how a data service or API is to be developed. Because contract testing is closely linked to a test-driven approach, teams need to think first what the consumers need from their API rather than starting the development of what an API can do and telling consumers about it afterward. This promotes teams to think from their users' perspectives as early as possible, ultimately improving the user experience.

2.5.3 Lack of buy-in

Contract testing requires a lot of collaboration across different teams. Therefore, getting everyone to contribute might be more difficult because it takes time to see the value of contract testing. To mitigate this, it's important that you address concerns, provide training and support, and create an environment that encourages open communication and shared responsibility.

As we mentioned, contract testing requires at least two teams—the consumer and the provider. If only one team is invested, then contract testing won't succeed. To avoid this situation, implement our suggestions from section 2.4. Overcoming any resistance to change and fostering a culture of collaboration and trust are essential for successful adoption.

2.5.4 More technical than other testing activities

Based on our experience, establishing a contract testing framework demands additional technical skills compared to writing integration or E2E tests. Contract tests are run like traditional unit tests, which are usually engineered by developers. Contract testing tools, such as Pact, often entail a steeper learning curve compared to other test automation frameworks. To fully harness the benefits of contract testing, it's necessary to grasp and implement key Pact concepts such as can-i-deploy, webhooks, and versioning, among others. In chapter 8, we'll guide you through the implementation of these advanced concepts, ensuring a comprehensive understanding of their usage and advantages.

Setting up a contract testing framework with tools such as Pact requires a solid understanding of the underlying concepts and practices specific to contract testing. While writing integration or E2E tests primarily revolves around interacting with the application interfaces, contract testing focuses on defining and validating the contracts between consumer and provider components. This distinction requires additional knowledge and familiarity with contract testing principles.

As a popular contract testing tool, Pact also provides advanced features and functionalities that require a deeper level of comprehension. Concepts such as *can-i-deploy* allow teams to determine whether a change to a consumer or provider system adheres to the existing contract, enabling confident deployment decisions. *Webhooks* facilitate real-time communication between consumer and provider systems, supporting changes to contract testing scenarios. *Versioning* ensures compatibility and contract management when systems evolve over time.

To fully use the benefits of contract testing and Pact, it's crucial to become proficient in implementing these advanced concepts. Chapter 8 serves as a comprehensive guide, walking you through the step-by-step implementation of these advanced features. We'll provide practical examples, explanations, and best practices to guide you with the necessary skills and understanding.

2.5.5 Difficult when there are external teams

Implementing contract testing becomes much easier when both consumer and provider teams are internal to the company. However, in many scenarios, collaborations involve external teams. This presents a challenge for contract testing, particularly when the data provider(s) are third-party or external services.

When dealing with external teams or third-party data providers, the process of implementing contract testing encounters additional complexities. External teams often operate independently and have their own established testing practices. They might also argue that they have a solid testing strategy in place already. Convincing them to adopt contract testing and integrate provider tests into their pipelines requires effective communication, collaboration, and an understanding of their existing workflows and concerns. They may also be reluctant to include provider tests in their CI pipelines due to factors such as time constraints, lack of resource allocation, and priority problems. Fortunately, the good news is that this challenge can be overcome through the adoption of bi-directional contract testing, a topic we'll delve into further in chapter 11.

Remember, introducing any new testing activity or tool requires patience, persistence, and clear communication. Engage your team members, address their concerns, and make sure to highlight the advantages of contract testing, but also be transparent about the challenges that come with contract testing.

2.6 A practical guide on introducing contract testing to projects

At this point, let's say you have a solid foundation on what contract testing is and have also successfully convinced your teams to try out contract testing. You understand the theory behind contract testing, but you still want a how-to guide to get started. Where to start, which tool to choose, and how to get there aren't always straightforward, especially if you don't already have much experience in contract testing. To help you lay out the plan for your contract testing journey, we've come up with the following high-level guide to help you incorporate contract testing into your existing and/or new projects:

- Research what tools to use.
- Identify your consumers and providers.
- Define the contract.
- Write a basic consumer and provider test.
- Add contract testing to your continuous integration/continuous delivery (CI/CD) pipelines.

2.6.1 Research what tools to use

There are a few tools that you can use to implement contract testing, which we'll cover in chapter 3, section 3.6. It's important to research how each tool can help you solve a problem rather than choosing a tool based on its popularity and adoption. While we focus on Pact in this book, it might be worthwhile to research other contract testing tools to see if they fit your context better. The following questions can be a starting point when looking for a contract testing tool:

- Can the tool support the programming language that your codebase is also using? We believe contract tests should be co-located in the consumer and provider codebase, so writing them in the same language increases their adoption.
- Can the tool support both the consumer and provider side adequately?
- Can the tool support different messages or communication types, for example, REST, GraphQL, and Kafka?
- Can the tool produce a contract that is generated from code instead of generating it outside the code?

- Are you looking at a more consumer-driven or provider-driven workflow? Some contract testing tools are more consumer-driven, while others are provider-driven.
- Do you want a contract testing tool that allows you to store the contracts on your own self-hosted infrastructure or to a fully managed cloud infrastructure?
- Are you looking for a tool that can also manage contract versions automatically?
- Can the tool integrate seamlessly in a CI pipeline?

By understanding the testing and technical requirements, you can then focus on how a tool can help you address their needs.

2.6.2 Identify your consumers and providers

Start by identifying who your consumers and providers are. If you're working on a team responsible for a public-facing website, then your team is a good candidate to be a consumer. From a consumer perspective, identify various APIs or data providers your website communicates with, and start with one of them. It's recommended to focus on one provider at a time and make sure that they are also willing to implement provider tests from their side because they need to verify the contract that you'll generate.

On the other hand, if you're working on a team responsible for providing data, your team is a good candidate to be a provider. Start speaking to one of your consumers and letting them know you're on board with verifying the contract tests.

It's also recommended to find allies or champions from both the consumer and provider teams so they can champion the idea of contract testing and communicate the work that will need to happen.

2.6.3 Define the contract

The contract process is slightly different in contract testing, especially in consumer-driven contract testing. The consumer defines the contract, which details the expectations they require from the provider. This also enforces an agreement going forward that the provider must meet the expectations defined by the consumer.

At this stage, it's perfectly fine to define the initial contract manually. For now, you can store this in a location that your team can access or a Microsoft Word document—whichever works for you. At this stage, just write the minimal contract that is needed by the consumer and provider. We'll automate the generation of the contract at a later stage when you write the consumer contract test, but it's still handy to have an initial understanding of how the consumer and provider will interact. An example contract is shown here:

ExampleApp and User API contract
  Consumer: ExampleApp
  Provider: User API

Given there is an "ExampleApp" that uses "User API"
When it sends a request to "/user/marie"
Then the "User API" should respond with a status code of 200
And the "User API" should return the following:
- ID (integer)
- Full name (string)
- Username (string)

Remember that the contract should only include the consumer expectations from the provider. It should check the format or the structure of the response and verify if there are any misunderstandings between a consumer and a provider. Your contract shouldn't cover any business logic or any side effects that might happen on other systems.

2.6.4 Write a basic consumer and provider contract test

Once you have a basic contract in place, it's time to write the consumer and provider test. We recommend using the same programming language used by the consumer and provider codebase for the contract test. Chapters 4 to 8 cover how to write contract tests for different types of consumers and providers. For now, the high-level contract testing process between a consumer and a provider is illustrated in figure 2.11.

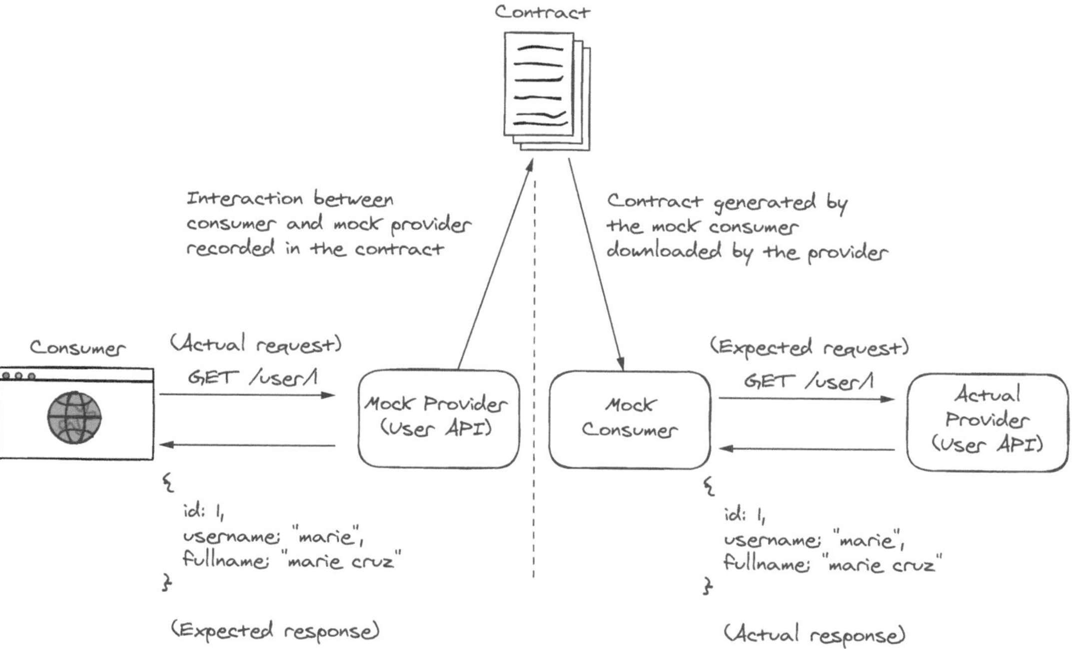

Figure 2.11 The contract testing process between a consumer and a provider

The illustration highlights how the interaction between a consumer and a provider is verified safely and reliably via a shared contract instead of needing to communicate with one another. This shows why contract testing offers the same faster execution as unit testing.

2.6.5 Add contract testing to your CI/CD pipelines

Once you've written your first consumer and provider tests and you're able to verify the interaction successfully by triggering the test locally, the next step is to add both the consumer and provider contract tests as part of your CI/CD pipelines so that the tests are triggered by new changes that respective teams are working on. Depending on which CI/CD pipelines you're using, the syntax of setting these tests up to run will be slightly different, but the workflow should remain the same.

Let's look at a basic contract testing workflow in your CI/CD, with manual triggers of the provider verification, which you can see in figure 2.12. We'll cover manual triggers for now to get you started, but we'll introduce you to an automatic trigger pipeline in chapter 10.

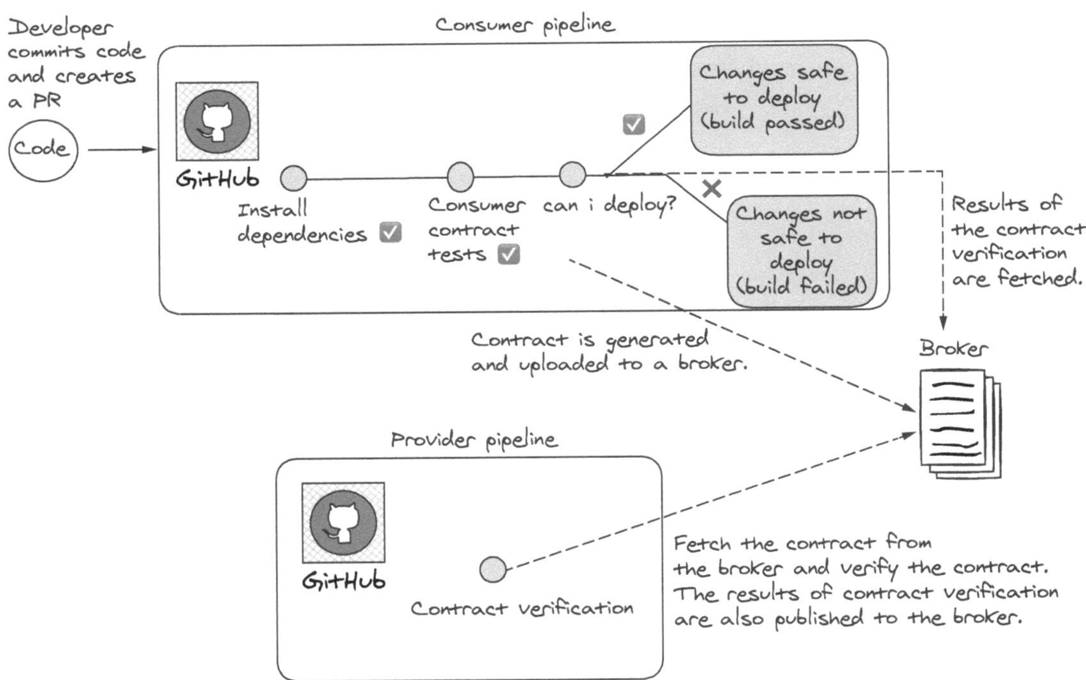

Figure 2.12 A basic consumer pipeline workflow that also includes a manual job for triggering contract verification on the provider pipeline

Let's break down what is happening here:

1. A developer pushes their code and creates a pull request on the consumer codebase.
2. The consumer contract test is triggered, and the consumer uploads the contract to a central place, called a broker, that the provider can also access.
3. The provider contract test is triggered manually from the provider pipeline. The provider retrieves the contract, replays the interactions, and verifies if the expected responses match the actual responses they provide.
4. If the provider verification is successful, the results of the verification are published, and the developer working on the consumer codebase gets feedback that their changes are safe to be deployed.
5. If the provider verification is unsuccessful, then the test fails. The developer working on the consumer codebase gets feedback that their changes aren't safe to be deployed.
6. The developer fixes the problem, and the steps are repeated again until the provider verification is successful.

From a provider pipeline, a basic contract testing workflow can look like the illustration in figure 2.13.

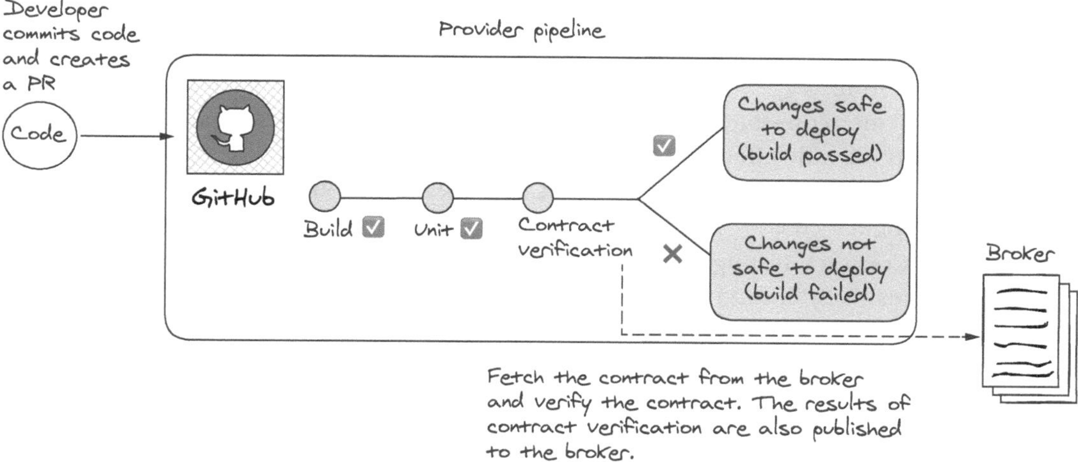

Figure 2.13 A basic provider pipeline workflow

Let's break down again what is happening here:

1. A developer pushes their code and creates a pull request on the provider codebase.

2. The provider contract verification test is triggered automatically. The provider retrieves the contract from a broker, replays the interactions, and verifies if the expected responses match the actual responses they provide.
3. If the provider verification is successful, the results of the verification are published, and the developer working on the provider codebase gets feedback that their changes are safe to be deployed.
4. If the provider verification is unsuccessful, then the test fails, and the changes can't be deployed.
5. The developer fixes the problem, and the steps are repeated again until the provider verification is successful.

Adding contract testing to your CI/CD pipelines requires a few configurations, especially if you want to trigger the provider job automatically every time there are contract changes published by the consumer.

It's recommended to continuously improve this process and introduce the concepts of webhooks, versioning, and environments incrementally, which we'll cover in more detail as part of chapter 10.

Summary

- Contract testing requires two sets of tests: one from the consumer and one from the provider. Without either of them, contract testing won't give you any real benefits.
- Contract testing combines the best qualities of unit testing and integration testing.
- Contract testing doesn't replace integration or E2E tests because it doesn't verify any side effects on the system's overall behavior.
- The red-green-refactor life cycle of TDD can also be likened to a contract testing life cycle.
- Contract testing improves the communication process between different teams by enforcing that any contract changes are verified before deploying to production.
- To get buy-in from the team, start with communicating why contract testing is needed.
- Start small by converting one integration test to a contract test and then continuously improve.
- Communicate the benefits and progress of your contract testing journey.
- Contract testing requires a team effort, so find allies or champions to help you.
- While there are many benefits, contract testing takes time and effort, so it might be challenging to implement it without the proper education.
- Contract testing is a highly technical activity and requires an understanding of advanced concepts not usually present in integration or E2E testing.

- Contract testing can be difficult to implement when you work with third-party or external services.
- When introducing contract testing, make sure to research the right tools for your context. Define the contract that needs to be adhered to by both consumer and provider, and plan your first test. Once you've written a small consumer and provider test, integrate them to a CI/CD pipeline and continuously make improvements as you go along.

3 A technical overview of contract testing

This chapter covers

- Defining consumers, providers, contracts, and contract brokers
- Contract testing life cycle
- Contract testing tools
- Contract testing approaches
- Communication types supported by contract testing

Before we walk through the implementation steps of contract tests (in later chapters), we'll first introduce the terminology and tooling. This chapter discusses what consumers and providers are in relation to software development. In addition, before writing contract test code, you must start conversations with key stakeholders regarding where to store the contracts.

In this chapter, we explain the core contract testing concepts. Then, we talk about deciding which contract testing approach to take. We cover the two approaches offered within the contract testing domain: consumer-driven contract testing (CDCT), often referred to as the traditional approach, and provider-driven contract testing (PDCT). We describe the pros and cons of CDCT and PDCT, guiding you to the best approach in your context.

Throughout the chapter, we compare contract testing to integration testing; therefore, a basic understanding or previous experience in the integration testing area is beneficial. Even though contract testing doesn't replace integration testing completely, comparing the two helps us understand the fundamental concepts of contract testing. Lewis Prescott (one of the authors) describes contract testing as flipping integration testing upside down, like reversing the integration testing process. The usual approach within integration testing is for the service team, for example, the API service, to implement the tests during the development process. Once the tests have passed, the API is deployed to an integration environment so that other teams can check if their integration will work successfully. I'm sure if you have experience in this, then you've run into challenges. At numerous conferences and meetups, we've asked this very question, with people stating challenges such as the following:

- Flaky dependencies, including third-party dependencies
- Environment setup and maintenance problems
- Bad seed data
- Environments down/unreliable

In an ideal world, if there were no budget constraints and a low level of complexity to spin up test environments, teams would use infrastructure as code or spin up the app within a local container. However, in our experience, development teams deal with the just-mentioned integration problems in several ways.

The first option is for teams to move away from the integration environment, add component tests that mock out the third-party dependencies, and remove the reliance on an unreliable environment. For example, teams containerize an integration environment on-demand using something like Docker. Containerized environments allow teams to test internally and in isolation, limiting the scope of their integration tests.

In the opposite direction to on-demand environments, we see teams focus on the fully integrated environment. Integration testing against a fully integrated environment gives the team the most confidence and represents a scenario closer to production. Due to the challenges around maintenance and expense with fully integrated environments, teams don't see the mocking option as a feasible solution. The confidence teams gain from a realistic environment setup outweighs the high maintenance and downtime.

However, we don't live in an ideal world because we don't all have limitless budgets or endless time to deliver the perfect solutions, so people turn to contract testing as a solution. Contract testing reduces the effort required compared with the first option and simulates the integration environment, retaining the confidence level from the second option.

We also walk through the technical details of the contract testing life cycle, particularly with the CDCT approach. While reading about the life cycle, also think about the human element of each step within software development, that is, who the people involved in the process are and what type of conversations you would have at each stage. The reason for mentioning human interactions is that contract testing is a great conversation starter for teams when there is an integration problem. The results from contract tests give teams the equivalent of a stack trace between systems.

Say we have a web application, and put yourself in the shoes of a team in charge. The team experienced an integration problem in the web application. For example, a data field in the response data has gone missing. A web developer starts by digging into their code to check that they are using the correct version of the API. Then, they check how they constructed the request and that everything has stayed the same. They can't see any changes to the specific HTTP request and confirm the API version. The only option left is for them to message the team who owns the API service to understand why the field has disappeared. The API team also doesn't think they have changed that HTTP response. However, they looked through their recent commits to find a trivial change has been made where the field naming convention has been changed from camel case to snake case to align with the existing API documentation. The API developer remembers sending technology-wide emails to notify the teams of the breaking change, but the web developer must not have seen the memo.

NOTE The lesson of this story is that humans will make mistakes, especially regarding communication. Any tools and processes enabling better communication can only be good.

This chapter also mentions different communication types, including API, GraphQL, and event-driven messaging. Contract testing is commonly associated with APIs but isn't applicable only to REST APIs. It also supports GraphQL-style and messages architecture. The same concepts apply to each communication type. Therefore, once you understand the core concepts described in this chapter, we suggest skipping to the chapter that covers your relevant kind of implementation.

3.1 What is a consumer?

Contract testing is built around the consumer and puts more control over their role than traditional integration testing. So, who is the consumer?

In day-to-day life, when you think about the consumer, what do you think about? Simply put, a *consumer* is a user of a product or a service. Think about all the products and services you use as a consumer, for example, the fridge and freezer that stores your food and the insurance policy you have to protect those products. Each person may use their products slightly differently or have different uses for their products. Fridges come in all different shapes and sizes, and many include freezer compartments. For example, one consumer may purchase a fridge to store their wine with a small freezer compartment for the ice. At the same time, another consumer buys a fridge freezer to store all their fresh ingredients and then needs the freezer to store the leftovers for reheating another time. The consumer is no different in software.

The consumer is usually a web or mobile app making requests to a backend service. However, a consumer can also be a service calling another backend service.

DEFINITION In terms of software, a consumer is anything that makes a request for another service whether to retrieve data, post an update, or consume an event.

The consumer-driven approach contains the word consumer because the consumer is driving the contract. For example, the frontend web application controls the user experience in a web application requesting user login data. Therefore, the web application dictates what data it requires to surface this information to the user. Of course, the service returning the data can input the type and structure of the data. However, in the actual user experience, the user doesn't care about how the data is structured. All they care about is being able to log in via the web application, which is why the consumer is so integral and should influence the expected data response. As shown in figure 3.1, the consumer request and expected response sets the data within the contract.

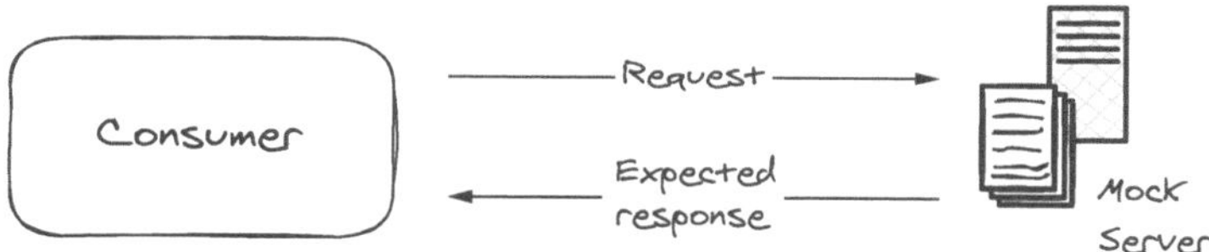

Figure 3.1 The consumer sets up request and response in the form of a contract, which gets created within a mock server.

Being the consumer in contract testing, in our experience, comes with its challenges as the driving force for the whole contract testing process. You have to be able to persuade the other teams to buy into the process. As the consumer, you can create the contract and publish it to the contract broker, but often, you depend on multiple teams to benefit from contract testing. In summary, a consumer is a service user that requests data from a service and is the driving force of contract testing.

3.2 What is a provider?

A *provider* is a "person or thing that provides" (https://mng.bz/NBaD). Using our retail consumer analogy from the previous section, an example of a provider is the energy supplier that provides the energy to power the fridge. The energy provider must be compatible with all the different types of consumer products, even though each product may have a different power usage or even different sockets.

On the other side of the request is a service collating and returning the relevant data. The provider, as described, "provides" some data to consumers. As shown in figure 3.2, the provider runs the consumer request against their local service and verifies the response.

In a CDCT approach, the consumer will mock out the provider, and the provider mocks out their downstream dependencies. The provider must add a test pointing to the consumer within the contract testing process and will automatically get any updates

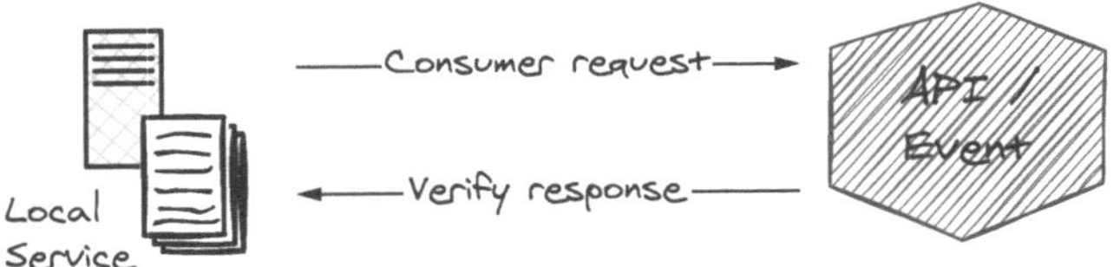

Figure 3.2 A provider replays the contract request and verifies the expected response against the local running service.

if they point to the latest version of the consumer contract. Teams will discuss test failures; either the consumer changes their interaction, or the provider changes their implementation. In summary, a provider makes a service available to someone who needs it, replays requests for their service, and becomes an ambassador for contract testing across the organization.

3.3 What is a contract?

Now, we've spoken a lot about the contract that sits between the consumer and the provider. However, we haven't described precisely what the contract is yet. A *contract* is "a legal document that states and explains a formal agreement between two different people or groups" (https://mng.bz/lrBy). The same applies within software development, apart from being a legal document. However, some engineers may hold you to the same level of demands. In addition, there is another layer in the software—the application and service involved—but people or groups still author these, so it's a pretty good definition in this context.

What's important to differentiate is the difference between a contract and a schema. A *schema* is as "an outline of a plan or theory" (https://mng.bz/Dp5E). As the definition suggests, a schema provides the outline, which will be defined in the planning phase before development starts so that both parties work toward the same schema definition using tools such as JSON Schema (https://json-schema.org/). A schema tool facilitates describing the JSON's structure and any rules and constraints to validate the data up front. It sounds very similar to contracts, right? However, the difference with contracts here is that a schema can't tell you how consumers use it and what fields aren't used. In addition, schemas require teams to create a mechanism for change and evolution. Contract testing inherently captures breaking changes to ensure no consumers get left behind.

The contract content contains request and response data and all the details in the contract testing context. The contract also includes the following:

- The name of the consumer and provider
- Any state or data requirements for the request
- Any matching rules for dynamic values
- A unique contract version
- Environment and deployment tags

Listing 3.1 shows a contract example for a login scenario.

Listing 3.1 Pact contract example

```
"consumer": {                  <--+
"name": "Web"                     |  Participants
},                                |
"provider": {                  <--+
    "name": "API"
},
"interactions": [           <-- Set of interactions
{
    "description": "GET user token",
    "providerState": "user authentication setup",
    "request": {
      "method": "GET",
      "path": "/token/1234",
      "headers": {
        "Accept": "application/json, text/plain, */*"
      }
     },
    "response": {
      "status": 200,
    "headers": {
        "Content-Type": "application/json"
      },
      "body": {
        "token": "bearer xxx"
      },
    "matchingRules": {          <--+ Matching rules to
      "$.body.token": {            | allow for more flexible
        "match": "type"            | matching of data
      }
    }
  }
}
],
  "metadata": {
    "pactSpecification": {
      "version": "4.0"
    }
  }
}
```

As shown in the JSON example, the contract has the names of both the consumer and provider, and you should start thinking about a naming convention for these, as the consumer and provider use these throughout the process. The contract also includes interactions, which lists all the information related to the request, expected response, description, provider states (covered in chapter 6), and matching rules (covered in chapter 4). The contract also includes the metadata associated with the Pact framework only.

In summary, a contract is a JSON object containing consumer and provider interactions, outlining the request details and expected response data, as well as the data setup details and dynamic response data rules.

3.4 What is a contract broker?

Where do the contracts get stored? Sharing the contracts between repositories and potentially different repository providers means there needs to be a central place to store the contracts. A *broker* is "a person who talks to opposing sides, especially governments, making arrangements for them or bringing disagreements to an end" (https://mng.bz/BgjJ).

Without a broker, passing around contracts can be tricky because of the different versions caused by code changes. Even if the contracts live in source control, a workflow must be active to notify other teams of updates, and there should also be a consistent storage structure.

Using the Pact Broker as an example, its purpose isn't to arrange but to organize and facilitate the contract life cycle, facilitating the sharing process of contracts among multiple software development teams. The broker builds the network of connections between teams and different data requirements from each other. In a CDCT approach, the consumer pushes their contract containing the version and other metadata up to the broker. The metadata allows the provider to pull down the contract version they need to verify. As shown in figure 3.3, the broker holds the information about the different consumers and providers, such as when the latest contract was published, webhook status, and when the provider last verified the contract.

Consumer ⇅	Provider ⇅		Latest pact published	Webhook status	Last verified	
GDS API Adapters	Account API		27 days ago	Create		···
GDS API Adapters	Asset Manager		27 days ago	Create		···
GDS API Adapters	Bank Holidays API		27 days ago	Create		···
GDS API Adapters	Collections Organisation API		27 days ago	Create		···
GDS API Adapters	Email Alert API		4 days ago	Create		···
GDS API Adapters	Imminence API		4 days ago	Create		···
GDS API Adapters	Link Checker API		27 days ago	Create		···
GDS API Adapters	Locations API		27 days ago	Create		···
GDS API Adapters	Publishing API		27 days ago	Create		···
Publishing API	Content Store		26 days ago	Create		···

Figure 3.3 A public version of Pact Broker provided by the UK Government (https://mng.bz/dZlQ) shows a real example of Pact Broker in use.

To enable consumers and providers to check if they can safely deploy their changes to production, Pact provides a command-line interface (CLI) tool called can-i-deploy, which enables consumers and providers to query the broker to determine the verification status of the contract. The broker is effectively cementing the agreement between a consumer and provider. The broker can also be seen as an alerting system that triggers conversations between consumers and providers when there are failures.

A real example illustrated in figure 3.4 shows how different versions of the API are used by different consumers at a large online fashion retailer. Both consumers were using an API endpoint that returned customer data. The mobile application consumes version 2 of the API, whereas the legacy desktop application still uses version 1 of the API. The customer support team responsible for the legacy desktop application had a release cycle that was six months long, and they had never prioritized migrating to version 2 of the customer data API service. The provider team had one core model, shared between version 1 and version 2, to avoid duplicate code and reduce the development time of updating two versions of the same API. When they identified that they were get-

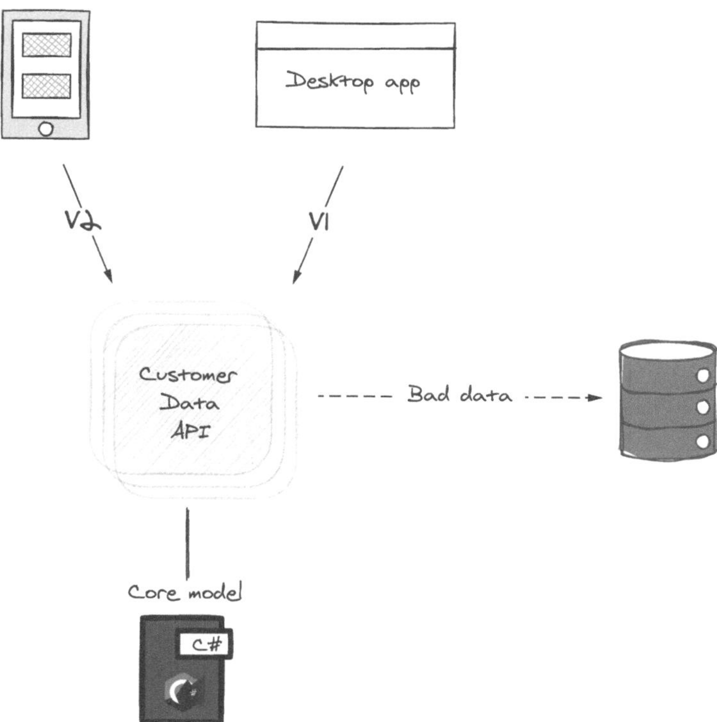

Figure 3.4 The mobile application consumes customer data API version 2, and the desktop application consumes customer data API version 1. The customer data API uses the core C# model, causing bad data in the customer database.

ting bad data into the customer database, they wanted to stop this by changing one of the fields to mandatory. The code changes were made, and tests within the API project now conform to the new mandatory field. However, the legacy desktop application wasn't available in the test environment as the integration wasn't working, and the release date was a couple of months away, so no one was looking into it. The legacy desktop application started erroring when releasing the API in production with the core model updates. Due to the API now requiring a mandatory field, their `PUT` request failed because it didn't contain this data. Due to the six-month release cycle of the legacy desktop application, the API team had to revert the changes and only change version 2.

This scenario signifies the importance of understanding all your consumers, especially those who can't quickly fix problems when they occur. In summary, a broker stores contracts centrally for consumers and providers to access, holds the status of the contract based on the version, and shows all the different consumer relationships for providers.

3.5 Consumer-driven contract testing life cycle

To introduce the core concepts of contract testing, we describe the life cycle of the CDCT approach. The example uses JavaScript and Java but applies to all other language combinations. Figure 3.5 shows the CDCT approach, and the process is also explained in the following steps:

1. The consumer maintaining a JavaScript application publishes the contract to a broker.
2. The provider maintaining a Java API or event service pulls down and verifies the contract from the broker.

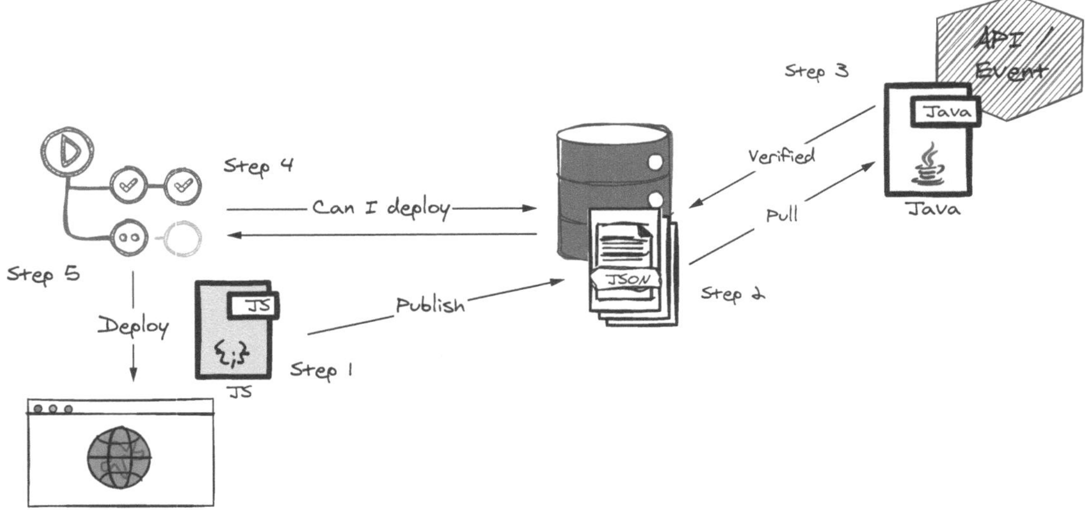

Figure 3.5 CDCT life cycle from a JavaScript web application, through the broker to Java API or event service, and finally using the can-i-deploy tool to verify the changes in the web application

3. The verification status is updated in the broker.
4. The consumer checks the contract verification status in the broker using the can-i-deploy tool.
5. The consumer deploys the changes.

The first step in the contract testing life cycle is to create the contract, whether generated from a web application, mobile application, or another service. The contract is generated from test code written in the consumer code and then published to the broker, which can also contain other consumer contracts, as shown in figure 3.6.

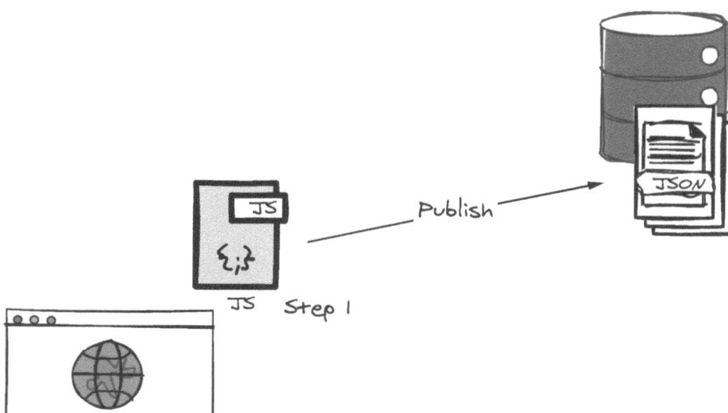

Figure 3.6 The contract is generated from the JavaScript test code and published to the broker.

Now that the contracts are available within the broker, the next step is for the provider to respond, as shown in figure 3.7. In this example, the provider pulls down the contract JSON document from the broker and replays the requests against their local service. When the provider tests run as part of a continuous integration (CI) pipeline, the contracts become successfully verified if there are no problems with consumer expectations and if the verification status for the specific version changes due to deployment is updated in the broker.

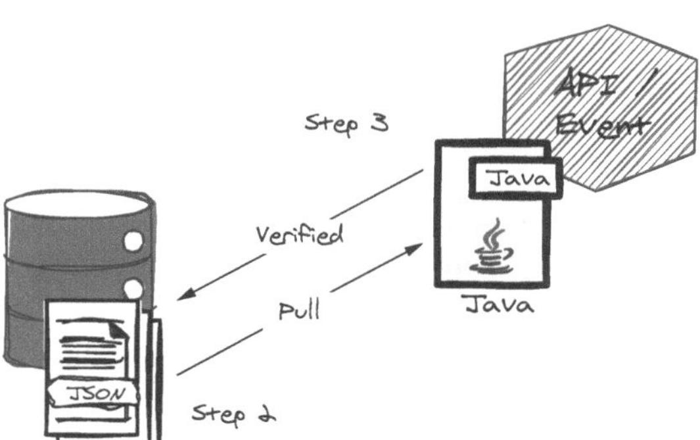

Figure 3.7 The provider Java test code verifies the contract and publishes the result to the broker.

Finally, we return to the consumer that created the contract. As part of the final step during the deployment of the JavaScript application CI pipeline, they check the broker to determine whether they can deploy their changes safely using the can-i-deploy tool, as shown in figure 3.8. The tool checks the verification status on the contract, ensuring that the Java API or event service has confirmed that their HTTP request is valid and matches the response they expected. Once the changes are confirmed, the consumer deploys the changes.

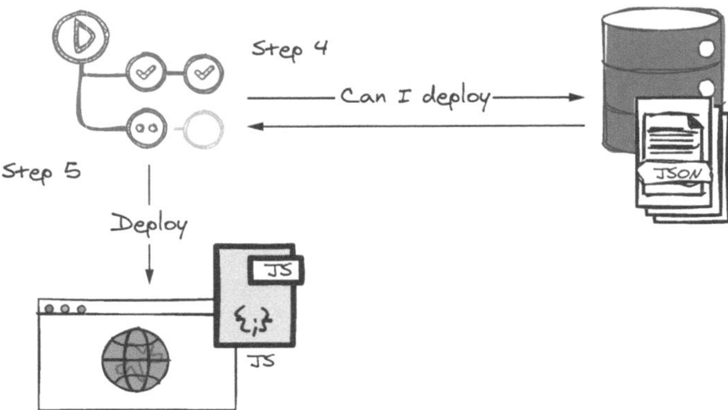

Figure 3.8 The consumer CI pipeline checks the contract status in the broker and can deploy the new changes to their application.

A few steps are involved in rolling out contract testing, which could seem daunting. However, each step involved within the life cycle in isolation is simple. Much of the complexity related to the contract testing process comes down to communication and collaboration. Imagine how cumbersome the steps described would be without a tool or framework to facilitate the process. For example, sharing contracts between development teams means someone needs to manage access to contracts between potentially many development teams. The contracts would live in source control, where the contracts need to be organized efficiently within the different project repositories. Luckily, this has already been solved by some incredible people at Pact (our thanks to the DiUS team, notably Ron Holshausen, Brent Snook, and Beth Skurrie, for making it happen in 2013 [https://docs.pact.io/history]).

The contract testing life cycle makes much sense when considering the challenges of modern software development, especially in microservices architecture. This type of architecture lends itself to siloed, distributed teams where communication isn't as accessible due to specific barriers. Barriers include physical location, separate backlogs of work, and code repositories. Now, with contract testing, teams can work in parallel when a contract is defined up front. Again, communication, as contract testing, helps facilitate intricate conversations about contract versions and backward compatibility.

3.6 Contract testing tools

Tooling is always a difficult decision in software, and deciding which tool is best for your context, the best documentation, and the shallowest learning curve are all key points to consider.

The beauty of contract testing is that the proposed process can be engineered with limited tooling. A custom solution was created to enable the contract testing life cycle in one of the author's projects. The architecture involved integrating with Oracle database processes, and the tricky part of implementing contract testing within this solution was that we were trying to confirm that the multiple processes were finished successfully. The solution can be explained in the following steps and also shown in figure 3.9:

1. A web application, which is the consumer, triggers a message that gets put on a queue.
2. The message content published on the queue acts as a contract and is stored in a GitHub repository to share with the database service team.
3. The database team posts the message contract onto their queue from the provider side, triggering the database processes.
4. Finally, the database is polled with a Status column indicating whether the message passed successfully.

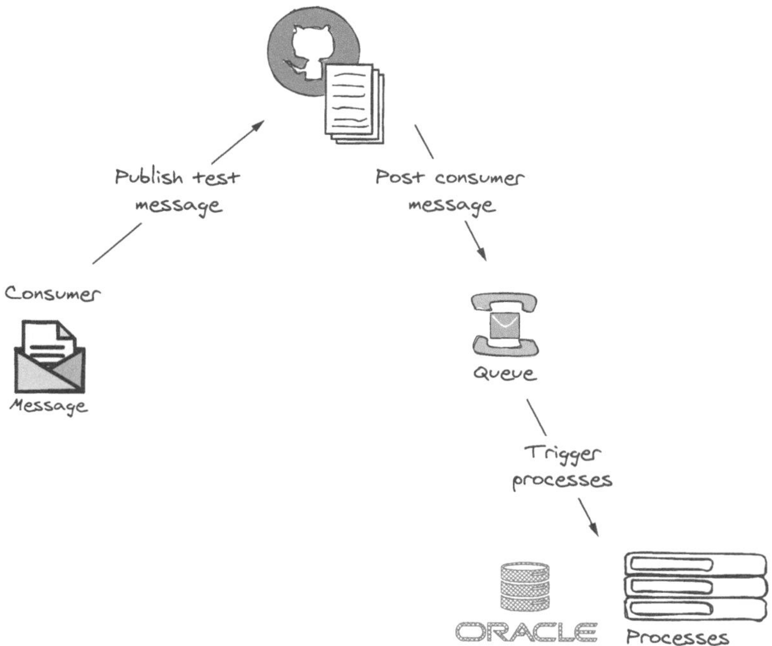

Figure 3.9 The consumer publishes a test message to GitHub. The consumer message is posted onto a queue that triggers the Oracle database processes.

This example shows how the contract testing flow can be applied simply using a GitHub repository and some custom code. Creating the boundaries of responsibility regarding who is in charge of testing each part of the end-to-end flow clarified things.

We've already mentioned the contract testing Pact framework as this will be the tool we use during the implementation chapters. However, there are other tools available, and more have been appearing in the market recently, notably SauceLabs contract testing (https://mng.bz/n0OK), Testsigma CDCT (https://mng.bz/r1RX), or ContractCase contracts by example (https://case.contract-testing.io/). Within this section, we touch on a few of the popular ones, which should cover the tools most people are using:

- Pact in the language of your choice (Java virtual machine [JVM] languages, Go, JavaScript, Python, .NET, PHP, Rust, and more)
- Spring Cloud Contract
- Postman
- JSON Schema (schema validation only)

Including schema validation presents the opportunity to compare the differences between schema validation and contract testing. The preceding list is incomplete; as mentioned, other tools/frameworks are available, but these are the ones we most commonly hear about.

3.6.1 Contract-based tools

Contract testing tools don't just offer the framework for creating and verifying contracts. They have an infrastructure for storing contracts and communicating with the broker to enable running in CI systems. Therefore, when considering which contract testing tool to choose, consider the whole end-to-end process and how the tool would fit into your existing infrastructure.

Choosing a tool depends on which language you use to develop the frontend and backend applications and what approach you want to take to start contract testing. As always, when deciding what tool to use for a specific task, such as evaluating open source test automation frameworks, there are many factors to consider. It's not just about the tool's performance but you must also consider community support when you need help. Another factor to consider is the learning curve required to train the team.

In a scenario where there may be an existing tool such as Postman that's already familiar to the team, it can be adapted to follow the contract testing process. A current tool could be the right choice while showing the value to management, and once proven, then the option to migrate to a native contract testing tool could be an easier transition.

We've chosen Pact as the preferred tool for the book due to its multilanguage support and high level of community support; we're also most familiar with Pact. However, writing contract tests without a tool is possible (see an example from one of the Pact authors at https://github.com/DiUS/diy-contract-example) if you want to take and implement the theory independently, but using a tool like Pact will make the process easier.

See appendix A, sections A.1 and A.2, for a brief description and review of the leading contract testing tools available. To conclude our findings on the tooling, there are a few different variants:

- Native contract testing tools such as Pact and Spring Cloud Contract (and probably others not mentioned here)
- Adapted integration testing tools such as Postman (and probably others not mentioned here)

3.7 Contract Testing Approaches

At the beginning of this chapter, we mentioned that there are two main approaches when it comes to contract testing:

- The traditional consumer-driven contract testing (CDCT) approach
- The provider-driven contract testing (PDCT) approach

Let's take a look at these two approaches in detail.

3.7.1 Consumer-driven contract testing

Ian Robinson first posted about the consumer-driven contract pattern in 2006 (https://mng.bz/V205). Ian described the challenges with schema versioning and breaking changes, showing the need for this style of testing more than 17 years ago. But still, CDCT isn't part of every testing strategy or on the radar for most projects. There is nothing much to say about CDCT in this section that hasn't already been mentioned throughout this chapter, so we'll now focus more on the PDCT approach.

3.7.2 Provider-driven contract testing

This chapter and previous chapters have detailed the "traditional" CDCT approach. For several reasons, PDCT has emerged as an option, primarily since the PactFlow team released bi-directional contract testing functionality (the terms provider-driven and bi-directional contract testing will be used interchangeably in this chapter). From our perspective, this has also been coming for a while, mainly because teams want to use the OpenAPI documentation they already have and extend it for contract testing to prevent breaking changes.

A perception of contract testing is that there is a steep learning curve and significant time investment required before seeing its value. Throughout this book, we aim to quickly break down each implementation step to provide value. However, another option to reduce the time investment and learning curve is PDCT or bi-directional contract testing by using Pact adaptors for consumers that integrate with different testing and mocking frameworks. With PDCT, providers can use their existing OpenAPI specifications as contracts, while consumers can use existing test mocks or stubs as consumer contracts. The contracts generated from mocks can then be published to the broker, like the CDCT approach. In a CDCT approach, only one contract is generated, whereas in a PDCT approach, two contracts are generated—one from the consumer and one from the provider. The PDCT life cycle is shown in figure 3.10 and explained in the following steps:

1. The consumer maintaining a JavaScript application publishes the contract to a broker.
2. Independently, the provider maintaining a Java API or event service also publishes its OpenAPI specification to the broker, which has been tested by the provider already using tools such as ReadyAPI, REST Assured, Dredd, or Postman.
3. A broker, such as PactFlow, compares the consumer contract against the provider OpenAPI specification, and the verification status is updated in the broker.
4. The consumer checks the contract verification status in the broker using the can-i-deploy tool.
5. The consumer deploys changes.

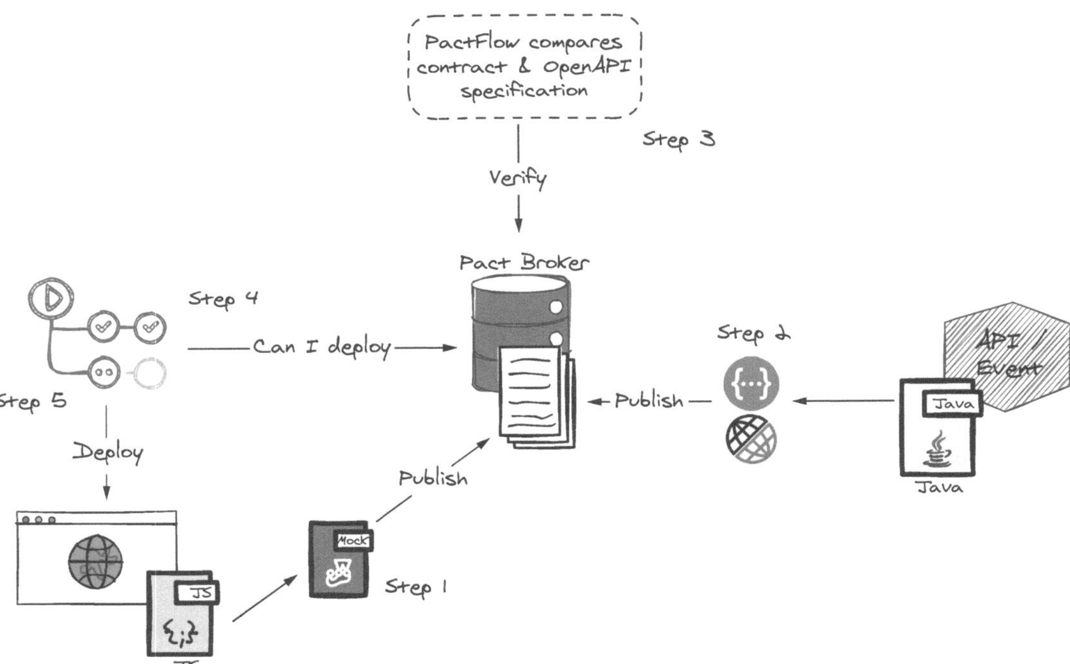

Figure 3.10 PDCT life cycle from JavaScript web application, including test mocks, through the broker to the Java API service with OpenAPI documentation, and finally using the can-i-deploy tool to verify the changes in the web application

In a CDCT approach, the first step is creating the contract, which happens when the HTTP request is made to the mock provider. However, in the PDCT example, the

HTTP response has already been mocked out using existing testing frameworks, such as Cypress, meaning this mock response becomes the expected response within the Pact contract, as shown in figure 3.11. The contract can then be published to the broker.

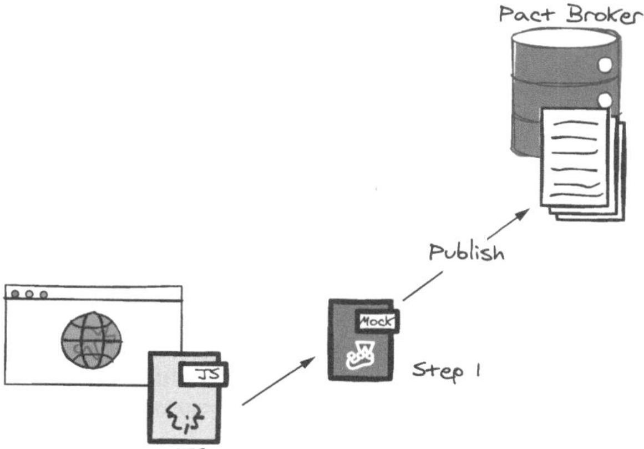

Figure 3.11 JavaScript web application, including the test mocks published contract to the pact broker

On the provider side, the Java API or event service generates its OpenAPI specification independently of the consumer web application. Then, the API tests, which capture all paths within the OpenAPI specification, run against the local running Java API or event service. The OpenAPI specification is then published to the broker, as shown in figure 3.12. One thing to note is that the PDCT or bi-directional approach is only supported by PactFlow's team plan.

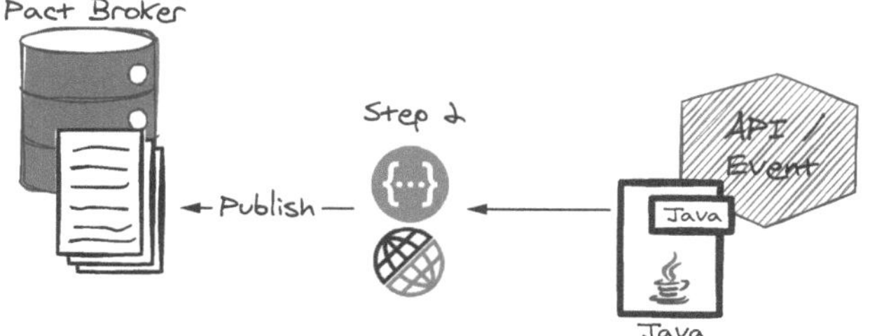

Figure 3.12 The Java API service publishes the OpenAPI documentation to the Pact Broker with test results.

Once the consumer and provider have published their contracts and test results to the broker, the broker compares the provider OpenAPI specification with the consumer contract, as shown in figure 3.13, and the provider test results also confirm the provider contract verification status (mentioned in the contract testing life cycle, section 3.1).

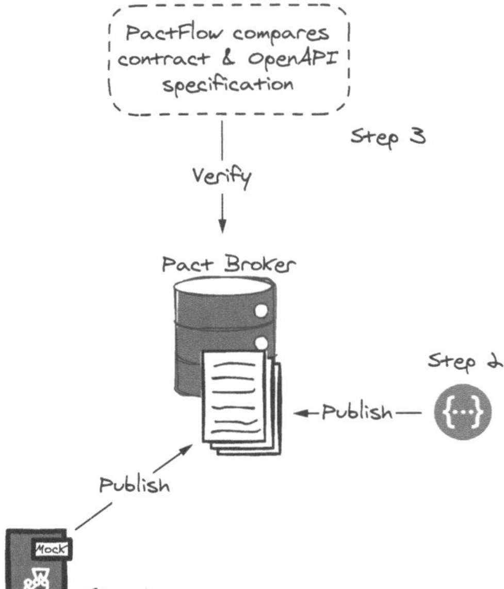

Figure 3.13 Pact Broker compares the consumer mocks with the OpenAPI specification test results to verify the contract.

Finally, the web application can check the contract verification status within its CI pipeline and determine whether deploying the app changes is safe, as shown in figure 3.14.

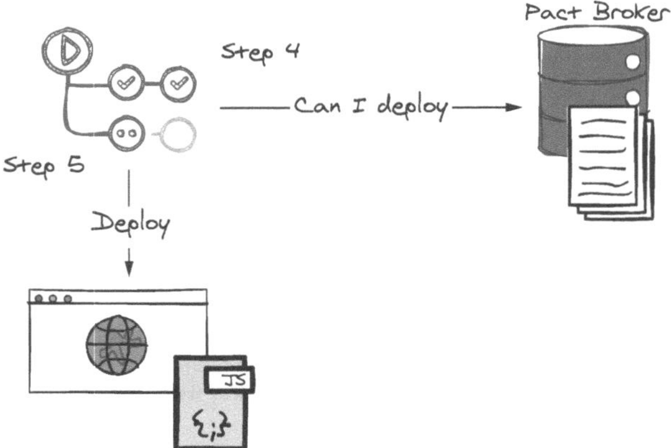

Figure 3.14 Using the can-i-deploy tool to verify the contract changes and deploy the web application

BENEFITS OF PDCT

With PDCT, existing mocks and stubs are used to generate contracts with minimal additional time and effort. PDCT also reduces the learning curve for teams that can adapt their existing mental models to include contract testing. Other benefits include the following:

- The ability to adopt contract testing with all integrated systems that expose an OpenAPI specification
- A natural progression for teams already using schema assertions
- The exciting potential of including third-party providers into this type of testing, with people we speak to often saying that third-party providers are a key challenge for them

Challenges of PDCT

With PDCT, consumers who use adapters to generate contracts from mocks lose out on the loose matching functionality. This functionality allows for more flexible data matching, which removes the friction of static response data, for example, date fields.

PDCT also offers much less assurance as the verification status is only a flag from the provider stating the test status for the OpenAPI specification interaction, instead of the deep comparison like with CDCT. In addition, PDCT doesn't provide insight into consumer usage of the API.

Using provider integration tools such as Postman requires spinning up the application independently of the tests themselves, making it less efficient than running the tests locally, like with the native Pact approach. In addition, if the tests live separately from the code, it may be more difficult to debug any problems that occur.

3.8 Communication types supported by contract testing

In chapter 1, we explained contract testing alongside REST APIs. However, there are other interfaces that the Pact framework can support. GraphQL and event-driven systems have gained popularity in recent years as well. Both still have interfaces between services that could require contract tests to verify their relationship.

3.8.1 GraphQL

GraphQL has an interface very similar to REST but with a query language to request and update specific pieces of data. This design allows consumers to be much more flexible with what they request. In the example of a web application, REST may receive data in the response it doesn't need. A proper consumer-driven approach, Pact offers a specific wrapper for GraphQL interactions, which we'll explore in chapter 7.

3.8.2 Event-driven systems

Messaging-based communication offers asynchronous capabilities for systems. The messages pass to a message queue consumed by another service that has subscribed to it. The language could be clearer because they also use the term *consumer*. So, explaining the relationship with contract testing could be quite tricky.

Events are a great starting point for implementing contract testing as they are small and concise objects passed around between applications. The only caveat to implementing contract testing with events is the prerequisite that you abstract the message object from the underlying event technology. It's important to separate the code responsible for dealing with the specific tool's protocol level stuff, for example, an AWS lambda handler, the Amazon Web Services (AWS) Simple Notification Service (SNS) topic, and the section of code that handles the message body.

The event-driven contract testing life cycle is shown in figure 3.15 and explained in the following steps:

1. The event consumer publishes the message content as a contract to a broker.
2. The event producer then pulls down the expected message from the contract store broker and verifies that against the message body produced.
3. The event consumer checks the contract verification status in the broker using the can-i-deploy tool.
4. The event consumer deploys the changes.

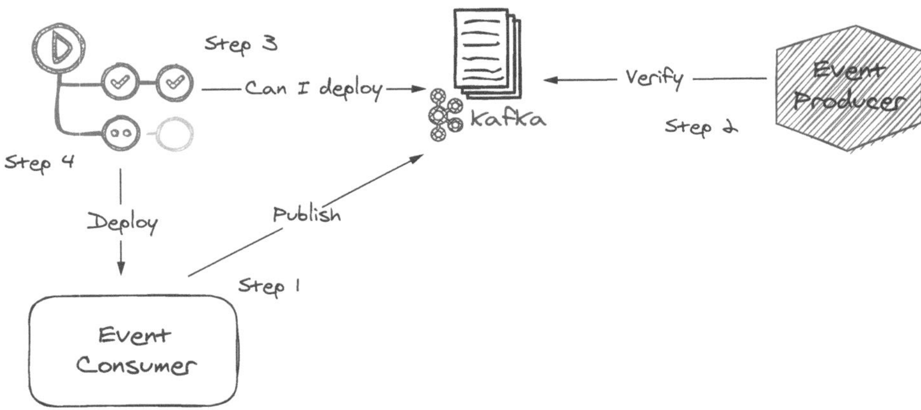

Figure 3.15 Event-driven architecture life cycle applied to PDCT using Kafka through the contract store broker, finally checking can-i-deploy in CI

As confusing as the crossover of terminology between event-driven architecture and contract testing is, contract testing provides a simple way to verify that the messages are in the right format and contain the right information. Tools such as Protocol Buffers (https://protobuf.dev/) can mitigate these problems as a static way to share the message format. We'll explore contract testing with event-driven architectures such as ActiveMQ, Kafka, and Rabbit in chapter 8.

Summary

- A consumer is a user of a service and the owner of the contract tests in PDCT.
- The provider makes the service available and gains confidence in its implementation by verifying consumer contracts.

- A contract is a representation of consumer interactions with the provider service.
- The broker is the central location for storing and keeping consumer and provider aligned.
- The contract testing life cycle integrates with the consumer and the provider CI workflows via a contract store.
- The PDCT life cycle passes a contract between teams, enabling confidence in integrations stably and reliably.
- Contract and schema testing tools aim to provide the framework and infrastructure across multiple languages and communication types.
- Pact is the most popular contract testing framework to implement PDCT, and PactFlow (team plan) supports PDCT.
- GraphQL requests are supported by wrapping the GraphQL layer.
- Event-driven systems are supported by mocking the message body independent of the messaging technology.

Part 2

Consumer-driven contract testing

At this stage, you must be itching to implement consumer-driven contract testing (CDCT) and get hands-on with all the technical implementation. This part of the book contains the most chapters, diving deep into implementing CDCT for different communication types, the various ways to store your contracts, and how to integrate contract testing as part of your continuous integration/continuous delivery (CI/CD) pipelines.

In chapter 4, you learn how to implement CDCT between a web application consumer and a data provider using the Pact framework in JavaScript. You also learn how to store the contract that the consumer generates into a Pact Broker.

As some of you work with mobile apps, we also have a chapter dedicated to implementing CDCT between an Android mobile app and a data provider. Chapter 5 explores this setup using the Pact framework in Java.

Because CDCT requires both tests to be written on the consumer and provider side, chapter 6 shows how the provider tests need to be set up, with the introduction of provider states. Chapter 7 demonstrates how to introduce contract testing for a GraphQL layer, while chapter 8 shows how to implement contract testing for event-driven architecture.

While we've chosen to use PactFlow as the Pact Broker for this book, there are other options for storing and hosting your contracts, which chapter 9 covers extensively. Finally, chapter 10 demonstrates how to set up contract testing in a CI/CD pipeline using GitHub actions. You learn the basic setup as well as more advanced configurations, such as using webhooks, using the can-i-deploy tool, recording releases or deployments, versioning, and more.

Some of these chapters also have chapter exercises to solidify your contract testing learning experience. By the end of this part of this book, you will have gained confidence in implementing CDCT in your work projects.

4 Implementing consumer-driven contract testing for web applications

This chapter covers

- Guidelines in writing consumer contract tests
- Contract testing tooling setup for the consumer
- Writing consumer contract tests between a web application and data provider
- Publishing contracts to a Pact Broker

At this point, we hope you're itching to start writing your first contract test! As mentioned in chapter 2, it's always better to start with the "Why" and to understand what pain points contract testing is trying to solve before you rush in to try it out just because someone told you to. Building on the Why, it's essential to have a solid understanding of the core concepts and principles of contract testing. If you feel that you want to read the previous chapters again to solidify your knowledge further, please go ahead. We'd rather you make sure you fully understand how contract testing works before trying out the implementation part.

If you have a solid grasp of the Why and the foundational concepts, it's time to get hands-on with contract testing. This technical chapter will guide you through the setup process step-by-step, ensuring that you can start implementing contract tests effectively. We'll first provide recommended practices to help you write consumer contract tests. Next, you'll learn how to set up the necessary tools and libraries for contract testing in your specific development environment using the Pact tool. As mentioned in chapter 3, we use Pact because it's the standard tool for writing contract tests. Pact (https://docs.pact.io/) is a code-first tool for testing HTTP and message integrations using contract tests.

Once your environment is configured, this chapter will cover how to write consumer contract tests between a web application and a data provider. If you're also interested in writing contract tests for other consumers such as a mobile and GraphQL client, we'll also cover these consumers, but in chapters 5 and 7. Finally, this chapter will show how you can publish your contract to a central repository, such as Pact Broker, for data providers to access and verify the contract.

By the end of this chapter, you'll not only understand the theory behind contract testing but also have practical experiences in implementing it, making you well-equipped to reap its benefits in your software development projects.

4.1 Guidelines in writing consumer contract tests

Before you start writing consumer contract tests, it's highly important that you take your time to understand recommended practices or guidelines so you don't end up with contract tests that are flaky and brittle. As we mentioned in chapter 2, a test is considered flaky when it produces inconsistent results without introducing any changes to the code. You might run a flaky test several times, and it will pass or fail. On the other hand, a test is considered brittle when it fails due to small code changes or changes from other systems, and it can also be difficult to maintain. Yes, even contract tests can be susceptible to flakiness and brittleness if you're not careful. What you don't want to happen is for your team to start losing confidence in your contract tests. Debugging and fixing flaky and brittle tests can consume valuable development time, slowing the release cycle and potentially causing delays in delivering new features or bug fixes.

Consumer contract tests serve as a critical safety net in your application. They are designed to ensure your services interact correctly and reliably with their data providers. If these tests aren't well-structured or don't follow the recommended practices, they can become unreliable, leading to false positives or negatives, which can also overlook any real problems. This can destroy your team's confidence in the test suite, making it difficult to trust the results. In this section, we'll discuss some recommended practices when writing consumer contract tests, and we'll cover the following topics:

- The focus of a consumer contract test
- The importance of using mocks instead of stubs
- Using loose matchers to avoid high coupling
- The importance of writing isolated contract tests
- Using can-i-deploy to verify that you can safely deploy to production

4.1.1 The focus of a consumer contract test

Consumer contract tests have one focus—to make sure that when a consumer asks for data from a provider service, everything goes according to their contract agreement. Imagine it as a way to check if the consumer's expectations match what the provider actually does. These tests don't dig into the nitty-gritty functional details of how the provider works; instead, they focus on what the consumer needs and checks if they get it.

Think of consumer contract tests as a security guard at a building entrance where security is high. They make sure that everyone follows the rules laid out in their working contract. A consumer contract test acts as a security guard to catch any mistakes or misunderstandings in how the consumer asks for data and what they expect in return from the provider.

A general rule of thumb that the Pact tool recommends (https://docs.pact.io/consumer) is to ask yourself this question: "If I don't include this scenario, what bug in the consumer or what misunderstanding about how the provider responds might be missed?" If the answer is none, don't include it.

4.1.2 The importance of using mocks instead of stubs

Mocks and stubs are two important techniques developers have used to write a unit test. They act as "test doubles," like a movie stunt double. These two techniques are different, and knowing the difference in contract testing is important.

A *mock* in testing is a substitute for a real component (e.g., a data provider or an object) that a singular function or method relies on. The mock imitates the behavior of the real component, but it doesn't have the actual functionality. When writing tests that need a mock, you normally have to set up the expectations for the component you're interacting with as part of your test.

On the other hand, a *stub* is a simplified version of a component that provides predetermined responses. It doesn't have the full component functionality but responds according to a predefined script or set of rules. When writing tests that need a stub, normally, the stub has already been created and has a preprogrammed response sitting outside your test.

From a consumer contract point of view, it's important to understand that you need mocks and not stubs, and that mocks are what tools such as Pact provide. A mock validates the behavior of your test, whereas a stub does not. When you write a consumer contract test, you follow this approach (see figure 4.1):

1. Initialize the setup of your mock provider.
2. Set the expectations that the consumer has against the mock provider.
3. Call the consumer against the mock provider. The mock provider validates the test, and, if successful, the contract is generated. If not successful, the test fails, and the contract isn't generated.

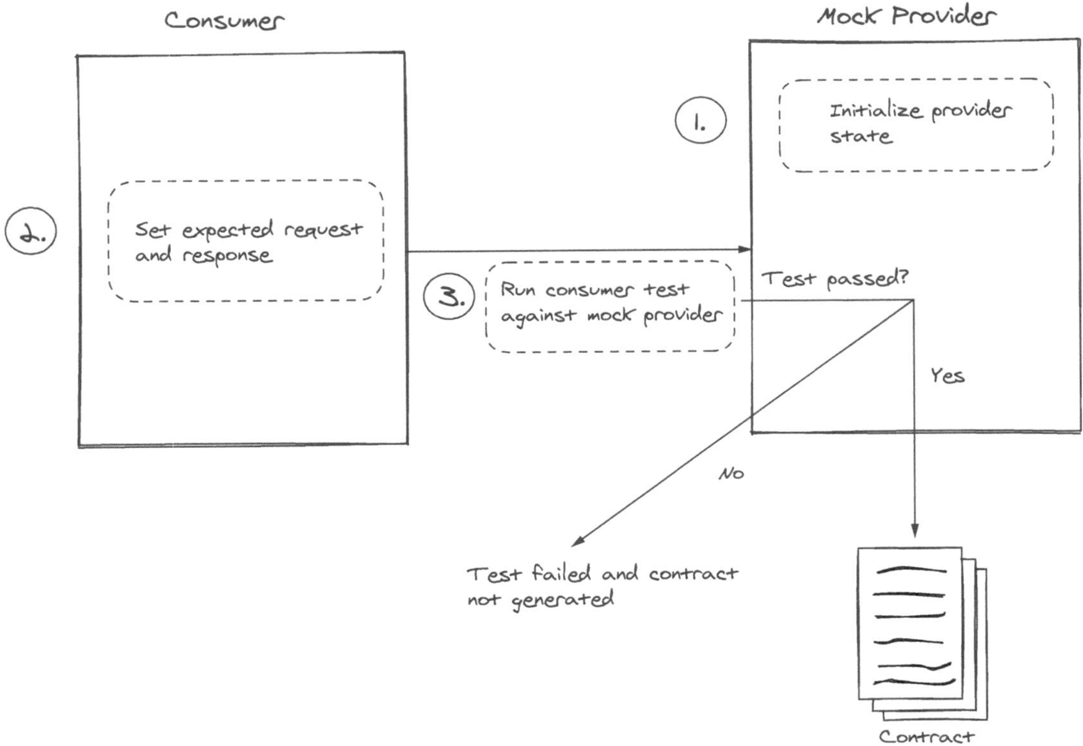

Figure 4.1 The flow of writing a consumer contract test using Pact

A mock provider will fail the consumer test if there are any errors in the interaction or expectation that you registered with the mock provider. A stub, on the other hand, will bypass this error, which totally defeats the purpose of contract testing. One of the reasons we decided to cover the Pact tooling as part of this book is because Pact provides you with a mock provider easily.

4.1.3 Using loose matchers to avoid high coupling

Another general recommendation when writing consumer contract tests is to be aware of the loose matchers concept to avoid high coupling. High coupling occurs when a change in one area affects other areas. Let's think of coupling in the context of LEGO blocks. In a *high coupling scenario*, the LEGO blocks are tightly interlocked, and removing or changing one block can cause the entire structure to collapse. These blocks depend heavily on each other to stay together, making it challenging to modify or maintain the structure. Imagine trying to replace one block in a tightly woven LEGO wall—it's difficult without disrupting the whole thing. On the other hand, in a *low coupling scenario*, each LEGO block is self-contained and doesn't rely heavily on other blocks to function. You can easily assemble and disassemble your structure because the blocks are loosely connected. In contract testing, high coupling occurs when a small change from the provider, even if it's just the data it returns, causes the consumer contract test to fail. This is one reason why a contract test might be flaky and brittle and, if you're not careful, will suffer the same fate as a flaky integration test. For more context on this, check out Martin Fowler's "Tolerant Reader" blog article (https://martinfowler.com/bliki/TolerantReader.html).

To combat flaky tests, tools such as Pact provide *loose matchers*, a functionality that allows for more flexible matching of data, to ensure that consumers verify the shape of the interaction rather than the actual data it returns. Loose matchers can be in the form of type-based matching, arrays, or even plain regular expressions. With type-based matching, you care more about the type of data a specific field returns, rather than the actual data itself. Here's an example code snippet:

```
const EXPECTED_BODY = {
  id: like(1),
  username: like('marie'),
  fullname: like('marie cruz')
}
```

This object represents the data shape the consumer expects from a data provider. If the consumer makes a `GET` request to get the details of a user, it only cares if the data of the expected fields are similar to the one we expect; in this case, an integer for the ID and string for the username and full name. If, for some reason, the ID is a string on the provider's side, our contract will fail. We'll cover in more detail how you can use loose matchers with Pact in this chapter.

Even though loose matching is recommended, this recommendation must be considered on a field-to-field basis. If you have specific fields where you care about the data being returned, then don't use loose matchers. Here's another question that the Pact tool recommends you consider: "If I made this looser/tighter, what bugs would I miss/prevent?"

4.1.4 The importance of writing isolated contract tests

From our revised test automation pyramid discussed in chapter 2, contract tests sit above unit tests, so they have similar qualities to a unit test. One of its similarities is that contract tests should be verified in isolation, with no context or dependency from previous interactions. Contract tests that depend on the outcome of previous tests are brittle and will land you in that same state of brittle integration tests.

However, some consumer interactions require providers to be in a certain state. Let's consider an example between a web application and a product API. If we want to write a contract test between a web application sending a `GET` request to retrieve a list of products, this test requires that products exist first. This is great if products always exist on the provider side. However, this might not always be the case. What happens if the provider's data has been refreshed? How can we achieve a reliable contract test?

Contract testing tools such as Pact provide functionalities for setting up provider states to ensure the provider is in the right state for the consumer contract test, as shown in figure 4.2.

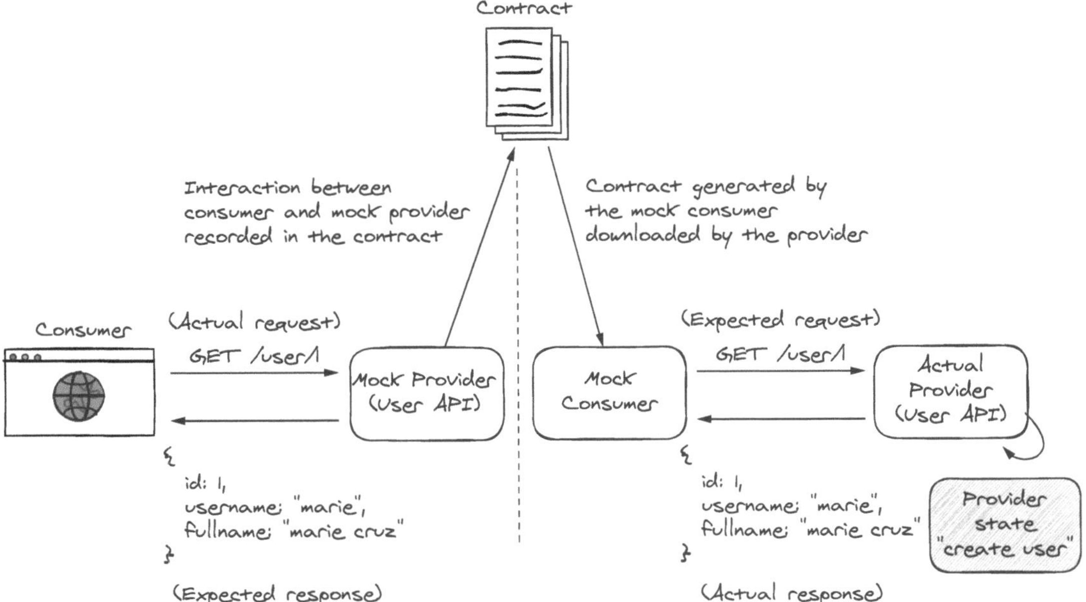

Figure 4.2 The important role of provider states in contract testing. Provider states are useful when the consumer expects providers to be in a certain state.

This ensures that the provider is in the right state or precondition to match the response that the consumer expects before the data provider verifies the contract. In figure 4.2, a provider state named "create user" is set up in the provider contract tests. This state will create the necessary data the consumer requires to ensure that when consumers send a `GET` request to retrieve a specific user, the correct data is always available. We'll explain provider states in more detail in chapter 6.

4.1.5 *Using can-i-deploy to verify that you can safely deploy to production*

One of the most important recommendations when integrating consumer contract tests is to ensure you can safely deploy the changes to production. For example, let's say that the consumer has changed their application code. To check that the changes are compatible, the contract tests are run. The provider has verified the new contract, and it's detected that the consumer change isn't compatible! To have a safety mechanism in place, the consumer can use the can-i-deploy command provided by Pact, as part of the contract verification, to confirm that their contract has been verified. In the example shown in figure 4.3, the contract verification failed, which means that they can't deploy the new changes to production. We'll discuss in more detail how to use the can-i-deploy tool in chapter 10.

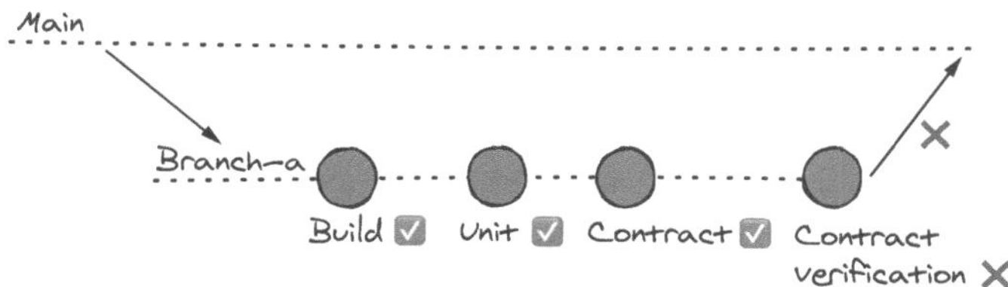

Figure 4.3 Consumer build pipeline with contract verification in place using the can-i-deploy tool

4.2 Contract testing tooling setup for the consumer

As mentioned, we'll use the Pact contract testing tool to show how to start with contract testing because this is the current de facto contract testing tool. Pact supports various programming languages such as Java, JavaScript, Go, Python, and many more (https://docs.pact.io/roadmap/feature_support). This means that if your consumer uses a different programming language than your data provider, which is common in many organizations, you can write the contract tests using the same language as the application code. This provides benefits such as ease of test maintenance and better collaboration with developers. After all, writing automated tests is a software development activity.

Because it will be difficult to cover all the programming languages that Pact supports, this chapter will focus on how to set up pact-js, which is the JavaScript version. As the online documentation is likely to be more up-to-date with implementation changes on how to use their API, make sure to always check their documentation for more information (https://mng.bz/5OGz).

4.2.1 Requirements

To follow along in this step-by-step tutorial, you need to have the following installed in your machines:

- Node (LTS version)
- Git and GitHub account (optional, but preferred to have so your changes are tracked)
- Visual Studio Code (VS Code; or other visual code editor, but we'll show the examples using VS Code)

For comprehensive installation details of Node and pact-js, refer to appendix B, specifically sections B.1 and B.2.

To make this easier, we've created an example GitHub project, https://github.com/mdcruz/pact-js-example/, that you can download or fork online using Git. Feel free to jump to the next section if you already know how to fork the project or download it. If you need additional guidelines on how to fork or download the project, refer to appendix B, specifically sections B.3 or B.4. Once you have a copy of this GitHub project in your local machines, switch to a new branch called `setup-contract-tests-consumer` by running the following command:

```
git checkout setup-contract-tests-consumer
```

4.3 Consumer contract tests between a web application and data provider

So far, we've been using the example of a web application and a user API that returns basic information about different users. In the GitHub project that we've provided, we'll now use a new example!

Let's imagine a web application communicating to a movies API. The web application is the consumer, while the movies API is the provider. The responsibility of the movies API is to return different movies and the year they were released to the web application. The web application contains different functions that query the movies API. For this example, we've decided to add both the consumer and provider in the same GitHub project to simplify the process, as shown in the following project structure:

```
> consumer-web
> data
> provider
package.json
package-lock.json
README.md
```

In the real world, this likely won't be the case. The consumers and data providers will live in separate projects, especially as more and more teams adopt a microservices architecture. But, to ease your understanding with contract testing, we've decided to keep everything in the same project so it's easier to follow.

4.3.1 Movies API overview

As mentioned, the movies API returns a list of movies to the consumer and has four important files:

- *movies.json*—A JSON file containing static data of movies
- *movies.js*—A class that represents a movie and what actions a user can perform
- *provider.js*—A class that contains all the logic to set up the example API
- *provider-service.js*—The main entry point to start the API

An overview of how the movies API was created is shown in figure 4.4.

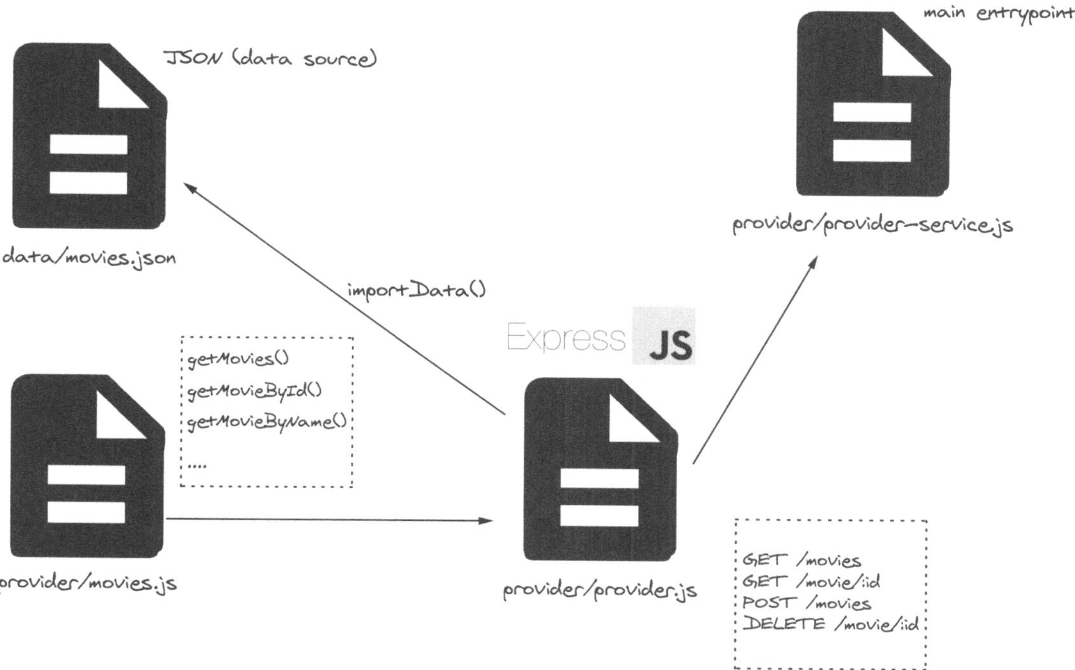

Figure 4.4 Provider project (movies API) at a glance with all the relevant files

MOVIES.JSON

To simplify the movies API's data source, the movies API in our example doesn't connect to a database. Instead, the movies API returns static data from a basic JSON file. The sample JSON file is found by expanding the data folder on your GitHub project. You should see a file named movies.json with the following content:

```
[
  { "id": 1, "name": "The Shawshank Redemption", "year": 1994 },
  { "id": 2, "name": "The Dark Knight", "year": 2008 },
  { "id": 3, "name": "Amelie", "year": 2001 },
  { "id": 4, "name": "Fight Club", "year": 1994 },
  { "id": 5, "name": "The Lion King", "year": 1994 }
]
```

MOVIES.JS

If you expand the provider folder on your GitHub project, you should also see a file named movies.js, which represents a movie and should have the following code:

```
class Movie {
  constructor() {
    this.movies = [];
  }
```

```
  getMovies() {
    return this.movies;
  }

  getMovieById(id) {
    return this.movies.find((movie) => parseInt(id) == movie.id);
  }

  getMovieByName(name) {
    return this.movies.find(movie => movie.name === name)
  }

  insertMovie(movie) {
    this.movies.push(movie);
  }

  getFirstMovie() {
    return this.movies[0];
  }
}

module.exports = Movie;
```

The file movie.js is exported as `Movie` so our provider can call functions such as the following:

- `getMovies` for retrieving all the movies
- `getMovieById` for finding a movie that matches the ID provided and returns the matched movie
- `getMovieByName` for finding the movie that matches the name provided and returns the matched movie.
- `insertMovie` for inserting a new movie
- `getFirstMovie` for retrieving the first movie

As this is just an example project, we've kept this as simple as possible, but in real projects, these functions will have error handling and unit tests!

PROVIDER.JS

The file provider.js contains most of the code logic and has two main responsibilities, as shown in figure 4.5:

- Create the function to import the example data set from our movies.json file.
- Create the movies API and expose the different endpoints.

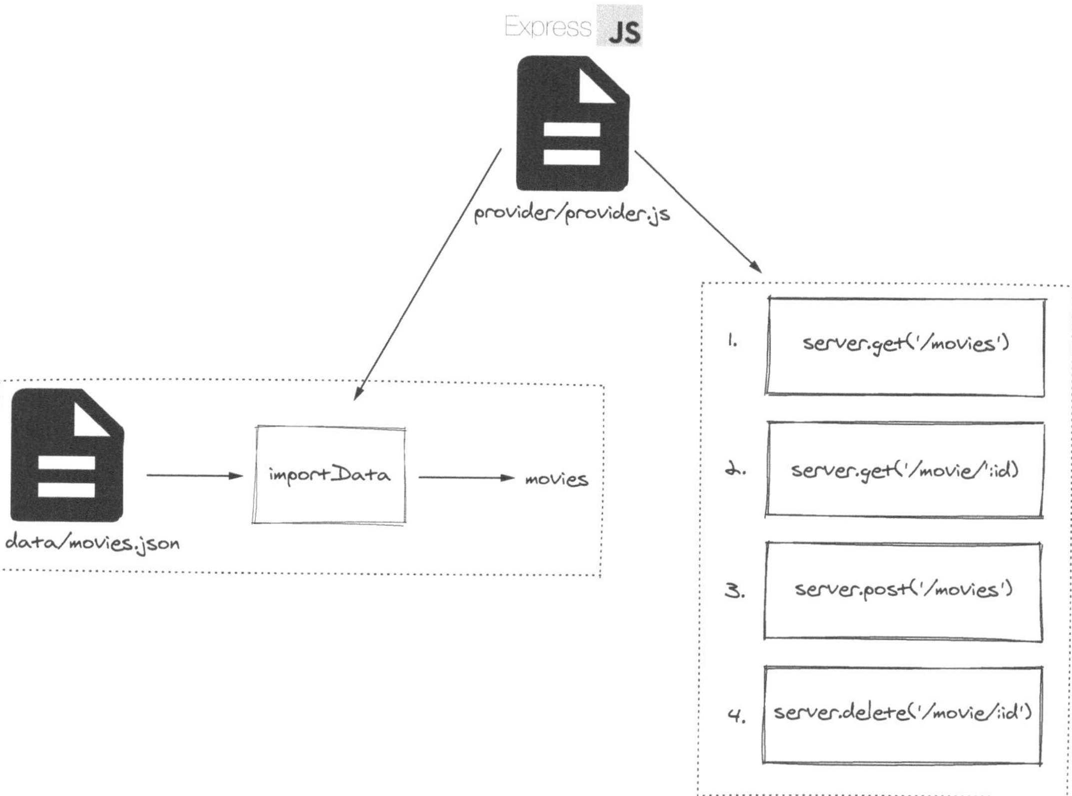

Figure 4.5 Code logic in provider.js exposes a function to import the data from our example data set and also exposes the different endpoints for the movies API.

The file provider.js exports a function called `importData` to import the example data set from our movies.json file and insert it into our `movies` class, which you can see in the following code snippet:

```
const importData = () => {
  const data = require('../../data/movies.json');
  data.reduce((a, v) => {
    v.id = a + 1;
    movies.insertMovie(v);
    return a + 1;
  }, 0);
};
```

Load default data into the Movies class

To create the movies API and expose the different endpoints, we've used the Express framework (https://expressjs.com/), a popular framework for creating backend applications in a client-server architecture. Express can be used to create and expose APIs for your clients to use. The provider.js also contains the code to set up the Express framework and the routes needed for the API to respond to the client's request. For example, the following code snippet registers two new `GET` requests to Express:

```
...

const movies = new Movies();

server.get('/movies', (req, res) => {
  res.send(movies.getMovies());
});

server.get('/movie/:id', (req, res) => {
  const movie = movies.getMovieById(req.params.id);
  if (!movie) {
    res.status(404).send('Movie not found');
  } else {
    res.send(movie);
  }
});

...
```

The first route registers that any `GET` requests made to `'/movies'` will respond by sending all the movies. The second route registers `GET` requests to `'/movie:id'`, with the ID as a route parameter. Route parameters capture the values provided at their position in the URL. For example, `'/movie/1'` should return the movie "The Shawshank Redemption" while `'/movie/1000'` should return an error with the message "Movie not found."

PROVIDER-SERVICE.JS

Finally, the file provider-service.js acts as our main entry point. It exposes the provider.js, calls the function to import the data, starts the server, and listens on the available port for connections:

```
const { server, importData } = require('./provider');
const port = process.env.PORT || 3000;

importData();

server.listen(port, () => console.log(`Listening on port ${port}...`));
```

To start, install the project dependencies by running `npm install` on your terminal. Once everything is installed, start the provider service locally by typing the following command:

```
npm run start:provider
```

Running the command should print the following message:

```
Listening on port 3001...
```

`start:provider` is a custom script that we've added within the scripts section of the package.json file, which contains the following command:

```
"scripts": {
    "start:provider": "cross-env PORT=3001 node provider/provider-service.js"
  }
```

The preceding command specifies an environment variable called `PORT` and sets the value to `3001`. We use the `cross-env` module to make sure that this command works regardless of the operating system you're using, especially if you're using a Windows machine. Then, using the `node` command, you're simply executing the code specified in the provider-service.js class. If you then open up your browser of choice and type in `localhost:3001/movies`, you should see the list of movies returned:

```
// 20231007002601
// http://localhost:3001/movies

[
  {
    "id": 1,
    "name": "The Shawshank Redemption",
    "year": 1994
  },
  {
    "id": 2,
    "name": "The Dark Knight",
    "year": 2008
  },
  {
    "id": 3,
    "name": "Amelie",
    "year": 2001
  },
  {
    "id": 4,
    "name": "Fight Club",
    "year": 1994
  },
  {
    "id": 5,
    "name": "The Lion King",
    "year": 1994
  }
]
```

You can modify the JSON file if you want to add more movies. To see the changes, press Ctrl-C to stop the provider service and then start the provider service again.

4.3.2 Web application overview

From the consumer perspective, we're also keeping it simple. A user interface (UI) will present a list of movies in real-world projects. In our simple project, we expose the functions the UI will need to display the data. To query the movies API, we've decided to use axios (https://axios-http.com/), which is a popular promise-based HTTP client for making HTTP requests. If you expand the consumer-web folder in your GitHub project, you should see a file named consumer.js which contains the following code snippet:

```
const axios = require('axios');

const fetchMovies = async (url) => {
  const response = await axios
    .get(`${url}/movies`)
    .then((res) => res.data)
    .catch((err) => err.response);
  return response;
};

...

const deleteMovie = async (url, id) => {
  const response = await axios
    .delete(`${url}/movie/${id}`)
    .then((res) => res.data.message)
    .cath((err) => err.response.data.message);
  return response;
};
```

The `fetchMovies` function makes a `GET` request to the URL passed in, followed by `'/movies'`. This should return the response from the `GET` request. If there are any errors, the error message is returned instead. On the other hand, the `deleteMovie` function makes a `DELETE` request to the URL passed in, followed by `'/movie/${id}'` where the `${id}` variable corresponds to the movie ID. If the movie is found, this should return a message that the movie has been deleted. If the movie doesn't exist, the `DELETE` request should return a message that the movie isn't found. Now that you have an overview of both the consumer and provider, let's get started with writing our first consumer contract test!

4.3.3 Consumer contract

If you remember from chapter 2, when starting with contract testing, especially consumer-driven contract testing (CDCT), the consumer should specify the contract. Let's imagine that the following scenarios are expected from the movies API, which forms the basis of the consumer contract:

1. **Scenario: Get all movies**
   Given there is a movies API
   When the consumer fetches all movies
   Then the movies API should return a status code of 200
   And for each movie, it should return the ID, name, and the year it was released.

2 **Scenario: Get a single movie**
   Given there is a movies API
   When the consumer fetches a single movie
   Then the movies API should return a status code of 200
   And the ID, name, and year the movie was released.
3 **Scenario: Add a new movie**
   Given there is a movies API
   When the consumer adds a new movie by specifying the movie name and date
   Then the movies API should accept the movie
   And return a status code of 201.
4 **Scenario: Add an existing movie**
   Given there is a movies API
   When the consumer adds an existing movie by specifying the movie name and date
   Then the movies API should return a status code of 409
   And the movies API should return a suitable error message.
5 **Scenario: Delete a nonexistent movie**
   Given there is a movies API
   When the consumer deletes a new movie that doesn't exist
   Then the movies API should return a status code of 404
   And the movies API should return a suitable error message
6 **Scenario: Delete an existing movie**
   Given there is a movies API
   When the consumer deletes an existing movie
   Then the movies API should return a status code of 200.

All these scenarios are great candidates for contract testing because they define the consumer's expectations from the data provider. The scenarios don't detail the provider's functional implementation because the consumer cares that they get the data shape they want from the contract agreement. For example, scenarios 4 and 5 define the provider to return the correct status code and a suitable error message. If the provider decides to update the error message, the contract should still pass because the consumer doesn't care about the actual value of the error message.

4.3.4 Writing the first consumer contract test

Let's start writing the consumer contract test for scenario 1. Writing the consumer contract test will be broken down into the following code:

- Importing the required dependencies
- Setting up the mock provider that the consumer will use

- Registering the expectation that the consumer has against the provider to the mock provider
- Calling the consumer against the mock provider
- Verifying the consumer test and generating the contract

IMPORTING THE REQUIRED DEPENDENCIES

In the consumer-web folder, create a new file called consumer-contract.spec.js, and add the following lines of code to import the required dependencies:

```
const path = require('path');
const { fetchMovies } = require('./consumer');
const { PactV3, MatchersV3 } = require('@pact-foundation/pact');
```

We require the `path` module to manage the file directory naming for our contract because we'll need to store the contract that Pact will generate. We also need the actual `consumer` and only need the `fetchMovies` function for now. Finally, we require both the `PactV3` and `MatchersV3` module from the Pact library.

SETTING UP THE MOCK PROVIDER

The next step that you need to do is to define the mock provider that Pact will use. Remember that when it comes to contract testing, the consumer doesn't directly interact with the provider, but instead interacts with the mock provider that Pact provides. To do that, add the following lines of code to your consumer-contract.spec.js file:

```
const provider = new PactV3({
  dir: path.resolve(process.cwd(), 'pacts'),
  consumer: 'WebConsumer',
  provider: 'MoviesAPI',
});
```

This code calls the `PactV3` constructor to create a new mock provider that we can use as part of our consumer contract test. As part of the constructor, we're passing parameters to define the directory for the contracts to be stored in the pacts folder of the current working directory. This will also create the folder if it doesn't exist yet. We also pass in the parameters to define the name of the consumer and the provider, which, in this example, are `'WebConsumer'` and `'MoviesAPI'`. These names will be used throughout the contract generation and when you upload the contract to a Pact Broker.

REGISTERING THE CONSUMER EXPECTATION

Let's now structure the first test by using Jest's describe block. If you're not familiar with Jest (https://jestjs.io/), Jest is a popular JavaScript testing framework that comes built-in with all the methods and utilities you need for testing your JavaScript code. Jest should have been installed in your local project as part of the project's requirements. If you haven't installed the GitHub project's dependencies, then make sure to do it by running `npm install`.

Now, add the following code into the consumer-contract.spec.js file after the provider configuration:

```
describe('Movies API', () => {
  describe('When a GET request is made to /movies', () => {
    test('it should return all movies', () => {

    });                                          Our first
  });                                            test here
});
```

A describe block in Jest is a way to organize the structure of your test. The top-level describe block explains that the test is for the movies API. The second describe block is for the specific scenario we want to test, which is scenario 1. For scenario 1, the consumer expects that when a GET request is made to the /movies/ endpoint, the provider should respond with all the movies. The test block represents the actual test itself. To register a new expectation or interaction, we need to set up the mock provider with the correct consumer expectations in Pact by using the following code:

```
test('it should return all movies', () => {
   provider
      .uponReceiving('a request to all movies')
      .withRequest({
         method: 'GET',
         path: '/movies',
       })
       .willRespondWith({
         status: 200,
         body: MatchersV3.eachLike(EXPECTED_BODY),
       });
     });
 });
```

With this interaction, we're calling the uponReceiving API and passing in the scenario name as a string. It's a recommended practice to keep the naming easy to understand. In this example, we're saying that the scenario name is 'a request to all movies'. Next, we call the withRequest API and pass in the HTTP request information, which, in this case, is a GET request to the '/movies' endpoint.

To represent the HTTP response details from the provider, we call the willRespondWith API and pass in the response details. In this example, the provider should respond with a status of 200. The response body is represented as a variable called EXPECTED_BODY. Let's first declare this variable outside our test:

```
const EXPECTED_BODY = { id: 1, name: "My movie", year: 1999 };
```

Feel free to update EXPECTED_BODY to be of any value, as long as the data type matches. Using Pact matchers, we're saying that the EXPECTED_BODY should have an

ID, the movie name should be something similar to "My movie", and the year should be something similar to the year 1999.

Remember that with contract testing, the consumer should care more about the shape of the data rather than the data itself. This is what we refer to as loose matching. We use the `MatchersV3.eachLike` matching rule to ensure the type matches all the values. This way, the test should still pass if the provider returns different values, but the types are similar. If, for whatever reason, the movie ID changes from an integer to a string, the matching rule will fail, and the contract test will throw an error.

CALLING THE CONSUMER AGAINST THE MOCK PROVIDER

The next step is to call the function the consumer created as responsible for fetching all the movies. In this example, the `fetchMovies` function is passed in as a callback function to `provider.executeTest`. A callback function is a function that is passed as an argument to another function executed by that function:

```
await provider.executeTest(async mockProvider => {
    const movies = await fetchMovies(mockProvider.url);
})
```

The `provider.executeTest` function provides a dynamic mock provider that is passed into `fetchMovies`. One available property of the mock provider is the URL itself, which we can pass into `fetchMovies`. Instead of the actual movies API URL, the `fetchMovies` will be tested against the URL of the mock provider, which could require some refactoring to make it more testable.

VERIFY THE TEST AND CONTRACT GENERATION

Once the `fetchMovies` function is called, we need to verify that the actual data returned by the consumer matches the expected data. We do this by comparing the actual data returned by the consumer and the expected data we defined. To do this in Jest, we can call the `expect` function and pass in the actual data received from the consumer. We then use the `toEqual` matcher and pass in the expected data:

```
await provider.executeTest(async mockProvider => {
    const movies = await fetchMovies(mockProvider.url);
    expect(movies[0]).toEqual(EXPECTED_BODY);
});
```

For your reference, the full test should look like this one:

```
const path = require('path');
const { fetchMovies } = require('./consumer');
const { PactV3, MatchersV3 } = require('@pact-foundation/pact');

const provider = new PactV3({
  dir: path.resolve(process.cwd(), 'pacts'),
  consumer: 'WebConsumer',
  provider: 'MoviesAPI',
});
```

```
const EXPECTED_BODY = { id: 1, name: "My movie", year: 1999 }

describe('Movies Service', () => {
  describe('When a GET request is made to /movies', () => {
    test('it should return all movies', async () => {
      provider
        .uponReceiving('a request to all movies')
        .withRequest({
          method: 'GET',
          path: '/movies',
        })
        .willRespondWith({
          status: 200,
          body: MatchersV3.eachLike(EXPECTED_BODY),
        });

      await provider.executeTest(async mockProvider => {
        const movies = await fetchMovies(mockProvider.url);
        expect(movies[0]).toEqual(EXPECTED_BODY);
      })
    });
  });
});
```

Now, you're ready to run the test! To run this test, let's create a new script in our package.json called `test:web:consumer`, which uses the `jest` command followed by the test file you want to execute:

```
"scripts": {
    "start:provider": "cross-env PORT=3001 node provider/provider-
     service.js",
    "test:web:consumer": "jest consumer-web/consumer-contract.spec.js"
  }
```

Make sure you save all the changes! To run the test, open your terminal and type in the following command:

```
npm run test:web:consumer
```

If everything has been set up well, running this command should return one passing test and it should provide the output shown in figure 4.6.

```
PASS consumer/consumer-contract.spec.jsun
onse
  Movies Service
    When a GET request is made to /movies
      ✓ it should return all movies (38 ms)

Test Suites: 1 passed, 1 total
```

Figure 4.6 Test output of running the consumer contract test

When the test run completes, Pact will also generate the contract, which is saved in the `pacts` directory. You should now see a similar folder structure output like this:

```
> consumer-web
> data
> pacts
  { } WebConsumer-MoviesAPI.json
> provider
package.json
package-lock.json
README.md
```

The contents of the contract should include information about the consumer and provider name, the interaction that has been registered, the request and response details expected from the provider, the matching rules specified, and any other relevant metadata. You should see a similar contract in JSON format, like this:

```
{
  "consumer": {
    "name": "WebConsumer"
  },
  "interactions": [
    {
      "description": "a request to all movies",
      "request": {
        "method": "GET",
        "path": "/movies"
      },
      "response": {
        "body": [
          {
            "id": 1,
            "name": "My movie",
            "year": 1999
          }
        ],
        "headers": {
          "Content-Type": "application/json"
        },
        "matchingRules": {
          "body": {
            "$": {
              "combine": "AND",
              "matchers": [
                {
                  "match": "type",
                  "min": 1
                }
              ]
            }
          }
        },
```

```
          "status": 200
        }
      }
    ],
    "metadata": {
      "pact-js": {
        "version": "12.1.0"
      },
      "pactRust": {
        "ffi": "0.4.9",
        "models": "1.1.11"
      },
      "pactSpecification": {
        "version": "3.0.0"
      }
    },
    "provider": {
      "name": "MoviesAPI"
    }
  }
```


4.3.5 Other programming languages

While we've chosen how to write consumer contract tests in JavaScript, Pact supports other programming languages as well, such as Java, C#, Ruby, and Python. Please refer to https://docs.pact.io/implementation_guides/ for specific implementations of Pact with other programming languages.

4.4 Publishing the contract to Pact Broker

After the contract is generated, the contract needs to be uploaded to a central place, called Pact Broker, as described in section 3.4. You can host your own Pact Broker, but for this example, we'll show you how to use PactFlow (https://pactflow.io/).

PactFlow is a fully managed Pact Broker to help you and your teams get started with Pact easily. PactFlow comes with a free starter plan that you can use (see chapter 9 to understand the difference between PactFlow and open source Pact Broker). It comes with managing up to two contracts and unlimited users. To get started, please sign up for a free starter plan account (https://pactflow.io/try-for-free/), and follow the instructions. Once you have an account, you should see an example landing page similar to figure 4.7.

When uploading the contract to PactFlow, you need to provide two values and export them as environment variables:

- PactFlow base URL
- PactFlow API token

These two values can be found by clicking the Settings icon in figure 4.7. Clicking this icon should direct you to the settings page, as shown in figure 4.8.

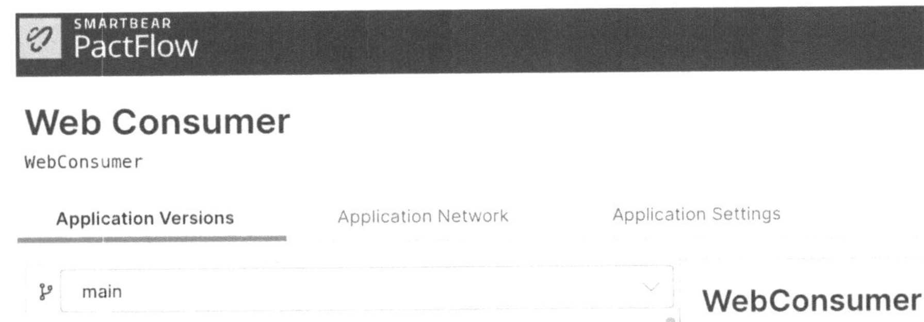

Figure 4.7 Landing page for PactFlow, a software as a service (SaaS) offering that helps you and your teams get started with Pact easily. When you create an account and navigate to the landing page, example contracts between different consumers and providers are provided to show how contract testing can work.

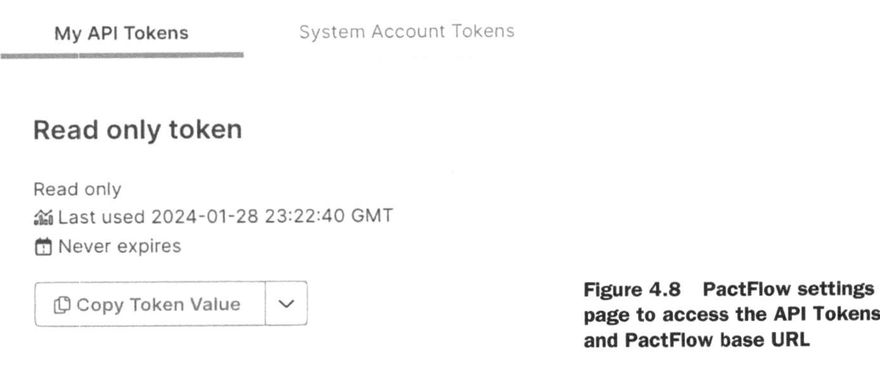

Figure 4.8 PactFlow settings page to access the API Tokens and PactFlow base URL

Once you've copied the base URL and API token, you can export them by typing the following in to your terminal:

```
# Mac
export PACT_BROKER_BASE_URL=<YOUR_BASE_URL>
export PACT_BROKER_TOKEN=<YOUR_TOKEN>
# Windows
set %PACT_BROKER_BASE_URL%=<YOUR_BASE_URL>
set %PACT_BROKER_TOKEN%=<YOUR_TOKEN>
```

If you're a Windows user, replace `export` with `set`. You can verify if the environment variables have exported correctly if you typed the following:

```
# Mac
echo $PACT_BROKER_BASE_URL
echo $PACT_BROKER_TOKEN
```

```
# Windows
echo %PACT_BROKER_BASE_URL%
echo %PACT_BROKER_TOKEN%
```

Now, you're ready to publish the contract! To do so, let's create a new script in our package.json called `publish:pact`, which uses the `pact-broker` command, which comes built-in when the Pact library has been installed:

```
"scripts": {
    "start:provider": "cross-env PORT=3001 node provider/provider-
     service.js",
    "test:web:consumer": "jest consumer-web/consumer-contract.spec.js",
    "publish:pact": "pact-broker publish ./pacts --consumer-app-
version=1.0.0 --tag=main --broker-base-url=$PACT_BROKER_BASE_URL
--broker-token=$PACT_BROKER_TOKEN"
  }
```

This command will publish the contract stored in my pacts folder to PactFlow. We'll use the `--consumer-app-version` flag and pass the `1.0.0` value to it for now. In chapter 10, we'll look at how to set better versions for our contracts. Next, we'll use the `--broker-base-url` and `--broker-base-token` flags and pass in the environment variables I set for my broker URL and token.

Make sure to save all the changes. To publish the contract, open your terminal, and type in the following command:

```
npm run publish:pact
```

You should see a message in your terminal, similar to figure 4.9:

```
→  pact-js-example git:(main) ✗ npm run publish:pact

> pact@1.0.0 publish:pact
> pact-broker publish ./pacts --consumer-app-version=1.0.0
er-token=$PACT_BROKER_TOKEN

Created WebConsumer version 1.0.0 with tags main
```

Figure 4.9 Output of publishing the contract to PactFlow

When you navigate back to PactFlow, you should now see a new contract that has been published, as shown in figure 4.10. Notice that the status of the contract is set to Unverified. This is because the provider hasn't yet verified the contract from their end.

And, there you have it! You've created your first consumer contract test and you've also published the contract to PactFlow. This is just one part of contract testing. The next stage is for the provider to verify the contract, which we'll explore in chapter 6.

WebConsumer
Version: f2a457875252ee7b666c7eadfd2658265dd87d18
Published 2024-05-17 13:25:45 GMT+1
main

Figure 4.10 New contract uploaded to PactFlow with the status set to Unverified

You'll also have the chance to write the contract tests for the other scenarios we defined in section 4.3.3. We haven't included it in this chapter because some of the scenarios required provider states to be set up, which we'll cover in chapter 6.

4.4.1 Committing all changes to GitHub

When you finish this chapter, don't forget to commit all the changes you've introduced locally to your forked GitHub project. To commit all your changes and push them up to your forked project, enter the following commands into your terminal:

```
git add .
git commit -m "added consumer contract tests"
git push origin setup-contract-tests-consumer
```

Summary

- The focus of contract testing is to verify what the consumer needs and check if they get it, based on the contract agreement.
- When writing consumer contract tests, you need to use a mock instead of a stub. A mock validates the behavior of your test, whereas a stub does not.
- Use loose matching, a functionality that allows for more flexible matching of data, when needed, to avoid flaky and brittle contract tests.
- Contract tests, similar to unit tests, should be isolated and not dependent on other tests.
- To follow the examples in the book, Node.js needs to be installed on your machine.
- Movies API is an example API that we've used to demonstrate how to write contract tests.
- Pact provides a set of functionalities for setting up the mock provider that the consumer interacts with, defining the expected interactions, and matching rules for a robust test.
- Pact also supports other programming languages such as Java, C#, Ruby, and Python.
- PactFlow, a commercial platform for sharing and managing contracts, is a great way to get started with using Pact Broker.

5 Implementing consumer-driven contract testing for mobile clients

This chapter covers

- Pact consumer setup for Android apps
- Android consumer test implementation
- Android consumer contract generation

Chapter 4 covered consumer-driven contract testing (CDCT) for web clients using Pact (specification version V3). However, if you're a mobile developer or tester, you'll want to understand how to implement CDCT in your native language. In this chapter, we'll use Kotlin and Gradle to walk through the implementation steps of CDCT in an Android-native application using Pact (specification version V4), from setting up the interaction and applying best practices to generating the consumer contract. Skip to chapter 6 if mobile isn't something you need at the moment.

If you have a strong understanding of the foundational concepts from chapter 3, it's time to start implementing contract testing. In our experience of working with mobile applications within a microservices environment, it's important to take care of external APIs interacting with the mobile app. Mobile apps are released in a bundled version at a point in time, but not every user updates the app at the same time. Good coverage around the contracts is key to providing a seamless experience for the user.

Imagine you're developing the mobile app for the new search feature, returning a list of movies. The API specification defines the `'/movies'` endpoint with an example response containing the ID, name, and release date. The API and mobile app are built based on the specification. Imagine the mobile app implementation changes the date field from a date type to a string in their tests that mock out the API service. They realize they only need to display the year of the movie's release, so there is no need to consume the raw date. However, due to time pressures, the API team forgot to make the change on their side. Once the API is deployed to a test environment and the mobile app Android Package Kit (APK) is available, then the misalignment will be detected. Figure 5.1 demonstrates how contracts can stray. Think about scenarios you've experienced that would benefit from a consumer contract test being implemented. This is a simple example but shows the importance of CDCT. Providing early feedback on these incidents can save time and reduce rework.

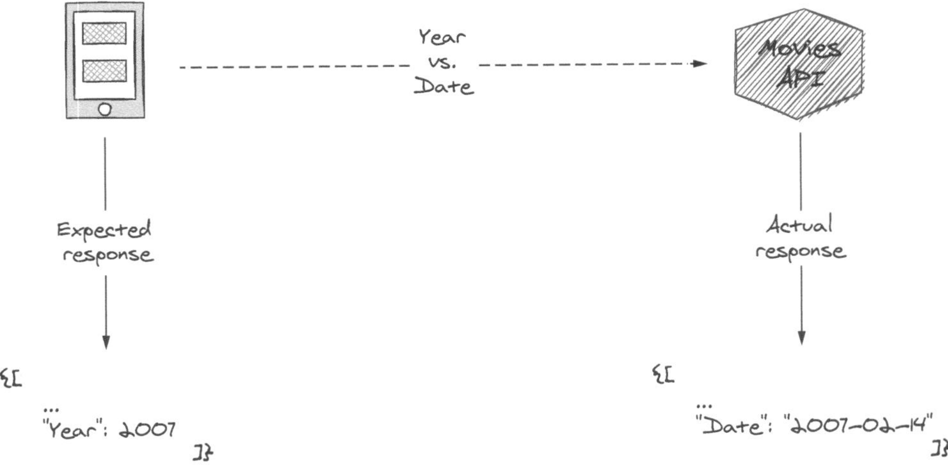

Figure 5.1 Mobile expected response with `Year` field and movies API actual response with `Date` field

In this chapter, we'll use CDCT for the following scenarios from the movies API:

1. **Scenario: Get all movies**
   Given a movie exists
   When a request is made to `GET` all movies
   Then the movies API should return 200 status code
   And the movies API response should return the ID, name, and year.
2. **Scenario: Add a new movie**
   Given the movie doesn't exist
   When a `POST` request is made to add a new movie

And body includes the movie name and release date
Then the movies API should return 201 status code.

5.1 Pact consumer setup for Android apps

Throughout the chapter, we'll reference a mobile app that searches via an API call to get a list of movies. We'll focus on the data layer of the mobile app, which communicates with the API service. We're not experts in mobile app development, so use the code in this chapter for reference, and apply your knowledge appropriately in your project.

In this chapter, we explain what you need regarding dependencies, test annotations, and all the intricacies of consumer Pact tests. We'll use the pact-jvm (https://github.com/pact-foundation/pact-jvm) implementation of the consumer-driven contract library Pact. Dependencies will be implemented using Gradle and Kotlin. The tests are written using the JUnit 5 framework. You can follow along with the code in the project repository (https://github.com/mdcruz/pact-js-example/).

5.1.1 Requirements

To follow along in this step-by-step tutorial, you need to have the following installed on your machine:

- Android Studio, Giraffe Version or above
- Git and access to GitHub

Navigate to the consumer-mobile folder in the GitHub project. The first thing we need is to add the dependencies to our Gradle project. build.gradle is implemented using Kotlin. First, import test logging for exception format and events. These will be referenced later in the build file.

Listing 5.1 build.gradle imports

```
import org.gradle.api.tasks.testing.logging.TestExceptionFormat.FULL
import org.gradle.api.tasks.testing.logging.TestLogEvent.FAILED
import org.gradle.api.tasks.testing.logging.TestLogEvent.PASSED
import org.gradle.api.tasks.testing.logging.TestLogEvent.SKIPPED
```

Second, add the Pact ID to the `plugins` section (check the latest version from the Gradle plugin portal: https://plugins.gradle.org/plugin/au.com.dius.pact). Pact JVM was originally created at DiUS.

Listing 5.2 build.gradle plugins

```
plugins {
    ...
    id("au.com.dius.pact") version "4.3.15"
}
```

Next, include the Pact JVM consumer package from Maven Central (https://mng.bz/6Yzy) as a test implementation dependency. JUnit 5 is part of the reference here, so make sure other JUnit 5 dependencies have also been included, such as junit-jupiter. Jupiter is a dependency for writing tests with Junit5. The latest version is available from the Maven repository (https://mng.bz/o09M).

Listing 5.3 build.gradle dependencies

```
dependencies {
    ...
    testImplementation("org.junit.jupiter:junit-jupiter:5.9.0")
    testImplementation("au.com.dius.pact.consumer:junit5:4.3.15")
}
```

Finally, add a task with type test and configuration, including using JUnit platform and test logging. In addition, add system properties to overwrite Pact files.

Listing 5.4 build.gradle tasks

```
tasks.withType<Test>().configureEach {
    useJUnitPlatform()
    testLogging {
      events(PASSED, SKIPPED, FAILED)
      exceptionFormat = FULL
      showExceptions = true
      showCauses = true
      showStackTraces = true
    }
    systemProperties["pact.writer.overwrite"] = true
}
```

5.1.2 Mobile app implementation

Now, we'll highlight some elements of the implementation within our example mobile app (located in the consumer-mobile folder in GitHub, https://mng.bz/n0KK). The code referenced in this section is only to provide some context for the implementation. Feel free to skip to section 5.2 if you want to jump to the Android consumer test implementation. For the mobile app implementation, let's look at the data layer within our mobile app (for reference in the GitHub example, see app/src/main/java/com/example/movie/data/repository/MovieRepositoryImpl.kt), as follows.

Listing 5.5 Movie repository implementation

```
class MovieRepositoryImpl @Inject
constructor(private val api: MovieAPI): IMovieRepository {
    override suspend fun getMovies(): MoviesDto {
        return MoviesDto(api.getMovies())
      }
    }
interface IMovieRepository {
    suspend fun getMovies(): MoviesDto
}
```

The implementation of the movie repository contains the API request to the external service. The constructor argument takes a `MovieAPI`-type object, as follows. The implementation contains one function, which gets all movies from the API.

Listing 5.6 `MovieAPI` object

```
interface MovieAPI {
    @GET("/movies")
    suspend fun getMovies(): List<Movie>
}

data class MoviesDto(
  val response: List<Movie>
)

data class Movie(
    val id: Int,
    val name: String,
    val year: Int,
)
```

The interface contains the API request, annotated with `retrofit2.http` request method `GET`, as shown in listing 5.6. The `getMovies` function returns a response with type `MoviesDTO`. The `MoviesDTO` data object returns the response list of the `Movie` object type. The `Movie` data object contains the ID, name, and year of the movie. This outlines how the mobile app will deserialize the JSON response from the movies API. Then, it can be passed to the presentation layer for display within the mobile app. The test hooks into the client, which exposes the API requests.

Listing 5.7 Movie client

```
fun MovieClient(url: String = BASE_URL): MovieAPI {
     return Retrofit.Builder()
     .baseUrl(url)
     .addConverterFactory(GsonConverterFactory.create())
     .build()
     .create(MovieAPI::class.java)
}
```

BASE_URL is an environment variable.

The movie client has been abstracted from the Dagger provider method binding (read more about Dagger basics at https://mng.bz/vJVM), which exposes an implementation of the API client. This has been abstracted so the URL can be passed as an argument to the function, which will become clear later when setting up the Pact mock server for the consumer tests. The movie client function returns the `MovieAPI` interface. Within the function, the retrofit builder defines the base URL and builds the instance of the `MovieAPI` client.

5.2 Android consumer test implementation

Now we can get to the main part of the chapter, which is implementing the contract tests for the data layer. We'll detail the implementation of the API repository and client hooks directly into the contract tests, which means that any change to the API implementation within the mobile app will automatically change the test implementation as well. Don't worry if you aren't familiar with the inner workings of Android native mobile apps. The important thing to take from the movie API client is that the client and repository implementation used within the test is the same as that used within the app. The only difference is that the URL has been replaced by the Pact mock server. This provides a significant benefit of implementing contract testing, linking back to some of the challenges we described in the introduction around API documentation becoming outdated. For example, the mobile app could filter the data returned from the movies API within the query parameters to the most recent 50 films to improve performance. To do that, the mobile app implementation can change the request in its code, and the Pact test automatically picks up the change. Therefore, an integration test is still recommended to test the real URL to verify that the configuration and authorization have been set up correctly.

Let's start writing consumer contract tests. As we're using Kotlin and JUnit 5, there are annotations that help us set up the test. The Pact consumer test sits along with the unit tests within the test projects, as shown in figure 5.2.

Figure 5.2 Android movie app folder structure showing the application com.example.movie folder. Under test folders, MoviesApiPactTest is highlighted.

In Android apps, the folders are split under the Java folder into application code; the presentation layer tests, which sit under the androidTest folder; and the logic layer tests, which live under the test folder. The Pact tests go with the logic tests in the test folder. Once the test file has been created, the class needs annotating with the Pact extension annotation, as follows.

Listing 5.8 Movie Pact class

```
import au.com.dius.pact.consumer.junit5.PactConsumerTestExt
import org.junit.jupiter.api.TestInstance
import org.junit.jupiter.api.extension.ExtendWith

@ExtendWith(PactConsumerTestExt::class)
@TestInstance(TestInstance.Lifecycle.PER_CLASS)
class MoviesApiPactTest {
```

The `ExtendWith` annotation takes the `PactConsumerTestExt` class as an argument to allow the test to enable Pact setup tasks. The Pact setup includes starting the mock server and methods to check that the class has all the right elements for the test to run successfully. `PactConsumerTestExt` comes bundled with the Pact JUnit 5 package, working with `ExtendWith` from the Junit Jupiter API package. Testing instance lifecycle `PER_CLASS` shares the test instance state between the test methods.

Once the class has been annotated, the next step is to build our Pact contract for the mock server when intercepting the request. To build the Pact contract, start with a `createPact` function. Remember from chapter 3, the consumer diagram shown in figure 5.3 is what we're going to set up in this chapter.

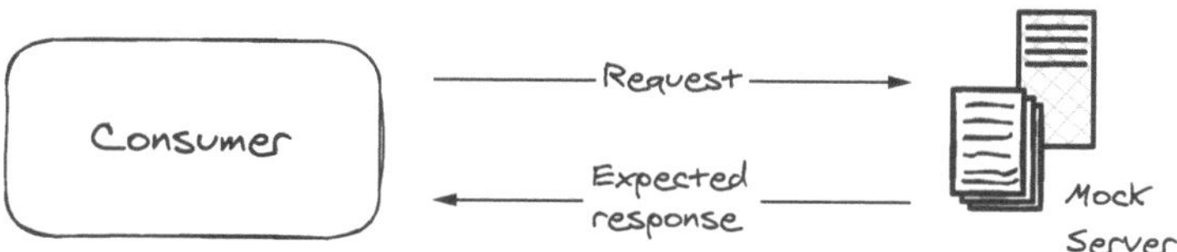

Figure 5.3 The consumer sets up the request and response in the form of a contract, which gets created within a mock server.

Create a function with the Pact annotation, along with parameters for the provider and consumer, shown in listing 5.9. The provider is the movie API service, and the consumer is the Android app. Each interaction will then be assigned to this consumer-provider relationship. Therefore, it's really important to keep the naming convention consistent and make sure the provider name is being referenced the same way across different consumers as well. The builder parameter is what we'll use to construct the Pact contract, and the output type of the builder will be V4Pact.

Listing 5.9 Create Pact

```
import au.com.dius.pact.consumer.dsl.PactDslWithProvider
import au.com.dius.pact.core.model.annotations.Pact
import au.com.dius.pact.core.model.V4Pact

@Pact(provider = "MoviesAPI", consumer = "MoviesAndroidApp")
fun createPact(builder: PactDslWithProvider): V4Pact {
```

V4Pact refers to version 4 (https://mng.bz/EOYO) of the Pact file format, supported in the Pact-JVM implementation. The V4 file format is a JSON text file with the following sections:

- consumer
- provider
- interactions
- metadata

The first two sections, the consumer and the provider, state which parties the contract is between. The third section, interactions, contains all the details of the consumer request and expected response. Think of an interaction as a test scenario. Each scenario is added to the contract for each consumer interaction with the provider. For example, the consumer wants to display all movies to the user by making a `GET` request to the `'/movies'` endpoint. The consumer also has an admin portal that adds movies to the list by making a `POST` request to the `'/movies'` endpoint. Each scenario has different request content and expected responses. The fourth section contains any metadata related to which version of the Pact file is being used and which implementation, for example, pact-jvm.

The builder parameter argument will form the core of the `createPact` function. The builder sets up the interaction related to the specific API request that will be tested, as shown in figure 5.4.

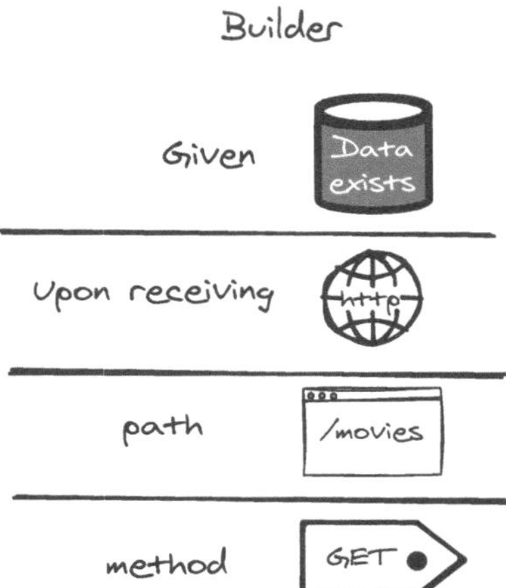

Figure 5.4 The Pact contract builder to be passed to the provider includes the given data upon receiving the HTTP request, URL path, and HTTP method.

There is a chain of steps to be performed using the builder: first setting the `given` statement, which takes a string argument. The given string sets out any prerequisites the provider service needs to set up before running the test. In the movie example app, this outlines that when requesting to get movies, there must be a movie that exists in the database. The string `"a movie exists"` is then used by the provider service to trigger the creation of movie data, as shown in listing 5.10. Following the given statement, the `upon receiving` method is a descriptive sentence relating to the request. This description is the start of the specific interaction with the provider service. Then, the subsequent methods define the URL path and HTTP method of the request.

Listing 5.10 Pact Builder, part 1

```
return builder
    .given("a movie exists")
    .uponReceiving("a request for all movies")
    .path("/movies")
    .method("GET")
```

The next part of building the Pact contract is the response methods, which will form what the consumer expects to receive from the provider service as shown in figure 5.5.

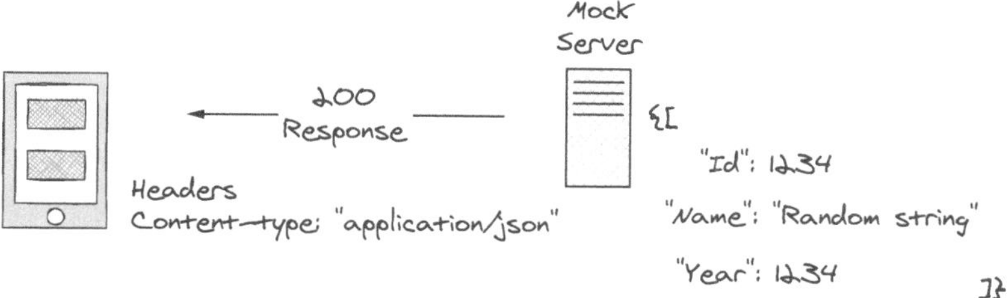

Figure 5.5 Pact response from the mock server with a 200 status code, header content type, and response body

The mock response contains everything you expect from the provider service, including the status code, headers, and response body. You'll set up the expected response within the Pact mock server with random values. The code in the following listing shows how these values are generated from the Pact domain-specific language (DSL).

Listing 5.11 Pact Builder, part 2

```
import au.com.dius.pact.consumer.dsl.DslPart
import au.com.dius.pact.consumer.dsl.PactDslJsonBody

    val body: DslPart = PactDslJsonArray.arrayEachLike()
        .integerType("id")
        .stringType("name")
        .integerType("year")
        .closeObject()!!
        ...
        .willRespondWith()
        .status(200)
        .headers(mapOf("Content-type" to "application/json"))
        .body(body)
```

Pact DSL matching methods

The following method chained to the Pact contract builder is `willRespondWith`, which starts the response section of the consumer interaction. The first part of the response section sets the HTTP status code with a number as an argument, for example, 200. Then, the `headers` method takes a map of two string elements. The header in this example sets the content type to JSON for the body of the response object. The `body` method supports different types of objects as arguments, such as `JSON` or `Document`. In this example, we're using the `DslPart` object type.

The body is constructed using the Pact DSL to build the JSON body, including Pact matchers. Matchers provide the ability to define the values of the JSON as the type of the value rather than the exact value itself. The movie's response contains an array of randomly generated objects with the ID, name, and year of the movie. Each part of the response is chained in the Pact DSL, and the movie elements are defined as their type, with the element key as the method argument. `Id` and `Year` are defined as integer types. `name` is declared as a string type. Each type method is a Pact DSL matching method; if no example value is provided within the method, then a random value will be generated. Find more matching methods available in the Pact documentation (https://mng.bz/4pYV). The final part of the builder adds the interaction to the Pact contract, as shown in the following listing.

Listing 5.12 Pact Builder, part 3

```
.toPact(V4Pact::class.java)
```

The final method, which finishes the consumer contract interaction, takes a Pact class argument. In this example, we're using the V4 Pact file format. Bringing it all together, we've created a consumer and provider interaction within a function that will generate a contract and form the mock within our consumer test, as shown in figure 5.6.

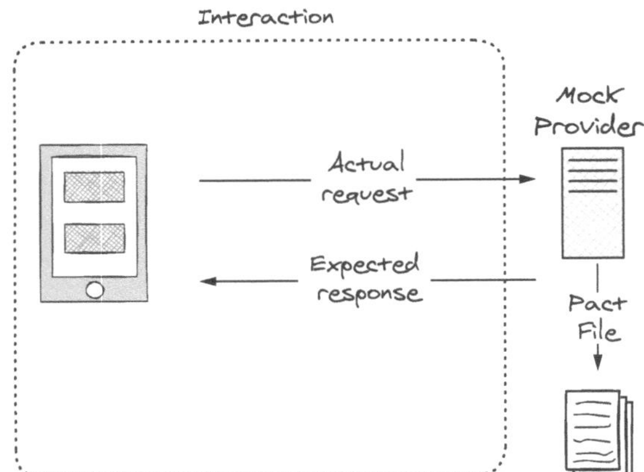

Figure 5.6 Pact interaction contains the mobile app's actual request intercepted and the expected response returned from the mock server. Finally, the interactions are converted to a Pact file.

Looking at the complete picture, the `createPact` function is annotated with the consumer and provider related to the specific request. The function takes `PactDslWithProvider` as an argument and returns the V4 Pact file format as the output. The body of the expected response is defined as a `DslPart` object. Finally, the builder chains all the request and response details needed to set up the contract, which maps directly to how the request is made in the code. The full version of the code is shown in the following listing, which shows the test and how it calls this function we've created.

Listing 5.13 `createPact` function

```
import au.com.dius.pact.core.model.annotations.Pact

@Pact(provider = "MoviesAPI", consumer = "MoviesAndroidApp")
fun createPact(builder: PactDslWithProvider): V4Pact {
```

```
    val body: DslPart = PactDslJsonArray.arrayEachLike()
        .integerType("id")
        .stringType("name")
        .integerType("year")
        .closeObject()!!
    return builder
        .given("a movie exists")
        .uponReceiving("a request for all movies")
        .path("/movies")
        .method("GET")
        .willRespondWith()
        .status(200)
        .headers(mapOf("Content-type" to "application/json"))
        .body(body)
        .toPact(V4Pact::class.java)
}
```

The test starts with a test annotation like any other JUnit test, as shown in listing 5.14. Then, the `PactTestFor` annotation provides the glue to connect the Pact setup we did earlier. This Pact test annotation takes multiple arguments. First, the provider names the same `"MoviesAPI"` provider given earlier when creating the Pact interaction. The second argument is the Pact method, which connects the function we created earlier (refer to listing 5.9). The third argument is the provider type. In this example, we're using an HTTP request; therefore, the `SYNCH` type is required for synchronous type requests.

Listing 5.14 Pact Test

```
import au.com.dius.pact.consumer.MockServer
import au.com.dius.pact.consumer.junit5.PactTestFor
import au.com.dius.pact.consumer.junit5.ProviderType
import org.junit.jupiter.api.Test

@Test
@PactTestFor(providerName="MoviesAPI",
pactMethod = "createPact",
providerType = ProviderType.SYNCH)
fun `should get movies response`(mockServer: MockServer) {
```

The reason for having a test within Pact is to make sure that the interaction that was built within the `createPact` method matches the actual request that is made from the mobile app. Then, if everything aligns between them, the contract will be created. To make this comparison, the test function takes a mock server provided by the Pact consumer package. Pact intercepts the request and returns the expected response within the Pact interaction build phase.

The test function contains the HTTP request and any assertions to check that the request has happened correctly, as shown in listing 5.15. The client is set up with the mock server URL, and, as shown earlier in listing 5.7, the function needs to overwrite the base URL for Pact to work. The response blocks the thread until its completion of the client call to get movies. The client method `getMovies` calls the `"/movies"` URL, as shown earlier in listing 5.6. The test asserts that the response data returned isn't empty, confirming the request has been mocked properly.

Listing 5.15 Assertion

```
import com.example.movie.data.di.AppModule.MovieClient
import org.junit.jupiter.api.Assertions.assertTrue

fun `should get movies response`(mockServer: MockServer) {
    var client = MovieClient(mockServer.getUrl())
    val response = runBlocking {
      client.getMovies()
    }
    assertTrue(response.isNotEmpty())
}
```

5.3 Android consumer contract generation

Running the test in Android Studio, you should see the green arrow icon by the test class or test function, as shown in figure 5.7.

```
class MoviesApiPactTest {

    @Test
    @PactTestFor(providerName="Movie
    fun `should get movies response`
```

Figure 5.7 Test class and test function with green arrows in Android Studio margin on the left

On completion of the test, if you get a green tick, then the Pact file should have been written to the pacts folder within the build folder, as shown in figure 5.8.

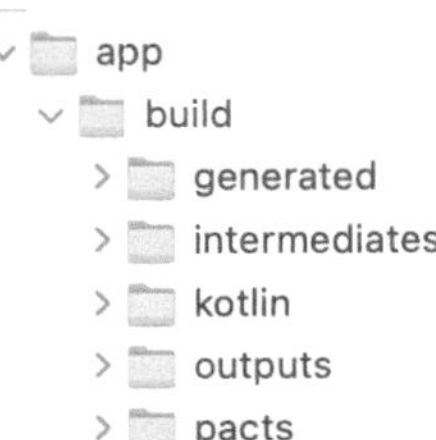

Figure 5.8 Android studio project folders app > build > pacts, with the pacts folder open showing the movie-android-app-movie-api.json file

The Pact JSON file that we built maps all the sections to JSON objects. Listing 5.16 shows the consumer and provider names. This creates the link in the Pact Broker for the interactions within the Pact file.

Listing 5.16 Android Movie Pact, part 1

```
"consumer": {
  "name": "MoviesAndroidApp"
},
```

```
"provider": {
  "name": "MoviesAPI"
}
```

Then, you'll see the array of interactions between the consumer and the provider. First, the `providerStates` array, which relates to the `given` method, is the state that the provider needs to be in before the test on their side. Following the response object is the `generators` object, containing each of the attributes defined as a specific type, for example, integer type. These types are part of the response body variable from listing 5.8. The `id` is given the `RandomInt` type, which generates a random integer for the contract in the correct format. Next is `matchingRules`, which come from the same methods. Returning matchers are used as part of the provider tests to match types against provider data types.

Listing 5.17 Android Movie Pact, part 2

```
"interactions": [
    {
      "description": "a request for all movies",
      "key": "95905108",
      "pending": false,
      "providerStates": [
        {
          "name": "a movie exists"
        }
      ],
      "request": {
        "method": "GET",
        "path": "/movies"
      },
      "response": {
        "body": {
          "content": [
            {
              "id": 100,
              "name": "string",
              "year": 100
            }
          ],
          "contentType": "application/json",
          "encoded": false
        },
        "generators": {
          "body": {
            "$[*].id": {
              "max": 2147483647,
              "min": 0,
              "type": "RandomInt"
            },
            "$[*].name": {
              "size": 20,
```

```
          "type": "RandomString"
        },
        "$[*].year": {
          "max": 2147483647,
          "min": 0,
          "type": "RandomInt"
        }
      }
    },
    "headers": {
      "Content-type": [
        "application/json"
      ]
    },
    "matchingRules": {
      "body": {
        "$": {
          "combine": "AND",
          "matchers": [
            {
              "match": "type"
            }
          ]
        },
        "$[*].id": {
          "combine": "AND",
          "matchers": [
            {
              "match": "integer"
            }
          ]
        },
        "$[*].name": {
          "combine": "AND",
          "matchers": [
            {
              "match": "type"
            }
          ]
        },
        "$[*].year": {
          "combine": "AND",
          "matchers": [
            {
              "match": "integer"
            }
          ]
        }
      }
    },
    "status": 200
  },
  "type": "Synchronous/HTTP"
 }
]
```

Finally, metadata is added to the Pact JSON file, which is taken from the package used and the Pact specification file format we defined.

Listing 5.18 Android Movie Pact, part 3

```
"metadata": {
  "pact-jvm": {
    "version": "4.3.15"
},
  "pactSpecification": {
    "version": "4.0"
  }
}
```

5.3.1 Pact matchers

Matchers are a key part of creating the mock objects within Pact (refer to section 4.1.3 for a detailed explanation). DSL matching methods range from generic string and integer types to specific date and IP address types. For more matcher types, see Pact JVM documentation (https://mng.bz/QVzj).

Listing 5.19 Matcher types example

```
PactDslJsonBody body = new PactDslJsonBody()
     .stringType("name", "Lewis")
     .integerType("no.")
     .date("todaysDate", "mm/dd/yyyy", date)
     .ipAddress("localAddress");
```

The matching types chain to the Pact DSL JSON body method. Some of the type methods can also take an optional argument, which is used as the example values within the Pact contract file. Matchers aren't exclusive to response bodies either. They can be applied to URL paths, headers, and query parameters.

Imagine we have an API that takes a movie name as the ID within the URL path, for example, "/movie/jaws". The `matchPath` method can be used to substitute the movie name with a regular expression. The method used in listing 5.7 path (`"/movies"`) earlier in the chapter would then be substituted with the `matchPath` method, as follows.

Listing 5.20 Match path

```
builder
  .given("test state")
  .uponReceiving("a movie id")
  .matchPath("/movies/[a-z]+")
```

Imagine the API exposes an endpoint to add a new movie to the database, and that this API endpoint requires an API token header to authorize the request. The `matchHeader` method can be used in this example for the provider to be able to substitute the API token with a real one when they run the test.

Listing 5.21 Match headers

```
.path("/movies")
.method("POST")
.matchHeader("API-Token", "xxx")
```

Imagine the `"/movies"` endpoint took a query parameter `"id"`. The `matchQuery` method can be used, taking three arguments: (1) the query parameter key value, (2) the regular expression for the value, and (3) the example value of the movie value. The provider will substitute the example value when running the test against their data set, as shown in listing 5.22. If you want to learn more about matching specifics, Pact documentation provides a detailed overview (https://mng.bz/XVE6).

Listing 5.22 Match query parameters

```
.path("/movies")
.method("GET")
.matchQuery("id", "[a-z]+", "jaws")
```

5.3.2 Pact POST requests

In listing 5.21 earlier, we touched upon an example that used a `POST` method. Of course, a `POST` request requires a body to accompany the request. As with the response body shown in listing 5.13 previously, the same can be applied after the request HTTP method as shown in listing 5.23. The `body` method chains off the HTTP method and takes a JSON body or Pact DSL object.

Listing 5.23 Request body

```
.method("POST")
.body("{\"name\": \"Lion King\", \"date\": \"2023-12-06\"}")
```

5.4 Chapter exercise

Now that you have a complete overview of how to create a consumer contract with Pact JVM, you can try and write more consumer tests for the `POST` endpoint scenario that we've provided:

1 **Scenario: Add a new movie**

Given the movie doesn't exist

When a `POST` request is made to add a new movie

And body includes the movie name and release date

Then the movies API should return the 201 status code.

Listing 5.24 `POST` request to add movie

```
@Headers("Content-Type: application/json")
@POST("/movies")
suspend fun addMovie(@Body movie: Add): JSONObject
```

Function in file: data/remote/MovieAPI

```
override suspend fun addMovie(movie: Add): JSONObject {
  api.addMovie(movie)
        return JSONObject()
   }

  data class Add(
    override val name: String,
    override val year: Int
  )
```

Function in file: data/repository/MovieRepositoryImpl

Class in file: domain/model/Movie

If you need any help, have a look at the main branch on GitHub in the consumer-mobile folder (https://mng.bz/n0KK).

Summary

- The Pact packages required to run Pact consumer tests include the Pact plugin and the Pact consumer test implementation dependency.
- Consumer contract tests target the data layer within Android mobile apps, implementing a modular architecture that improves contract testing testability.
- The Pact Builder constructs the request data and response expectations, forming the contract test interactions for the provider.
- Pact tests with JUnit5 annotations generate contracts on completing a successful test run, represented in the Pact specification to be published to the Pact Broker.
- The PactV4 specification contains four main parts—consumer, provider, interactions, and metadata—enabling the improved support for matching features.
- Pact JVM matchers support URL paths, query parameters, headers, and body objects, allowing data flexibility for the provider for all dynamic values.

6 Implementing consumer-driven provider contract tests

This chapter covers

- Guidelines in writing consumer-driven provider contract tests
- Contract testing tooling setup for the provider
- Provider contract tests between a web application and a data provider
- Provider contract tests between a mobile app and a data provider

In chapters 4 and 5 of this book, our primary focus was on creating the contract tests designed for various consumers. It's essential to keep in mind that in contract testing, there are two sets of tests that you need to write—one set encompassing consumers and the other encompassing providers. Based on our practical experience, we found that when it comes to setting up provider contract tests, this phase typically demands less code than its counterpart, the consumer contract tests.

Within the scope of consumer-driven contract testing (CDCT), we observed that most of the contract testing efforts belong to the consumer teams. After all, it's the consumer teams that essentially lay down the terms of the contract that providers must adhere to. Nevertheless, this shouldn't devalue the significance of provider tests. In fact, provider tests hold equal weight in contract testing. Without properly executed provider tests, the contract testing life cycle can't function as intended.

To better illustrate this, consider the house-buying analogy, previously mentioned in chapter 1. When buying a house, both the buyer and the seller must collaborate effectively to ensure that both parties are content and satisfied before proceeding with the buying and selling. In this analogy, the provider, much like the seller in the house-buying scenario, is tasked with verifying the contract generated by the consumer. This verification is essential to confirm that the provider fully understands and is agreeable to the terms and conditions outlined in the contract.

This chapter serves as a guide to provider contract tests, with a particular focus on the movies API, which was initially introduced in chapter 4. Before explaining the hands-on part, we provide some guidelines in writing provider contract tests. We then look into how you can pull the contract generated by consumers from a central repository, such as a Pact Broker, and subsequently guide you through the process of verifying the contents of the contract and publishing the results.

This chapter is still part of the CDCT approach, even though we guide you with the provider tests. It's not to be confused with the provider-driven contract testing (PDCT) approach, which we explore in chapter 11.

By the end of this chapter, you'll have more insights into the inner workings of CDCT, from the perspective of both consumers and providers, giving you more confidence to introducing contract testing to your teams.

6.1 Guidelines in writing provider contract tests

Similar to consumer contract tests, there are also a few guidelines when writing provider contract tests. Before you start the process of writing provider tests, the provider API should be available and ready to be tested because we'll be running the tests against the real provider API and not a mock one. In this section, we discuss some recommended practices in writing provider contract tests and cover topics such as the following:

- The focus of a provider contract test
- Using provider states effectively
- Using can-i-deploy to verify that you can safely deploy to production

6.1.1 The focus of a provider contract test

The primary focus of a provider contract test is to verify the contract that the consumer generated. Contract testing tools, such as Pact, provide a framework for allowing data providers to pull the contract and replay the interactions that the consumer registered as part of the contract. The interactions are run against the actual service, so any other features or functionality that the data provider provides but that aren't needed by the consumer shouldn't be tested as part of contract testing.

Let's explain this with a simple scenario using the movies API and web application consumer, first introduced in chapter 4. One of the scenarios that the web consumer expects is when they send a `GET` request to the `movies` endpoint, the movies API should return the ID, name, and year the movie was released, as shown in figure 6.1.

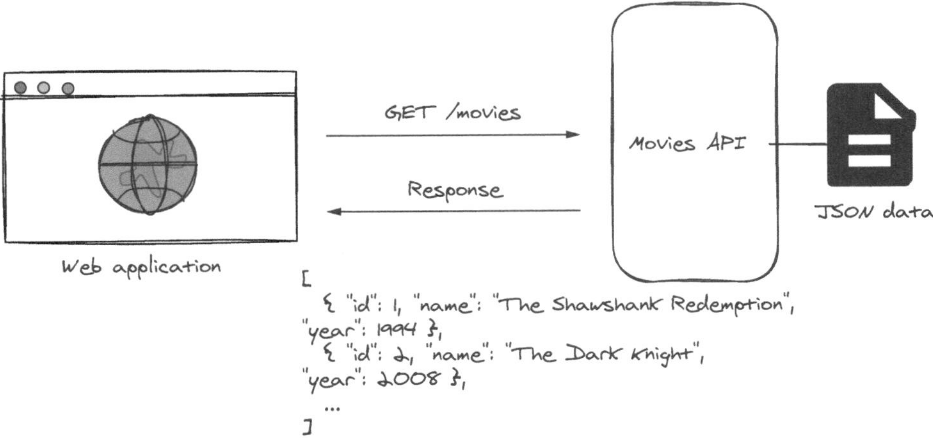
GET /movies
Response
Movies API
JSON data
Web application
[
{ "id": 1, "name": "The Shawshank Redemption",
"year": 1994 },
{ "id": 2, "name": "The Dark Knight",
"year": 2008 },
...
]

Figure 6.1 A web application sending a request to the movies API and the response it's expecting

A CDCT approach forces the data provider to develop only the consumer's required features. If the movies API introduces a breaking change that will update the `id` field from an integer to a string, the provider contract test should verify this change against the contract before deploying it to production.

As we first mentioned in chapter 2, contract testing allows the provider to develop features independently and safely. If the movies API introduces a new field, `reviewRating`, for a future feature that the web consumer doesn't need but a different consumer requires, then the provider contract test should be able to verify that the movies API can develop this feature safely.

However, a provider contract test shouldn't include tests verifying its business logic and other functionality. A different set of tests should cover the functionality, ideally on the unit level. For example, let's look at a different scenario where the consumer tries to add a movie. From a consumer perspective, their consumer contract tests should only be that when they add a new movie that doesn't exist, the provider should return the correct status code and that the new movie has been added successfully. If the provider has a few business rules regarding the movie's name, such as the character limit, then this needs to be covered as a separate unit test, as shown in table 6.1.

Table 6.1 Example business rules that should be covered in a unit test instead of a contract test

Business Rule	Unit	Contract
Movie name should have a minimum of 2 characters.	Yes	No
Movie name should have a maximum of 35 characters.	Yes	No

Table 6.1 Example business rules that should be covered in a unit test instead of a contract test *(continued)*

Business Rule	Unit	Contract
Movie name should only be alphanumeric.	Yes	No
Movie name shouldn't be empty.	Yes	Yes

Notice that a contract test covers the last business rule, which is also a major one. From a consumer perspective, this business rule makes the most sense for them, and they have built a shared understanding with the provider. If the other three business rules are also covered in a contract test, then if the provider changed their business rule that the movie name should now have a maximum of 30 characters instead of 35, the contract test will fail. Ideally, small changes in the business rules shouldn't break the contract with the consumers because it should have been picked up on the provider's unit tests. From a consumer perspective, they need to know how the provider responds if they send something wrong. All other functionalities the consumer doesn't care about should be covered by other types of tests from the provider side.

6.1.2 Using provider states effectively

As we mentioned in chapter 4, section 4.1.4, contract tests should be isolated and run without any dependencies because they sit above unit tests. However, what if a contract test requires some data that already exists on the provider? In some cases, you don't need to worry about this, but there are scenarios where consumers require an interaction in which the provider needs to be in a certain state. For example, in our web application and movies API scenario, the web application might send a `GET` request to the `/movie/2` endpoint to retrieve a specific movie. For the contract test to be stable, the data provider should always be in the same state of having the correct data set up before this interaction is verified. This step is crucial to avoid flaky contract tests. Imagine if the data provider was reset, and a contract test was run without ensuring the data provider was in the right state. The contract test will fail, not because of actual problems between the consumer and provider contract, but because the provider wasn't in the right state.

To ensure that providers are set up correctly before verifying the contract, contract testing tools, such as Pact, introduced the concept of provider states. Provider states allow data providers to define the state they need to be in to verify the interaction from the consumer contract successfully.

When you write a provider contract test with provider states, you need to also make sure that the provider state is provided from the consumer. In a nutshell, you follow this approach:

1. Set up the consumer contract test with a provider state.
2. Define the state on the provider.

This can also be visualized in the following code. Don't worry about the details of the code, but just pay attention to the flow of the test on both consumer and provider:

```
...

const EXPECTED_BODY = { id: 1, name: "My movie", year: 1999 };

const testId = 100;
EXPECTED_BODY.id = testId;

...

provider
  .given('a movie with specific ID', {          Sets up consumer
    id: 100,                                    contract test with a
  })                                            provider state
  .uponReceiving('a request to a specific movie')
  .withRequest({
    method: 'GET',
    path: '/movie/100',
  })
  .willRespondWith({
    status: 200,
    body: {
      id: integer(testId),
      name: string(EXPECTED_BODY.name),
      year: integer(EXPECTED_BODY.year)
    }
  })
})
...

stateHandlers: {
    'a movie with specific ID': (parameters) => {
      movies.getFirstMovie().id = parameters.id;
      return Promise.resolve({ description: `Movie with ID
${parameters.id} added!` });
    }
  }

...
```

Sets up the provider state on the provider side

We explain this code in more detail in section 6.3.2, but briefly, the state `'a movie with specific ID'` ensures that the provider is in the right setup before verifying the contract. In the preceding example code, we're making sure that the movie ID the consumer has specified as part of the contract exists on the provider side. When the provider replays the interaction from the contract, the provider will have the movie ID the consumer wants to test.

6.1.3 Using can-i-deploy to verify that you can safely deploy to production

As we first mentioned in chapter 4, when you integrate consumer tests into your pipeline, you need to make sure that any code changes from the consumer can be safely deployed to production. The same guideline can also be said for the provider contract tests. If the provider made some code changes and wants to deploy their changes to production, the can-i-deploy tool should also be used on the provider side to deploy these changes confidently and safely.

6.2 Contract testing tooling setup for the provider

As we mentioned already and you first saw in chapter 4, we use the contract testing tool Pact (https://pact.io/) to show how to start with contract testing because this is the current de facto contract testing tool. Because it will be difficult to cover all the programming languages that Pact supports, this chapter focus on how to set up pact-js, which is the JavaScript version.

> **NOTE** While we've chosen how to write provider contract tests in JavaScript, Pact supports other programming languages as well, such as Java, C#, Ruby, and Python. Specific implementations of Pact with other programming languages are listed at https://docs.pact.io/implementation_guides/.

As the pact-js online documentation is likely to be more up-to-date with API implementation changes, make sure to always check their documentation for more information (https://mng.bz/j0NP). If you've already followed the setup instructions in chapter 4, section 4.2, you don't need to do much setup in this chapter, apart from saving any local changes you have and switching to a new branch called `setup-contract-tests-provider`.

We'll still be using the example GitHub project that we've created, https://github.com/mdcruz/pact-js-example/, that you can download or fork online using Git. If you need additional guidelines on how to fork or download the project, see appendix B, specifically sections B.3 and B.4. Now, you're ready to verify the contract that the web application consumer created from chapter 4.

6.3 Provider contract tests between a web application and data provider

Let's revisit the consumer contract test that our web application from chapter 4 has created:

```
...

const EXPECTED_BODY = { id: 1, name: "My movie", year: 1999 };

describe('Movies Service', () => {
  describe('When a GET request is made to /movies', () => {
    test('it should return all movies', async () => {
      provider
        .uponReceiving('a request to all movies')
        .withRequest({
          method: 'GET',
```

```
            path: '/movies',
          })
          .willRespondWith({
            status: 200,
            body: MatchersV3.eachLike(EXPECTED_BODY),
          });

        await provider.executeTest(async mockProvider => {
          const movies = await fetchMovies(mockProvider.url);
          expect(movies[0]).toEqual(EXPECTED_BODY);
        });
      });
    });
  });
```

So far, we have one interaction to verify, but further in this chapter, we'll create one more consumer test to demonstrate provider states. In this interaction, the movies API provider is expected to respond with a status code of 200 and a body that is similar to `EXPECTED_BODY`.

6.3.1 Writing the provider test

Let's start writing the provider contract test. This will be broken down into the following code and shown in figure 6.2:

1. Importing the required dependencies
2. Running the provider service
3. Setting up the provider verifier options
4. Writing the provider contract test
5. Running the provider contract test

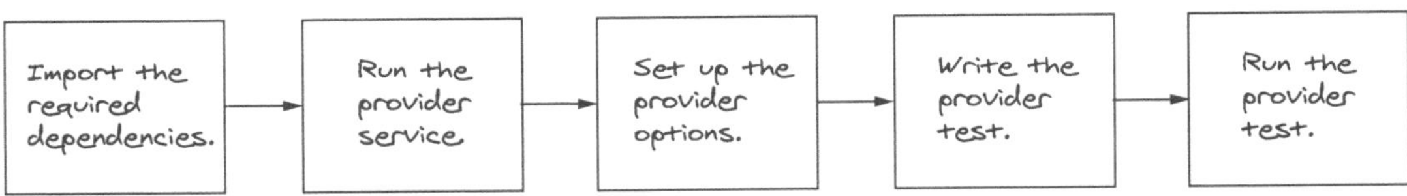

Figure 6.2 Steps in writing a provider contract test

IMPORTING THE REQUIRED DEPENDENCIES

In the provider folder, create a new file called provider-contract.spec.js, and add the following lines of code to import the required dependencies:

```
const { Verifier } = require('@pact-foundation/pact');
const { importData, server } = require('./provider')
```

First, we need the `Verifier` module from the Pact library. We also need the `importData` function and the `server` instance from the `provider.js` class.

Running the provider service

In a provider test, we need to make sure that the provider is up and running before we verify the contract. To start the provider as part of your test, add the following code after your import statements:

```
importData();

const port = '3001';
const app = server.listen(port, () => console.log(`Listening
on port ${port}...`));
```

This is essentially the same code found in provider-service.js. If you don't want to add this code, an alternative is to open another terminal window and run the command `npm run start:provider` before running your provider contract test. Just make sure that the movies API is up and running locally!

Setting up the provider verifier options

Pact provides an interface called `Verifier` to represent the provider for our test. To create the options for our provider, add the following code:

```
const options = {
  provider: 'MoviesAPI',
  providerBaseUrl: `http://localhost:${port}`,
  pactBrokerUrl: process.env.PACT_BROKER_BASE_URL,
  pactBrokerToken: process.env.PACT_BROKER_TOKEN,
  providerVersion: '1.0.0',
  publishVerificationResult: true,
  consumerVersionTags: ['main'],
};

const verifier = new Verifier(options);
```

In addition to these options, the `options` object contains other pieces of metadata:

- The `provider` name, `MoviesAPI`, should be the same name per the consumer contract.
- `providerBaseUrl` represents how to access our provider.
- `pactBrokerUrl` and `pactBrokerToken`, which we first set up in chapter 4, are required to download the consumer contract.
- `providerVersion` is hard-coded to `1.0.0` for now. We'll look at how to provide better versions in chapter 8.
- `publishVerificationResults` is set to `true` and will publish the verification results to our pact broker.
- `consumerVersionTags` is an array of consumer versions that we're going to verify. In this setup, the consumer version is set to `main`.

Once the options have been defined, we create a new instance of `Verifier` and pass in the options to that instance.

WRITING THE PROVIDER CONTRACT TEST

After setting up the provider verifier options, let's write the actual provider contract test using the Jest testing framework:

```
describe('Pact Verification', () => {
  test('should validate the expectations of movie-consumer', () => {
    return verifier
      .verifyProvider()
      .then(output => {
        console.log('Pact Verification Complete!');
        console.log('Result:', output);
        app.close();
      })
  });
});
```

The `describe` block explains that the test is for Pact verification. The test block represents the actual test itself. Within the `test` block, we're calling the `verifier` instance that we created previously and calling the `verifyProvider` method. This will replay the interaction from the contract and run it against the actual provider. For your reference, the full test in provider-contract.spec.js should look like this:

```
const { Verifier } = require('@pact-foundation/pact');
const { importData, server } = require('./provider')

importData();

const port = '3001';
const app = server.listen(port, () => console.log(`Listening
on port ${port}...`));

const options = {
  provider: 'MoviesAPI',
  providerBaseUrl: `http://localhost:${port}`,
  pactBrokerUrl: process.env.PACT_BROKER_BASE_URL,
  pactBrokerToken: process.env.PACT_BROKER_TOKEN,
  providerVersion: '1.0.0',
  publishVerificationResult: true,
  consumerVersionTags: ['main'],
};

const verifier = new Verifier(options);

describe('Pact Verification', () => {
  test('should validate the expectations of movie-consumer', () => {
    return verifier
      .verifyProvider()
      .then(output => {
        console.log('Pact Verification Complete!');
        console.log('Result:', output);
```

```
        app.close();
      })
  });
});
```

Running the provider contract test

To run the provider contract test, let's add a new script in our package.json file called `test:provider`, which uses the `jest` command followed by the test file you want to execute:

```
"scripts": {
      "test:provider": "jest provider/provider-contract.spec.js
--testTimeout=20000"
  }
```

The `--testTimeout` flag is added to make sure that the movies API service is up and running before running the test. If the service isn't up for 20 seconds, then a test timeout error will be thrown.

Before running the test, make sure you've exported the environment variables for your Pact Broker URL and Pact Broker token, which you can get from PactFlow's setting page, as first discussed in chapter 4, section 4.4. In addition, set the provider version to GitHub commit Secure Hash Algorithm (SHA). You can export them by typing the following into your terminal:

```
# Mac
export PACT_BROKER_BASE_URL=<YOUR_BASE_URL>
export PACT_BROKER_TOKEN=<YOUR_TOKEN>
export GITHUB_SHA=$(git rev-parse HEAD)
# Windows
set %PACT_BROKER_BASE_URL%=<YOUR_BASE_URL>
set %PACT_BROKER_TOKEN%=<YOUR_TOKEN>
set %GITHUB_SHA%=$(git rev-parse HEAD)
```

If you're a Windows user, replace `export` with `set`. To run the test, open up your terminal, and run the following command:

```
npm run test:provider
```

Alternatively, you can also add these two environment variables as part of your .bash_profile file so you don't have to export the Pact Broker token and URL every time. After running the command, you should see an output similar to figure 6.3.

When you navigate back to PactFlow, you should see that the following contract has now been verified, as shown in figure 6.4.

```
Verifying a pact between WebConsumer and MoviesAPI

  a request to all movies (2s 746ms loading, 390ms verification)
    returns a response which
      has status code 200 (OK)
      includes headers
        "Content-Type" with value "application/json" (OK)
      has a matching body (OK)

  console.log
    Pact Verification Complete!

      at log (provider/provider-contract.spec.js:32:17)

  console.log
    Result: finished: 0

      at log (provider/provider-contract.spec.js:33:17)

PASS provider/provider-contract.spec.js (5.4 s)
  Pact Verification
    ✓ should validate the expectations of movie-consumer (4868 ms)

Test Suites: 1 passed, 1 total
Tests:       1 passed, 1 total
Snapshots:   0 total
Time:        5.426 s, estimated 6 s
Ran all test suites matching /provider\/provider-contract.spec.js/i.
```

Figure 6.3 Example provider test run output

Figure 6.4 Consumer contract from WebConsumer verified by MoviesAPI provider

6.3.2 *Introducing provider states*

Now that you've verified the contract, things will get more interesting! If you remember from the scenarios that the web consumer defined in chapter 4, one of the scenarios was that they needed to request a specific movie. Let's revisit the scenario:

1. **Scenario: Get a single movie**
   Given there is a movies API
   When the consumer fetches a single movie
   Then the movies API should return a status code of 200
   And the ID, name, and year the movie was released.

When the consumer writes a contract test for this, most of the time, when the provider verifies the contract, the test will pass. But, in certain situations, this test could become flaky due to the movie being deleted by another team member or the test database being cleared. You don't necessarily want the contract test to fail when this situation arises. To solve this problem, we'll introduce provider states. Setting up provider states includes the following steps:

1. Writing a new consumer contract test
2. Using a provider state
3. Running the consumer contract test
4. Uploading the new contract
5. Setting up a `stateHandler` on the provider codebase
6. Running the provider contract test

Writing a new consumer contract test

Let's start with structuring and adding a new test in the consumer-web/consumer-contract.spec.js file:

```
describe('When a GET request is made to a specific movie ID', () => {
    test('it should return a specific movie', async () => {

    });
  });
```

Within the `test` block, let's set up the new interaction that we want to register to the mock provider:

```
const EXPECTED_BODY = { id: 1, name: "My movie", year: 1999 };

...

const testId = 100;
EXPECTED_BODY.id = testId;

 provider
    .uponReceiving('a request to a specific movie')
    .withRequest({
       method: 'GET',
       path: `/movie/${testId}`,
     })
     .willRespondWith({
       status: 200,
       body: {
         id: integer(testId),
         name: string(EXPECTED_BODY.name),
         year: integer(EXPECTED_BODY.year)
       }
     });
```

This is similar to the first consumer contract test introduced in chapter 4, except we've updated the path to `/movie/${testId}`. Next, you need to import and call the function the consumer created that is responsible for fetching a specific movie and passing in the URL of the mock provider and the test ID. Once the `fetchSingleMovie` function is called, you need to verify that the actual data returned by the consumer matches the expected data:

```
const { fetchMovies, fetchSingleMovie } = require('./consumer');

...

await provider.executeTest(async mockProvider => {
  const movies = await fetchSingleMovie(mockProvider.url, testId);
  expect(movies).toEqual(EXPECTED_BODY);
});
```

USING A PROVIDER STATE

To use a provider state, you need to call the `given` method and pass in the name of the provider state and any arguments we want to pass. The naming of the provider state is important because this needs to be the same name from the provider side:

```
provider
  .given('Has a movie with specific ID', { id: testId })
  .uponReceiving('a request to a specific movie')
  .withRequest({
    method: 'GET',
    path: `/movie/${testId}`,
  })
```

When Pact registers this interaction, it will also register the name of the provider state as well as any arguments the consumer passes. For your reference, the file consumer-web/consumer-contract.spec.js should now look like this:

```
const path = require('path');
const { fetchMovies, fetchSingleMovie } = require('./consumer');
const { PactV3, MatchersV3 } = require('@pact-foundation/pact');

const {
  eachLike,
  integer,
  string,
} = MatchersV3;

const provider = new PactV3({
  dir: path.resolve(process.cwd(), 'pacts'),
  consumer: 'WebConsumer',
  provider: 'MoviesAPI',
});

const EXPECTED_BODY = { id: 1, name: "My movie", year: 1999 };
```

```
describe('Movies Service', () => {
  describe('When a GET request is made to /movies', () => {
    test('it should return all movies', async () => {
      provider
        .uponReceiving('a request to all movies')
        .withRequest({
          method: 'GET',
          path: '/movies',
        })
        .willRespondWith({
          status: 200,
          body: eachLike(EXPECTED_BODY),
        });

      await provider.executeTest(async mockProvider => {
        const movies = await fetchMovies(mockProvider.url);
        expect(movies[0]).toEqual(EXPECTED_BODY);
      });
    });
  });

  describe('When a GET request is made to a specific movie ID', () => {
    test('it should return a specific movie', async () => {
      const testId = 100;
      EXPECTED_BODY.id = testId;

      provider
        .given('Has a movie with specific ID', { id: testId })
        .uponReceiving('a request to a specific movie')
        .withRequest({
          method: 'GET',
          path: `/movie/${testId}`,
        })
        .willRespondWith({
          status: 200,
          body: {
            id: integer(testId),
            name: string(EXPECTED_BODY.name),
            year: integer(EXPECTED_BODY.year)
          }
        });

      await provider.executeTest(async mockProvider => {
        const movies = await fetchSingleMovie(mockProvider.url, testId);
        expect(movies).toEqual(EXPECTED_BODY);
      });
    });
  });
});
```

Running the consumer contract test

In your terminal, use the same command found in the package.json file to run the consumer contract test:

```
npm run test:web:consumer
```

This should generate the same output as shown in figure 6.5.

```
PASS  consumer-web/consumer-contract.spec.js) pact_models::pact: Note: Existing pact is an older specif
  Movies Service
    When a GET request is made to /movies
      ✓ it should return all movies (26 ms)
    When a GET request is made to a specific movie ID
      ✓ it should return a specific movie (5 ms)

Test Suites: 1 passed, 1 total
Tests:       2 passed, 2 total
Snapshots:   0 total
Time:        0.943 s, estimated 1 s
Ran all test suites matching /consumer-web\/consumer-contract.spec.js/i.
```

Figure 6.5 Test output of running the consumer contract test

UPLOADING THE NEW CONTRACT

Because there are now two interactions registered, this will generate a new contract containing the expectations for the second test. Use the same command found in the package.json file to upload the new contract to PactFlow. Usually this would run as part of continuous integration (CI) only and requires GitHub commit SHA and GitHub branch environment variables to be set:

```
# Mac
export GITHUB_SHA=$(git rev-parse HEAD)
export GITHUB_BRANCH=<MAIN_BRANCH>
# Windows
set %GITHUB_SHA%=$(git rev-parse HEAD)
set %GITHUB_BRANCH=<MAIN_BRANCH>

npm run publish:pact
```

You might notice a similar output message in figure 6.6, which states that the contract wasn't successfully uploaded to PactFlow because of versioning problems. When contract changes are made, Pact recommends a unique version number to avoid any unreliable results with contract verification.

```
  Next steps:
    * Configure separate GraphQLProvider pact verification build and webhook to trigger it when the pact
 content changes. See https://docs.pact.io/go/webhooks
Cannot change the content of the pact for MoviesAPI version 1.0.0 and provider MoviesAPI, as race condit
ions will cause unreliable results for can-i-deploy. Each pact must be published with a unique consumer
version number. Some Pact libraries generate random data when a concrete value for a type matcher is not
 specified, and this can cause the contract to mutate - ensure you have given example values for all typ
e matchers. For more information see https://docs.pact.io/go/versioning
```

Figure 6.6 Test output of trying to upload a new contract to PactFlow. PactFlow recommends having a unique consumer version every time the contract is updated.

To fix this problem, we'll update the `--consumer-app-version` for now, but in later chapters, we'll show you how to use better versioning. This will normally be the commit number from version control in real-life projects. Go ahead and update the version manually as part of the `publish:pact` command found in package.json:

```
"publish:pact": "pact-broker publish ./pacts --consumer-app-
version=1.0.1 --tag=main --broker-base-url=$PACT_BROKER_BASE_URL
--broker-token=$PACT_BROKER_TOKEN"
```

Once the `publish:pact` command has the updated version number, save the file, and run the command again. You should now see a similar output as shown in figure 6.7.

```
Created WebConsumer version 1.0.1 with tags main
  Next steps:
    Configure the version branch to be the value of your repository branch.
Pact successfully published for WebConsumer version 1.0.1 and provider MoviesAPI.
  View the published pact at https://mariecruz.pactflow.io/pacts/provider/MoviesAPI/consumer/WebConsumer
/version/1.0.1
  Events detected: contract_published, contract_content_changed (pact content has changed since the last
 consumer version tagged with main)
  Next steps:
    * Configure separate MoviesAPI pact verification build and webhook to trigger it when the pact conte
nt changes. See https://docs.pact.io/go/webhooks
→  pact-js-example git:(main) ✗
```

Figure 6.7 Test output of uploading a new contract to PactFlow

SETTING UP A STATE HANDLER ON THE PROVIDER CODEBASE

The next step is to set up the provider state on the provider codebase. To do this, you need to set up the `stateHandlers` as part of the provider options in the provider/provider-contract.spec.js file. The `stateHandlers` define the different provider states before all the contract verification. The names of the `stateHandlers` must match the names of the provider states defined in the consumer contract test:

```
const options = {
  provider: 'MoviesAPI',
  providerBaseUrl: `http://localhost:${port}`,
  pactBrokerUrl: process.env.PACT_BROKER_BASE_URL,
  pactBrokerToken: process.env.PACT_BROKER_TOKEN,
  providerVersion: '1.0.0',
  publishVerificationResult: true,
  consumerVersionTags: ['main'],
  stateHandlers: {
    'Has a movie with specific ID': (parameters) => {

    }
  }
};
```

Within this state handler, the specific movie ID the consumer uses as part of their contract test must exist before calling the provider verification. There will be multiple ways of doing this, but as part of this code walkthrough, we've kept it simple by getting the first movie and updating its movie ID:

```
const { importData, movies, server } = require('./provider')

...

'Has a movie with specific ID': (parameters) => {
   movies.getFirstMovie().id = parameters.id;
   return Promise.resolve({ description: `Movie with ID
${parameters.id} added!` });
 }
```

The `getFirstMovie` function returns the first movie, and we're simply updating its ID with the ID that the consumer has used as part of their contract, represented by `parameters.id`. For your reference, the file provider/provider-contract.spec.js file should now look like this:

```
const { Verifier } = require('@pact-foundation/pact');
const { importData, movies, server } = require('./provider')

const port = '3001';
const app = server.listen(port, () => console.log(`Listening
on port ${port}...`));

importData();

const options = {
  provider: 'MoviesAPI',
  providerBaseUrl: `http://localhost:${port}`,
  pactBrokerUrl: process.env.PACT_BROKER_BASE_URL,
  pactBrokerToken: process.env.PACT_BROKER_TOKEN,
  providerVersion: '1.0.0',
  publishVerificationResult: true,
  consumerVersionTags: ['main'],
  stateHandlers: {
    'Has a movie with specific ID': (parameters) => {
      movies.getFirstMovie().id = parameters.id;
      return Promise.resolve({ description: `Movie with
ID ${parameters.id} added!` });
    }
  }
};

const verifier = new Verifier(options);

describe('Pact Verification', () => {
  test('should validate the expectations of movie-consumer', () => {
    return verifier
      .verifyProvider()
      .then(output => {
        console.log('Pact Verification Complete!');
        console.log('Result:', output);
```

As the provider isn't uploading the contract, the version remains similar. In chapter 10, we'll use an automated version number.

```
        app.close();
      })
    });
  });
```

RUNNING THE PROVIDER CONTRACT TEST

To run the provider verification, run the following command in your terminal again:

```
npm run test:provider
```

You should now see that two requests have been verified successfully by the provider. If you also look at the logs closely, you'll see a similar output as in figure 6.8.

```
2023-12-01T13:13:37.819737Z  INFO ThreadId(09) pact_verifier: Running setup provider state change handler '
Has a movie with specific ID' for 'a request to a specific movie'
2023-12-01T13:13:37.936919Z  INFO ThreadId(09) pact_verifier: Running provider verification for 'a request
to a specific movie'
2023-12-01T13:13:37.936952Z  INFO ThreadId(09) pact_verifier::provider_client: Sending request to provider
at http://127.0.0.1:65170/
2023-12-01T13:13:37.936954Z  INFO ThreadId(09) pact_verifier::provider_client: Sending request HTTP Request
 ( method: GET, path: /movie/100, query: None, headers: None, body: Missing )
```

Figure 6.8 Test logs explaining that the provider state change handler was run first before running the provider verification.

When you finish this chapter, don't forget to commit all the changes you've introduced locally to your forked GitHub project.

6.4 Provider contract tests between a mobile app and data provider

From chapter 5, we also created a consumer contract between a mobile app and the movies API. Because we provided the same provider name as part of the mobile consumer setup, as shown in the following code snippet, no additional steps are required to verify the mobile contract:

```
class MoviesApiPactTest {
  @Pact(provider = "MoviesAPI",
consumer = "movies-android-app")        <-- MoviesAPI provider name as part of the mobile consumer contract setup

  ...

}
```

If you also remember from the provider verification setup, we also used the same provider name when we defined the provider options:

```
const options = {
  provider: 'MoviesAPI',        <-- MoviesAPI provider name as part of the provider verification setup
```

```
    ...
};

const verifier = new Verifier(options);
```

When the provider verification is run, all contracts associated with the `MoviesAPI` provider will be pulled down from the Pact Broker and run against the local `MoviesAPI` service. This is one of the many benefits of using a Pact Broker because the provider can pull the relevant contracts they need to verify from different teams, ensuring that their contracts are verified before the provider pushes any of their changes to production.

6.5 Chapter exercise

Now that you have a complete overview of how to verify a contract from the provider side and also use provider states effectively, you can try and write more web or mobile consumer tests for the following scenarios that we've provided as part of the contract agreement and verify the new scenarios from the provider side:

1. **Scenario: Add a new movie**

   Given there is a movies API

   When the consumer adds a new movie by specifying the movie name and date

   Then the movies API should accept the movie

   And return a status code of 201.
2. **Scenario: Add an existing movie**

   Given there is a movies API

   When the consumer adds an existing movie by specifying the movie name and date

   Then the movies API should return a status code of 409

   And the movies API should return a suitable error message.
3. **Scenario: Delete a new movie**

   Given there is a movies API

   When the consumer deletes a new movie that doesn't exist

   Then the movies API should return a status code of 404

   And a suitable error message.
4. **Scenario: Delete an existing movie**

   Given there is a movies API

   When the consumer deletes an existing movie

   Then the movies API should return a status code of 200.

For the first and second scenario, because this is a `POST` request, the provider setup should look slightly different, with the addition of providing the request body:

```
provider
    .uponReceiving('a request to add a new movie')
```

```
.withRequest({
    method: 'POST',
    body: YOUR_BODY_HERE
    path: '/movies',
  })
```

When you've written the additional tests, don't forget to update the `--consumer-app-version` as part of the `publish:contract` script, and run the following command in your terminal to run the test:

```
npm run test:consumer
npm run publish:contract
```

If you encounter any problems with your tests and want to generate the contract found in WebConsumer-MoviesAPI.json, you can always delete the json file. The contract will be generated again after running the `npm run test:consumer` command.

Once the contract has been published to PactFlow, run the command to run the provider verification test. If you get stuck at any point, check out the main branch of the original GitHub project for assistance at https://github.com/mdcruz/pact-js-example/tree/main, or check out appendix C for the answers.

Summary

- The focus of provider contract tests is to verify the contract generated by their consumers.
- Contract testing shouldn't cover all the provider's business rules because contract testing isn't the same as functional testing and should be handled by a separate set of tests on the provider codebase.
- Provider states allow data providers to define the state they need to be in to verify the interaction from the consumer contract successfully.
- Pact provides a set of functionalities for the provider verification through the `Verifier` interface.
- To effectively set up provider states, the name of the provider state from the consumer must match the name of the state handler from the provider.
- When contract changes are made, Pact recommends a unique version number to avoid any unreliable results with contract verification.

7 Contract testing for GraphQL

This chapter covers

- A brief introduction to GraphQL
- GraphQL application overview
- Consumer contract tests between a consumer and GraphQL layer
- Provider contract tests between a consumer and GraphQL layer

In previous chapters, you've seen how to write contract tests for web and mobile consumers, but the underlying data provider has always been a representational state transfer (REST) API, which is quite common. However, you might work on a project involving GraphQL instead of REST. While REST APIs have been seen as the de facto standard for companies providing APIs, many companies are switching to GraphQL as an alternative. However, REST APIs and GraphQL can also work together, so GraphQL shouldn't be seen as a competitor or a complete replacement of REST. A common approach the authors have seen in work projects is using GraphQL as a middle layer between consumers and various backend data services using REST or other APIs such as gRPC or Simple Object Access Protocol (SOAP).

In this chapter, we provide a brief introduction to GraphQL and explain how to introduce contract testing to GraphQL applications, covering both the consumer and provider tests. As in previous chapters, we'll be using the sample movies application.

As a disclaimer, we aren't experts in GraphQL and are drawing from our personal experiences instead, having worked with our development team. If you want to know more about GraphQL and how to integrate it with different frontend and backend technologies, feel free to check out this free and open source tutorial: www.howtographql.com/.

7.1 A brief introduction to GraphQL

GraphQL (https://graphql.org/) is an API standard that provides a more efficient, powerful, and flexible alternative to REST. Facebook initially developed it, but it's now maintained by a large open source community.

Unlike REST APIs, GraphQL allows the request to describe the desired structure of the response, which is why a single API endpoint can be used for multiple purposes. To explain the difference, let's consider the scenario of fetching data. In the context of our movie application, let's say the consumer wants to create a landing page for each movie. The landing page will have data about the movie, the different actors from the movie, and other movies they have starred in. With a REST API, because an endpoint returns a fixed set of data structures, consumers would need to make different `GET` requests to multiple endpoints to retrieve all the data that they need, as illustrated in figure 7.1.

On the other hand, in GraphQL, consumers can send a single query and specify the data structure themselves, as shown in figure 7.2. In a GraphQL setting, consumers have full control of the data they want the server to return. This also eliminates the problem of under-fetching or over-fetching of data, which can also improve performance because consumers aren't making multiple requests.

GraphQL defines the data they expose through their own type language which is called the GraphQL schema definition language (SDL). This schema can be seen as the contract that the consumers need to abide by when making queries. An example schema for our movie is shown here:

```
type Movie {
  id: Int
  name: String
  year: Int
}
```

As we first mentioned in chapter 3, a schema provides the outline or the structure of a JSON file as an example. The `type Movie` doesn't expose any functionality yet, but it only defines the structure of a movie. In GraphQL, the behavior of the API is defined separately and is done by a resolver function. Resolvers are responsible for

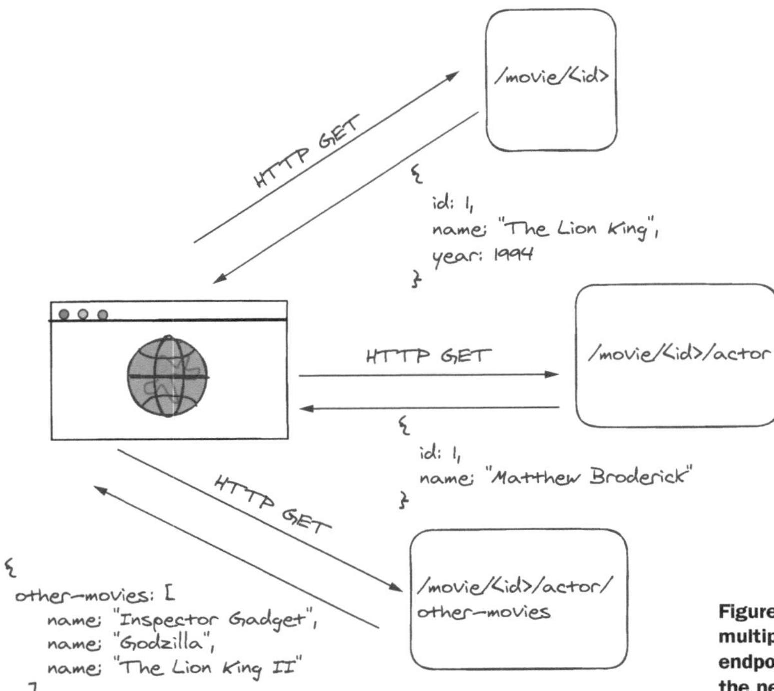

Figure 7.1 A web consumer making multiple `GET` requests to different endpoints via the REST API to get all the necessary data can lead to under-fetching or over-fetching of data.

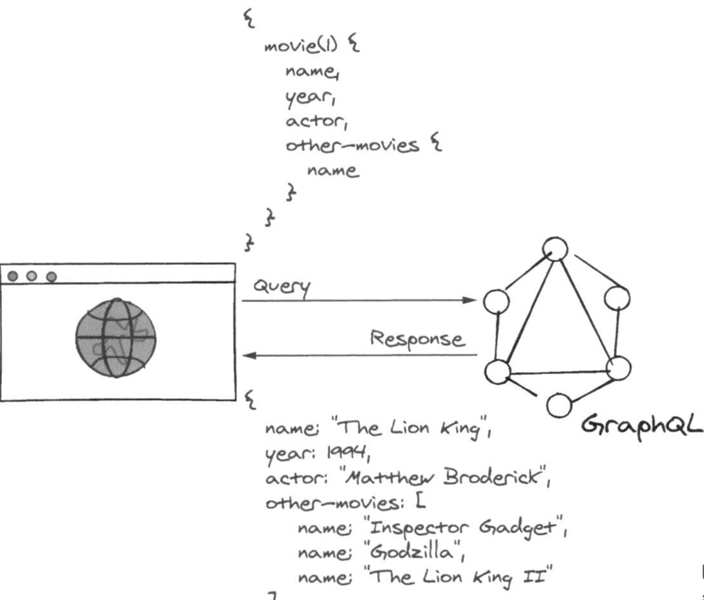

Figure 7.2 A web consumer making a single query to a GraphQL endpoint to retrieve all the data they require

knowing which data to fetch. An example resolver for getting a single movie is shown here:

```
const resolvers = {
  Query: {
    movie: (root, { movieId }, { dataSources }) => {
      return dataSources.movieApi.getMovieById(movieId);
    }
  }
}
```

With the schema and resolvers defined, if a consumer adds "rating" as part of their query, but the GraphQL SDL doesn't include "rating," then the query will fail.

Because the structure of a query can be defined with a schema, should you still do contract testing? Yes, you should! With contract testing, teams maintaining the GraphQL API can understand the following:

- How different consumers are using the API
- What query from consumers produces bad output
- What query from consumers produces different status codes, such as 401 or 403

If you would like to learn about GraphQL in more detail, check out the following resources:

- *GraphQL in Action* by Samer Buna (Manning, 2021): www.manning.com/books/graphql-in-action
- *Microservice APIs* by José Haro Peralta (Manning, 2022): www.manning.com/books/microservice-apis
- "Introduction to GraphQL": https://graphql.org/learn/
- GraphQL tutorials: www.apollographql.com/tutorials/

7.2 GraphQL application overview

To demonstrate how contract testing can be used in a GraphQL setting, we've also created an example application that you can play around with based on our movies API, which you can find in the same GitHub project (https://github.com/mdcruz/pact-js-example) that we've been referencing. If you need additional guidelines on how to fork or download the project, refer to appendix B, specifically sections B.3 and B.4. Once you have a copy of this GitHub project in your local machines, switch to the setup-contract-tests-graphql branch.

We're using Apollo (www.apollographql.com/), which is a collection of tools for working with GraphQL applications. On the server side, we're using Apollo Server, a JavaScript library for building GraphQL APIs, while on the client side, we're using Apollo Client, a JavaScript library for consuming GraphQL APIs on the frontend.

All the code for this chapter is in the graphql folder, as shown in this folder structure:

```
> consumer-mobile
> consumer-web
```

```
> data
> graphql
> pacts
> provider
```

In the real world, this project structure would be unlikely because consumers and providers will probably live in different projects. We've kept everything in a single project just to make the learning experience a bit easier.

The contract testing approach that we'll follow in this chapter will introduce contract testing between a consumer and a GraphQL layer. So, in this case, the GraphQL layer will be the provider. However, with other projects we've worked on, we've also seen contract testing approaches where the GraphQL layer was the consumer and different data sources as providers. GraphQL as a consumer approach is also valid, but we'll focus on a consumer interacting with a GraphQL endpoint for this chapter.

NOTE When GraphQL acts as the consumer, the same principles of contract testing that we've discussed in this book still apply.

7.2.1 GraphQL server overview

The GraphQL server consists of two important files:

- *data-source.js*—A file representing the data source for our GraphQL server, which at the moment, is the movies API. This file can be easily extended to also support other data sources.
- *graphql-server.js*—The main entry point to start the GraphQL server. The file consists of the GraphQL SDL, the resolver, and all the other setup to start our GraphQL server.

An overview of how the GraphQL server works is shown in figure 7.3.

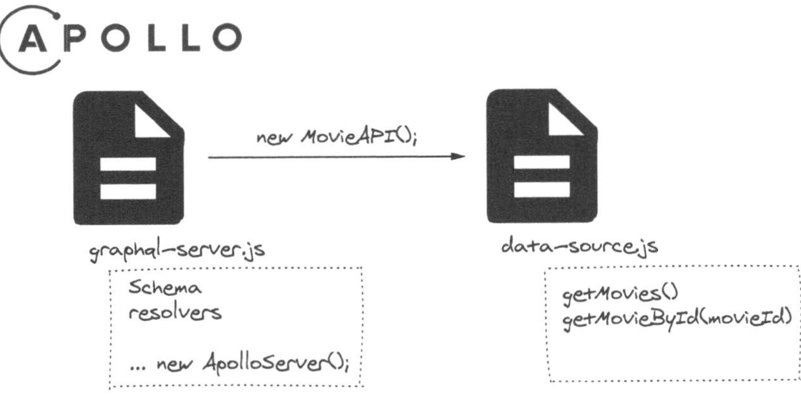

Figure 7.3 GraphQL API at a glance with all the relevant files

An overview of data-source.js

Inside the graphql folder, you should see another folder named provider. If you expand the provider folder, you should see a file named data-source.js, which should have the following code:

```
const { RESTDataSource } = require('@apollo/datasource-rest');

class MovieAPI extends RESTDataSource {
  baseURL = 'http://localhost:3001';

  async getMovies() {
    return this.get('/movies');
  }

  async getMovieById(movieId) {
    return this.get(`/movie/${movieId}`);
  }
};

module.exports = MovieAPI;
```

The package `@apollo/datasource-rest` exports a class called `RESTDataSource`, which is used to fetch data from REST APIs easily. `RESTDataSource` provides built-in methods such as `this.get()` to perform HTTP requests. The file exports the `MovieAPI` so the GraphQL server can use the `getMovies` and `getMovieById` functions.

An overview of graphql-server.js

Within the provider folder, there is another class named graphql-server.js, which represents the code to set up our GraphQL server. Let's break down the code into different parts:

```
const { ApolloServer } = require('apollo-server');
const { startStandaloneServer } = require('@apollo/server/standalone');
const MovieAPI = require('./data-source.js');
const gql = require('graphql-tag');
```

First, we import all the required packages needed to set up our GraphQL server. The `apollo-server` package is an open source library for server-side GraphQL, which exports the `ApolloServer` class.

> **NOTE** We're using Apollo Server 4 for this project. If you're familiar with Apollo Server 3, there are significant changes between the two versions, which we won't cover as part of this book. However, if you're interested in migrating from Apollo Server 3 to 4, then check out this useful migration guide from Apollo at www.apollographql.com/docs/apollo-server/migration.

Because we're using Apollo Server 4, we also need to export the `startStandaloneServer` function from `@apollo/server/standalone`, which is a recommended change.

We're also exporting the `MovieAPI` for our data source and the `gql` template literal tag from `graphql-tag`, a helpful utility for parsing GraphQL queries and defining our GraphQL schema. Next, we define our GraphQL schema:

```
const typeDefs = gql`

  type Movie {
    id: Int
    name: String
    year: Int
  }

  type Query {
    movie(movieId: Int!): Movie
    movies: [Movie]
  }
`;
```

Movie type containing three fields: id, name, and year

Query type defining all the queries allowed in our GraphQL server

The `typeDefs` object represents our GraphQL schema and contains two types:

- `Movie`—Represents a movie with the different fields it contains: `id`, `name`, and `year`.
- `Query`—Represents the queries allowed in our GraphQL server. The `movie` query represents a single movie and requires a mandatory `movieId`. There is also the query `movies`, which represents a list of movies.

To define the behavior of our queries, we define the `resolvers`:

```
const resolvers = {
  Query: {
    movies: (root, args, { dataSources }) => {
      return dataSources.movieApi.getMovies();
    },
    movie: (root, { movieId }, { dataSources }) => {
      return dataSources.movieApi.getMovieById(movieId);
    },
  },
}
```

Calls the getMovies() to get all the movies

Calls the getMovieById() and passes in the movieId to get a specific movie

The resolvers call the `getMovies` and `getMovieById` functions we defined in the class. To define our GraphQL server using Apollo, we create a new instance of `ApolloServer` and pass in our defined schema and the resolvers, as well as our data source. Once the GraphQL server is all set up, it's time to start the server as shown in the following code:

```
async function startServer() {
  const server = new ApolloServer({
    typeDefs,
    resolvers,
  });
```

Our GraphQL schema via the typeDefs object

Our GraphQL resolver via the resolvers object

```
  const { url } = await startStandaloneServer(server, {
    context: async () => {
      return {
        dataSources: {
          movieApi: new MovieAPI()
        }
      }
    }
  });

  console.log(` GraphQL server ready at ${url}`);
}

startServer();
```

Our movieAPI data source to fetch the data

Starts the GraphQL server

7.2.2 Running the GraphQL server

To run the GraphQL server, we've created a new script. Open your terminal, and run the following command:

```
npm install
npm run start:graphql:server
```

The command installs the package dependencies in case you haven't installed the dependencies required for this project and starts the GraphQL server. After running the command, you should see the following message printed to your terminal:

```
GraphQL server ready at http://localhost:4000/
```

When you navigate to `http://localhost:4000/`, you should see the GraphQL Playground, as shown in figure 7.4. Feel free to run some example queries to familiarize yourself with the GraphQL Playground.

`start:graphql:server` is a custom script that we've added within the scripts section of the package.json file, which contains the following command:

```
"scripts": {
    "start:provider": "cross-env PORT=3001
node provider/provider-service.js",
    "start:graphql:server": "npm run start:provider &
node graphql/provider/graphql-server.js"
  }
```

The command also starts the movie API provider because our GraphQL server has a dependency on it.

Figure 7.4 The GraphQL Playground is a graphical, interactive, in-browser GraphQL IDE that you can use for GraphQL development.

7.2.3 Consumer overview

From the GraphQL consumer perspective, we're also keeping it simple. A user interface (UI), typically using React, which is a popular JavaScript framework for building web applications, presents a list of movies in real-world projects. In our simple GraphQL project, we expose the functions the UI needs to display the data.

Inside the graphql folder, you should see another folder named consumer, which contains a file called graphql-client.js. Let's break down the code into two parts, with the first part focused on setting up the `ApolloClient`:

```
const { ApolloClient, InMemoryCache, gql, HttpLink }
= require('@apollo/client');

const client = new ApolloClient({
  cache: new InMemoryCache({
    addTypename: false,
  }),
  link: new HttpLink({
    fetch: require('node-fetch'),
    uri: 'http://127.0.0.1:4000/graphql',
  }),
});
```

Initializes ApolloClient so we can fetch data from our GraphQL server

The next part of the code defines the queries that we need to fetch all the movies and a single movie from our GraphQL server:

```
const getMovies = async () => {
  const response = await client
    .query({
      query: gql`
        query MoviesQuery {
          movies {
            id
            name
            year
          }
        }
      `,
    })
    .then((result) => result.data)
    .catch((err) => err.response);

  return response;
};

const getMovieById = async (movieId) => {
  const response = await client
    .query({
      query: gql`
        query Movie($movieId: Int!) {
          movie(movieId: $movieId) {
            id
            name
            year
          }
        }
      `,
variables: {
  movieId,
},
    })
    .then((result) => result.data)
    .catch((err) => err.response);

  return response;
};

module.exports = {
  getMovies,
  getMovieById,
};
```

The query for retrieving all movies from our GraphQL server

The query for retrieving a single movie from our GraphQL server

The `getMovies` function queries our GraphQL server to retrieve all the movies. This should return the `id`, `name`, and `year`. If there are any errors, the error message is returned instead. On the other hand, the `getMovieById` function queries our GraphQL server to retrieve a single movie. It's expecting a `movieId` as a variable corresponding to the movie ID. If the movie is found, this should return the `id`, `name`, and `year` of the movie. If the movie doesn't exist, the error message is returned instead. Now that you have an overview of both the GraphQL provider and consumer, let's begin writing our first consumer contract test for our GraphQL application!

7.3 Consumer contract tests between a consumer and GraphQL layer

Let's start writing the consumer contract test for scenario 1, as defined again here:

1. **Scenario: Get all movies**

   Given there is a movies API

   When the consumer fetches all movies

   Then the movies API should return a status code of 200

   And for each movie, it should return the ID, name, and year it was released.

Because GraphQL can be seen as a wrapper for our movies API, writing the consumer contract test follows the same pattern as a standard consumer contract test, as we've first explored in chapter 4. For familiarity, the steps to write the GraphQL consumer contract test will be broken down into the following steps:

1. Importing the required dependencies
2. Setting up the mock provider that the consumer will use
3. Registering the expectation that the consumer has against the provider to the mock provider
4. Verifying the consumer test, and generating the contract
5. Publishing the contract to the Pact Broker

7.3.1 Importing the required dependencies

In the consumer folder, create a new file called graphql-client-contract.spec.js, and add the following lines of code to import the required dependencies:

```
const path = require('path');
const { getMovies } = require('./graphql-client.js')
const { Pact, GraphQLInteraction, Matchers }
= require('@pact-foundation/pact');
const { eachLike } = Matchers;
```

We need the path module to manage the file directory naming for our contract because we'll need to store the contract that Pact will generate. We also require the actual query we need to test, which is the `getMovies` function from the graphql-client.js file. Finally, we require the `Pact` and `Matchers` modules from the Pact library, as well as `GraphQLInteraction`, a lightweight wrapper provided by Pact, to make GraphQL contract testing easier.

Unlike the consumer contract testing you first saw in chapter 4, the GraphQL interaction uses PactV2 instead of PactV3. There are breaking changes introduced in

PactV3, which you can find at https://mng.bz/Bgq8, but the overall concept of writing the contract test remains the same in PactV2. As of writing this book, there is currently an open request from the community for GraphQL to support PactV3, which you can see at https://mng.bz/NBE1.

7.3.2 Setting up the mock provider

The next step is to define the mock provider that Pact will use, which you should now be familiar with. Add the following lines of code to your graphql-client-contract.spec.js file:

```
const provider = new Pact({
  port: 4000,
  dir: path.resolve(process.cwd(), 'pacts'),
  consumer: 'GraphQLConsumer',
  provider: 'GraphQLProvider',
});

describe('GraphQL example', () => {
  beforeAll(() => provider.setup());

  ...
});
```

This code calls the `Pact` constructor to create a new mock provider that we can use as part of our GraphQL consumer contract test. As part of the constructor, we're passing parameters to define the port for the mock provider and the directory for the contracts to be stored in the pacts folder of the current working directory. We're also passing the parameters to define the name of the GraphQL consumer and provider, which, in this example, are `GraphQLConsumer` and `GraphQLProvider`. These names will be used throughout the contract generation and when you upload the contract to Pact Broker.

To structure the outline of our test, the preceding code also adds a `describe` block, first introduced in chapter 4 and provided by the Jest testing framework, as well as a `beforeAll` block to set up the mock provider by calling `provider.setup()`.

7.3.3 Registering the consumer expectation

To register a new consumer expectation or interaction, we need to set up the mock provider with the correct consumer expectations. We can set this up by adding the following code after the first `beforeAll` block:

```
beforeAll(() => provider.setup());

describe('When a query to list all movies on /graphql is made', () => {
  beforeAll(() => {

    const graphqlQuery = new GraphQLInteraction()
      .uponReceiving('a movies request')
      .withQuery(
        `
```

```
        query MoviesQuery {
          movies {
            id
            name
            year
          }
        }
        `
      )
      .withOperation('MoviesQuery')
      .withVariables({})
      .withRequest({
        method: 'POST',
        path: '/graphql',
      })
      .willRespondWith({
        status: 200,
        headers: {
          'Content-Type': 'application/json; charset=utf-8',
        },
        body: {
          data: {
            movies: eachLike(EXPECTED_BODY),
          },
        },
      });
    return provider.addInteraction(graphqlQuery);

  })
});
```

With this interaction, we're creating a new instance of `GraphQLInteraction`, calling the `uponReceiving` method and passing in the scenario name as a string. In this example, we say the scenario name is `'a movies request'`. Next, we call the `withQuery` method and pass in the GraphQL query to retrieve all movies. Because we have provided `MoviesQuery` as our operation name, which is optional, we also call the method `withOperation` and pass the operation name. The `withVariables` method represents any variables we need to pass to our query, which in this case is none, so we pass an empty object. We call the `withRequest` method to make the request, passing in the `/graphql` endpoint.

To represent the query response details from the mock provider, we call the `willRespondWith` API and pass in the response details. In this example, the mock provider should respond with a status of 200 and the correct header type. The response body is represented as a variable called `EXPECTED_BODY`. Let's declare this variable outside our test:

```
const EXPECTED_BODY = { id: 1, name: "My GraphQL movie", year: 1999 };
```

Feel free to update `EXPECTED_BODY` to be of any value, as long as the data type matches. Using Pact matchers, we're saying that `EXPECTED_BODY` should have an ID, the movie name should be something similar to "My GraphQL movie", and the year should be something similar to the year 1999.

Remember that with contract testing, the consumer should care more about the shape of the data rather than the data itself. We use the `eachLike` matching rule to ensure the type matches all the values. This way, the test should still pass if the provider returns different values, but the types are similar.

7.3.4 Verifying the consumer test and generating the contract

The next step is to call the function the GraphQL consumer created, responsible for fetching all the movies. In this example, the `getMovies` function is called and stored in the `response` variable:

```
test('returns the correct response', async () => {
  const response = await getMovies();
});
```

Once the `getMovies` function is called, we need to verify that the actual data returned by the GraphQL consumer matches the expected data. We do this by comparing the actual data returned and the expected data we defined:

```
test('returns the correct response', async () => {
  const response = await getMovies();
  expect(response.movies[0]).toEqual(EXPECTED_BODY);
});
```

To verify the consumer expectation against Pact and to generate the contract, we need to add the following methods in our test:

```
provider.verify();
provider.finalize();
```

For your reference, the full test should look like this one:

```
const path = require('path');
const { getMovies } = require('./graphql-client.js')
const { Pact, GraphQLInteraction, Matchers }
= require('@pact-foundation/pact');
const { eachLike } = Matchers;

const provider = new Pact({
  port: 4000,
  dir: path.resolve(process.cwd(), 'pacts'),
  consumer: 'GraphQLConsumer',
  provider: 'GraphQLProvider',
});

const EXPECTED_BODY = { id: 1, name: "My GraphQL movie", year: 1999 };

describe('GraphQL example', () => {

  beforeAll(() => provider.setup())
```

```
describe('When a query to list all movies on /graphql is made', () => {
  beforeAll(() => {
    const graphqlQuery = new GraphQLInteraction()
      .uponReceiving('a movies request')
      .withQuery(
        `
        query MoviesQuery {
          movies {
            id
            name
            year
          }
        }
      `
      )
      .withOperation('MoviesQuery')
      .withVariables({})
      .withRequest({
        method: 'POST',
        path: '/graphql',
      })
      .willRespondWith({
        status: 200,
        headers: {
          'Content-Type': 'application/json; charset=utf-8',
        },
        body: {
          data: {
            movies: eachLike(EXPECTED_BODY),
          },
        },
      });
    return provider.addInteraction(graphqlQuery);
  });

  it('returns the correct response', async () => {
    const response = await getMovies();
    expect(response.movies[0]).toEqual(EXPECTED_BODY);

    provider.verify();
    provider.finalize();
  });
 });
});
```

Now, you're ready to run the test! To run this test, let's create a new script in our package.json file called **`test:graphql:consumer`**, which uses the `jest` command followed by the test file you want to execute:

```
"scripts": {
   "test:graphql:consumer": "jest
graphql/consumer/graphql-client-contract.spec.js"
 }
```

Make sure you save all the changes! To run the test, open your terminal, and type in the following command:

```
npm run test:graphql:consumer
```

If everything has been set up well, running this command should return one passing test and an output similar to that shown in figure 7.5.

```
→ pact-js-example git:(update-packages) ✗ npm run test:graphql:consumer

> pact@1.0.0 test:graphql:consumer
> jest graphql/consumer/graphql-client-contract.spec.js


 RUNS  graphql/consumer/graphql-client-contract.spec.js
 RUNS  graphql/consumer/graphql-client-contract.spec.js
2023-12-22T20:01:53.245733Z  INFO tokio-runtime-worker pact_mock_server::hyper_server: Received request PO
ST /graphql
2023-12-22T20:01:53.246551Z  INFO tokio-runtime-worker pact_matching: comparing to expected HTTP Request (
 method: POST, path: /graphql, query: None, headers: Some({"Content-Type": ["application/json"]}), body: P
resent(206 bytes, application/json) )
2023-12-22T20:01:53.251380Z  INFO tokio-runtime-worker pact_mock_server::hyper_server: Request matched, se
nding response
 PASS  graphql/consumer/graphql-client-contract.spec.jsels::pact: Note: Existing pact is an older specific
  GraphQL example
    When a query to list all movies on /graphql is made
      ✓ returns the correct response (24 ms)

Test Suites: 1 passed, 1 total
Tests:       1 passed, 1 total
Snapshots:   0 total
Time:        0.658 s, estimated 1 s
Ran all test suites matching /graphql\/consumer\/graphql-client-contract.spec.js/i.
```

Figure 7.5 Test output of running the GraphQL consumer contract test

When the test run completes, Pact will also generate the contract, which is saved in the `pacts` directory. If you also generated the web consumer contract from chapter 4, you should now see a similar folder structure output like this:

```
> consumer-mobile
> consumer-web
> data
> graphql
> pacts
  { } GraphQLConsumer-GraphQLProvider.json
  { } WebConsumer-MoviesAPI.json
> provider
```

7.3.5 Publishing the contract to Pact Broker

To publish the GraphQL consumer contract to the PactFlow Pact Broker, we'll use the same script `publish:pact` that we created in chapter 4. Make sure you've exported your Pact Broker URL and token, as first explained in chapter 4, section 4.4, and then run the following command:

```
npm run publish:pact
```

You should see a message in your terminal, similar to figure 7.6, with two published contracts—one for the web consumer and one for GraphQL.

```
> pact@1.0.0 publish:pact
> pact-broker publish ./pacts --consumer-app-version=1.0.2 --tag=main --broker-base-url=$PACT_BROKER_BASE_
URL --broker-token=$PACT_BROKER_TOKEN

Updated GraphQLConsumer version 1.0.2 with tags main
  Next steps:
    Configure the version branch to be the value of your repository branch.
Pact successfully republished for GraphQLConsumer version 1.0.2 and provider GraphQLProvider with no conte
nt changes.
  View the published pact at https://mariecruz.pactflow.io/pacts/provider/GraphQLProvider/consumer/GraphQL
Consumer/version/1.0.2
  Events detected: contract_published
  Next steps:
    * Configure separate GraphQLProvider pact verification build and webhook to trigger it when the pact c
ontent changes. See https://docs.pact.io/go/webhooks
Updated WebConsumer version 1.0.2 with tags main
  Next steps:
    Configure the version branch to be the value of your repository branch.
Pact successfully republished for WebConsumer version 1.0.2 and provider MoviesAPI with no content changes
.
  View the published pact at https://mariecruz.pactflow.io/pacts/provider/MoviesAPI/consumer/WebConsumer/v
ersion/1.0.2
  Events detected: contract_published
  Next steps:
    * Configure separate MoviesAPI pact verification build and webhook to trigger it when the pact content
 changes. See https://docs.pact.io/go/webhooks
```

Figure 7.6 Output of publishing the contracts to PactFlow

7.4 Provider contract tests between a consumer and GraphQL layer

In chapter 6, we introduced how to write the provider contract tests between a web consumer and a REST API. The setup for provider contract testing between the GraphQL consumer and GraphQL provider is similar. One thing to note, though, is that our GraphQL server depends on the movies API, as shown in figure 7.7.

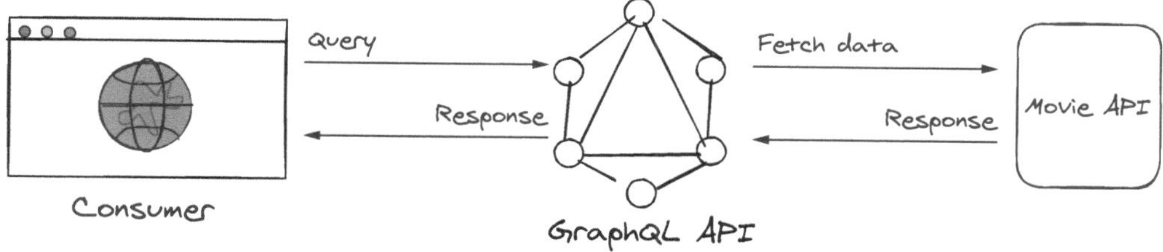

Figure 7.7 Consumer sending a query to the GraphQL server, which also has a dependency on Movies API

We can introduce contract testing in a few ways with this setup:

- Create a contract test between the GraphQL server and movies API, where the GraphQL server is the consumer, and the movies API is the provider. With this approach, the GraphQL server needs to have some form of collaboration with its consumers to make sure that their expectations will be covered.
- Create a contract test between the consumer and GraphQL server as the provider, and stub out the call to the movies API.
- Create a contract test between the consumer and GraphQL server as the provider, and make sure the movies API is up and running.

When choosing the approach, use what makes the best sense to you and your team. Because our example project is simple, we've decided to follow the last approach and make sure that the movies API is running.

To create the provider contract test, create a new file in the provider folder called graphql-server-contract.spec.js. The provider contract test will look similar to the one you first saw in chapter 6, apart from the `provider` and `providerBaseUrl` values:

```
const { Verifier } = require('@pact-foundation/pact');

const options = {
  provider: 'GraphQLProvider',
  providerBaseUrl: `http://localhost:4000/graphql`,
  pactBrokerUrl: process.env.PACT_BROKER_BASE_URL,
  pactBrokerToken: process.env.PACT_BROKER_TOKEN,
  providerVersion: '1.0.0',
  publishVerificationResult: true,
  consumerVersionTags: ['main'],
};

const verifier = new Verifier(options);

describe('Pact Verification', () => {
  test('should validate the expectations of GraphQLConsumer', () => {
    return verifier
      .verifyProvider()
      .then(output => {
        console.log('Pact Verification Complete!');
        console.log('Result:', output);
```

```
      });
    });
  });
```

To run this test, let's add a new command to our package.json file to run the GraphQL provider verification and call the command `test:graphql:provider`:

```
"scripts": {
    "start:provider": "cross-env PORT=3001
node provider/provider-service.js",
    "start:graphql:server": "npm run start:provider
& node graphql/provider/graphql-server.js",
    "test:graphql:provider": "npm run start:graphql:server
& jest graphql/provider/graphql-server-contract.spec.js --testTimeout=20000"
  }
```

The command `test:graphql:provider` runs the command `start:graphql:server` to start the GraphQL server as well as the movies API. When you run the `test:graphql:provider` command, you should see an output similar to figure 7.8.

```
RUNS  graphql/provider/graphql-server-contract.spec.js
The pact at https://mariecruz.pactflow.io/pacts/provider/GraphQLProvider/consumer/GraphQLConsumer/pact-ver
sion/41e368c38beb297e0f52c693b0e6887bbd8a8772 is being verified because the pact content belongs to the co
nsumer version matching the following criterion:
    * latest version tagged 'main' (1.0.2)

Verifying a pact between GraphQLConsumer and GraphQLProvider

  a movies request (2s 501ms loading, 429ms verification)
    returns a response which
      has status code 200 (OK)
      includes headers
        "Content-Type" with value "application/json; charset=utf-8" (OK)
      has a matching body (OK)

  console.log
    Pact Verification Complete!

      at log (graphql/provider/graphql-server-contract.spec.js:20:17)

  console.log
    Result: finished: 0

      at log (graphql/provider/graphql-server-contract.spec.js:21:17)

 PASS  graphql/provider/graphql-server-contract.spec.js (5.142 s)
  Pact Verification
    ✓ should validate the expectations of GraphQLConsumer (4576 ms)
```

Figure 7.8 Example test run output of pact verification between GraphQLConsumer and GraphQLProvider

When you navigate back to PactFlow, you should see that the GraphQL contract has now been verified, as shown in figure 7.9.

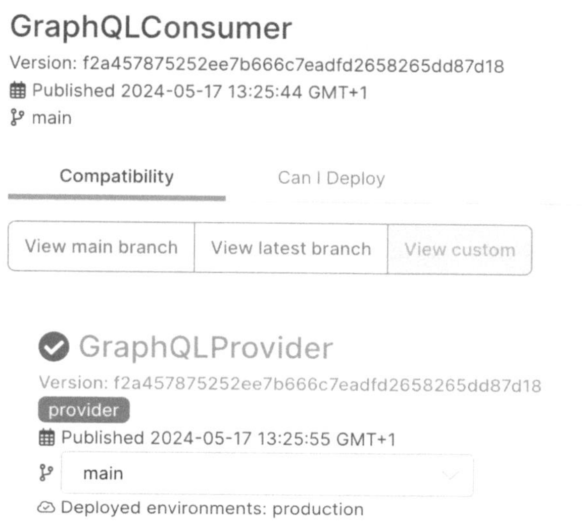

Figure 7.9 Consumer contract from GraphQLConsumer verified by GraphQLProvider as denoted by the success status

7.5 Chapter exercise

Now that you have a complete overview of how to perform contract testing with GraphQL, you can try writing more consumer tests for the following scenarios as part of the contract agreement and verifying them on the provider side:

1. **Scenario: Get a single movie**
   Given there is a movies API
   When the consumer fetches a single movie
   Then the movies API should return a status code of 200
   And the ID, name, and year the movie was released.

When you've written the additional tests, remember to update the `--consumer-app-version` manually as part of the `publish:contract` script, and then run the following commands in your terminal to run the consumer test, publish the contract, and run the provider verification:

```
npm run test:graphql:consumer
npm run publish:contract
npm run test:graphql:provider
```

You can also use the `afterAll` and `afterEach` blocks from Jest to avoid repeating any code duplication when it comes to verifying and generating the contract.

```
afterAll(() => provider.finalize());
afterEach(() => provider.verify());
```

When you finish this chapter, remember to commit all the changes you've introduced locally to your forked GitHub project. If you get stuck at any point, check out the file graphql/consumer/graphql-client-contract.spec.js from the main branch of the original GitHub project for assistance (https://github.com/mdcruz/pact-js-example/tree/main) or check out appendix C for the answers.

Summary

- GraphQL is a new API standard that provides a more efficient, powerful, and flexible alternative to REST.
- Contract testing provides value to teams working with GraphQL because they can understand how consumers are using their data, what queries produce bad output, and what queries produce different status codes.
- Apollo is a collection of tools for working with GraphQL applications.
- To fetch data from REST APIs, use the `@apollo/datasource-rest` package to perform HTTP operations easily that can be used by your GraphQL server.
- The `apollo-server` package is an open source library for creating a server-side GraphQL.
- The `@apollo/client` package is an open source library for creating a client-side GraphQL and provides built-in integration with React, a popular JavaScript framework for building web applications.
- Pact provides support for GraphQL contract testing through the `GraphQL-Interaction` wrapper.

8 Contract testing for event-driven architecture

This chapter covers

- Introduction to asynchronous API testing
- Pact consumer message setup with Kafka
- Kafka consumer implementation
- Event handler consumer test implementation
- Event consumer contract generation
- Kafka producer implementation
- Event producer test implementation

Chapter 4 covered the implementation of consumer-driven contract testing (CDCT) with APIs. However, if you work with an event-driven architecture, you'll want to understand how to implement CDCT with messages. In this chapter, we'll use Node.js and Kafka to walk through the implementation steps of CDCT in an event-driven application, from setting up the project and applying best practices to generating the consumer contract.

If you understand the foundational concepts from chapter 3, it's time to start implementing contract testing. In our experience of working with event-driven applications within a microservices environment, it's important to take care of event consumers interacting with the service. Event messages are often provided to update many consumers asynchronously. Ensuring no breaking changes occur within the message contracts is key to providing a seamless experience for the services consuming the events.

To provide more context regarding why contract testing is relevant in the world of events, consider the following: The structure of the event messages can evolve throughout the development process; therefore, the version of the event message will change. The contents of the message can be backward compatible, but imagine when a breaking change needs to be introduced. The subscribers of the event message need to be informed and implement the code they need to cope with the breaking change. Using contracts, the event producer can ensure that all consumers have adopted the new major version before deprecating the previous version of the event message. Figure 8.1 shows the event message with a breaking change between contract versions.

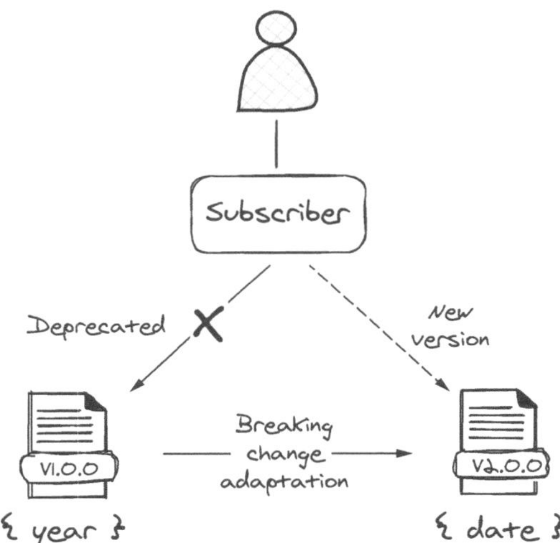

Figure 8.1 When breaking changes are introduced to events, the subscriber needs to migrate from version 1 to 2 by implementing the new message contract changes.

8.1 Introduction to asynchronous API testing

Throughout the chapter, we'll reference an event infrastructure that is just an adaptation of the movies example used in previous chapters. In an event-oriented system using the adapted movies example, instead of making calls to API endpoints, messages are published to topics, which are received by components that have subscribed to those topics. The Pact framework is built around HTTP requests, which is a limitation of the tool when implementing message-based communication. We'll focus on a scenario that updates movie data via an event broker called Kafka. Kafka is an open source distributed messaging system. Each part of the contract testing framework will sit alongside different parts of the events infrastructure, so it's important to understand the events implementation. For example, a web client publishes a message to add a new movie. The mobile client sends an asynchronous message to the "movies" Kafka topic. A backend service subscribes to the "movies" topic and adds the new movie data to the database. The next time a user searches for movies, they will be able to see the new movie data in the search. To explain it another way, with all the different components shown in figure 8.2, the producer publishes an event to trigger the addition of a movie on the Kafka message broker. The message broker job is to pass data between data sources. In this example, the message broker attaches it to a specific topic. Then, the service subscribed to the topic receives a message to create a movie. The subscriber will then process the message and perform the required steps to add the movie.

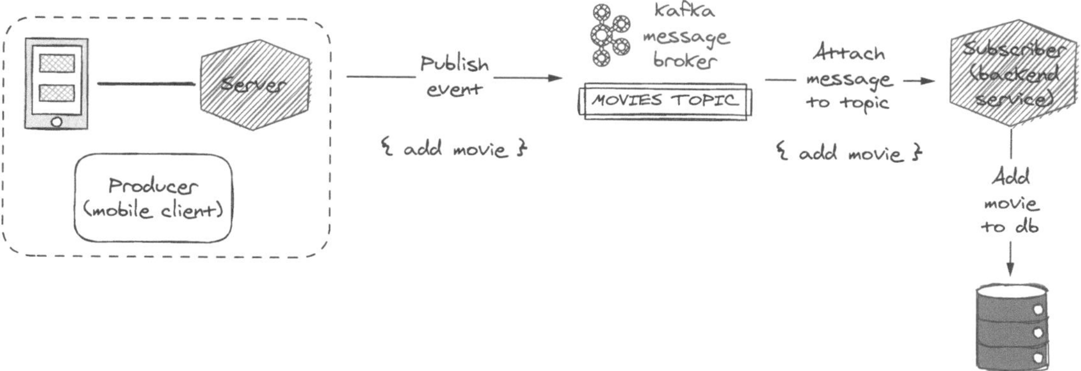

Figure 8.2 Event-driven architecture communicates via the Kafka message broker passing the message for CDCT from the producer via the "movies" topic to the subscriber.

In this chapter, we'll use CDCT for the following scenarios from the "movies" event service:

1. **Scenario: Add a new movie**
   Given that the movie doesn't exist
   When a producer publishes a message to add a new movie
   And the body includes the movie name and release date
   Then the message is published to the "movies" topic.

Concerning contract testing definitions, the subscriber relates to the consumer, and the producer equates to the provider, as shown in figure 8.3. The event consumer will publish the Pact contract to the Pact Broker with the expectations of the message contents. Then, the provider will replay the contract message contents against the real implementation to verify the Pact contract within the Pact Broker.

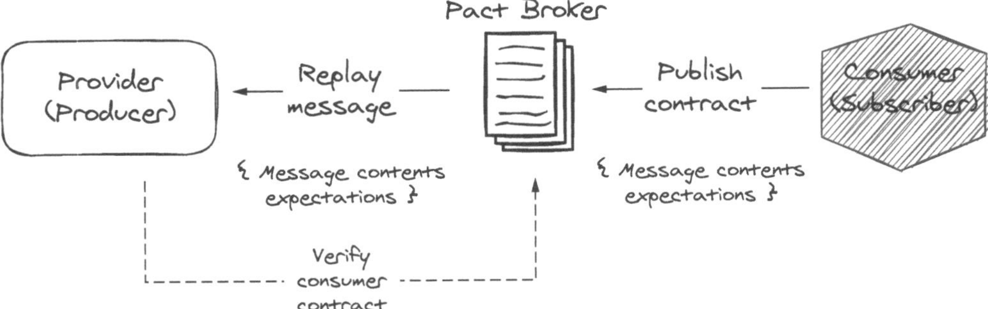

Figure 8.3 Showing the CDCT terminology and reversing the event flow with the Pact Broker in the middle

8.2 Pact consumer message setup with Kafka

We'll first focus on the construction of the event message by the producer and the consumer's handling of the event message. Focusing on the construction of the message and the message handler will answer the question of where the contract tests fit within the event code. We aren't experts in event architecture, so use the code in this chapter for reference, and apply your knowledge appropriately in your project. This section explains what you need regarding dependencies, asynchronous test functions, and all the steps of building consumer message Pact tests:

1. Use the pact-js (https://github.com/pact-foundation/pact-js) implementation of the consumer-driven contract library Pact.
2. Install dependencies using Node.js and npm.
3. Write the tests using the Jest framework.

You can follow along with the code in the project repository (https://github.com/mdcruz/pact-js-example/).

8.2.1 Requirements

To follow along in this step-by-step tutorial, you need to have the following installed on your machine:

- Node.js
- Git and access to GitHub
- Docker (optional, only if you want to run the Kafka cluster)

To get started, navigate to our project's root folder in GitHub. We've added the dependencies to our package.json file, as shown in listing 8.1. The package to add is Pact from Pact foundation, Jest, and kafkajs.

Listing 8.1 package.json

```
"dependencies": {
    ...
    "kafkajs": "^2.2.4"
},
"devDependencies": {
    "@pact-foundation/pact": "12.1.0",
    "jest": "29.7.0"
}
```

8.3 Kafka consumer implementation

Now, we'll explain the implementation within our example event consumer. It's important to understand the code surrounding the section that consumes the message, so that it's clear what is tested via contract testing and what still needs to be tested by unit or integration tests. Let's look at the event handler within our service to provide context for the implementation, as shown in listing 8.2. This function (see figure 8.4) handles the following:

1. Taking the event message received
2. Converting it to the `Movie` object
3. Inserting the data into the database

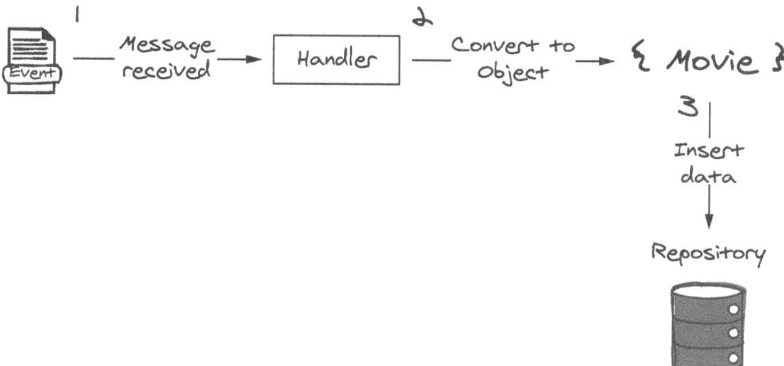

Figure 8.4 Steps to handle the event from receiving the message to inserting data into database

Listing 8.2 `Movie` handler

```
const repository = require("./movie.repository");
const Movie = require('./movie');

const handler = (message) => {        ◁ Takes the event message
  return Promise.resolve(
  repository.insert(                  ◁ Converts the message
                                        to the Movie object
```

```
    new Movie(message.name, message.year)      <-- Inserts data into
  )                                                 the database
)
}

module.exports = handler
```

The implementation of the movie handler, shown in listing 8.2, contains references to the movie model object and movie repository. The movie repository contains the `insert` method, which takes the `movie` object type (see listing 8.3) as an argument. The event message produced by the provider only sends the name and year as the consumer generates the ID.

Listing 8.3 `Movie` object type

```
class Movie {
    constructor(id, name, year) {
        this.id = id;
        this.name = name;
        this.year = year;
    }
}

module.exports = Movie;
```

The repository example in listing 8.4 sets the map value, but this is where the database code would go. The movie repository generates the `id` value and passes the event data to the data source.

Listing 8.4 Movie repository

```
class MovieRepository {

    constructor() {
        this.movies = new Map([]);
    }

    async insert(movie) {                    Updates the
        const id = 100;                 <--  database id
        return this.movies.set(id, movie.name, movie.year);
    }
}

module.exports = new MovieRepository();
```

Once the movie handler is defined, we need to set up the Kafka service, which contains the unique identifier for the client with the client ID and the topic subscription "movies" in this example. Upon receiving an event, handle each message by passing the message from the event as a JSON object.

Listing 8.5 Kafka service

```
const { Kafka } = require('kafkajs');

const clientId = 'movie-event';

const kafka = new Kafka({
  clientId: clientId,
  brokers: ['localhost:9092']
});

const consumer = kafka.consumer({ groupId: clientId });

const consumeMovieStream = async (handler) => {
  await consumer.connect();
  await consumer.subscribe({ topic: 'movies', fromBeginning: false });
  await consumer.run({
    eachMessage: async ({ topic, partition, message }) => {
      try {
        await handler(JSON.parse(message.value.toString()));
      } catch (e) {
        console.error('unable to handle message', e);
      }
    },
  })
}

module.exports = consumeMovieStream;
```

The `consumeMovieStream` function exported in listing 8.5 takes an argument, which will be the movie handler function shown previously in listing 8.2. Call the consume movie function within the server initialization function, as follows.

Listing 8.6 Server

```
const app = require('express')();
const cors = require('cors');
const consumeMovieStream = require('./src/service/kafka');
const streamHandler = require('./src/movies/movie.handler');
const port = 8080;

const init = () => {
    app.use(cors());

    consumeMovieStream(streamHandler);

    return app.listen(port, () =>
      console.log(`Provider API listening on port ${port}...`));
};

init();
```

Figure 8.5 shows the whole event handler implementation together, from the point at which the event is produced to the insertion of the data to the database.

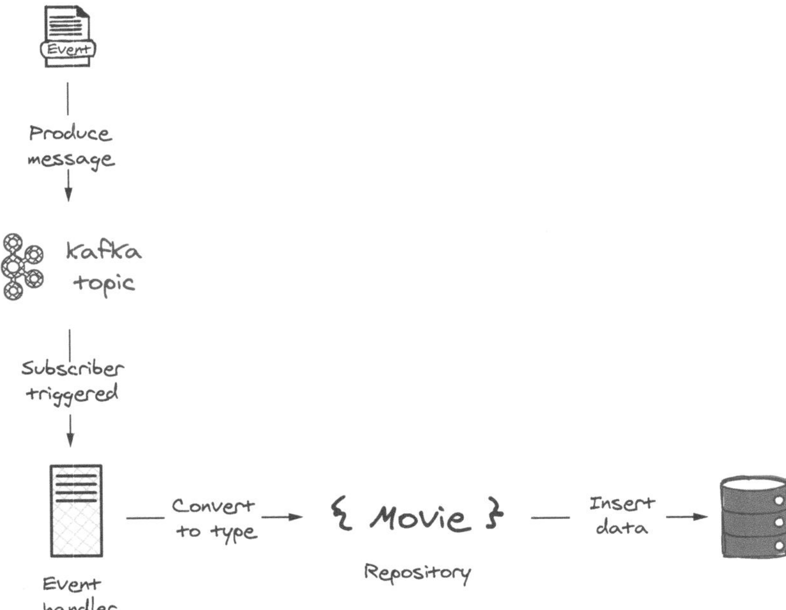

Figure 8.5 When event handlers that are subscribed to a Kafka topic are triggered, the event is produced. The event message must be in the right format as it needs to be converted to the `Movie` object for inserting into the database.

If you want to run the Kafka service alongside the tests to see how the actual Kafka implementation works, then read on or skip to section 8.4 as this information is optional. Ensure you have Docker installed, as stated in the requirements in section 8.2.1. Start the Kafka cluster with Docker Compose by running the script from the command line:

```
npm run start:kafka
```

Launch the docker-compose file, which contains the Kafka instance, Kafka UI, and `init` script, to set up the "movies" topic. A snippet showing the core components is provided in the following listing.

Listing 8.7 Docker Compose Kafka cluster

```
version: '3.8'

services:
  kafka:
    image: confluentinc/cp-kafka:6.0.14
    platform: linux/amd64
    depends_on:
      - zookeeper
```

```
  ports:
    - '29092:29092'
    ...

init-kafka:
  image: confluentinc/cp-kafka:6.0.14
  depends_on:
    - kafka
...

kafka-ui:
  image: provectuslabs/kafka-ui:latest
  ports:
    - 8085:8080
...

zookeeper:
  image: confluentinc/cp-zookeeper:6.0.14
  platform: linux/amd64
  ports:
    - '22181:2181'
...
```

The Kafka UI is available on port 8085, which shows the local Kafka cluster running with the "movies" topic available, as shown in figure 8.6.

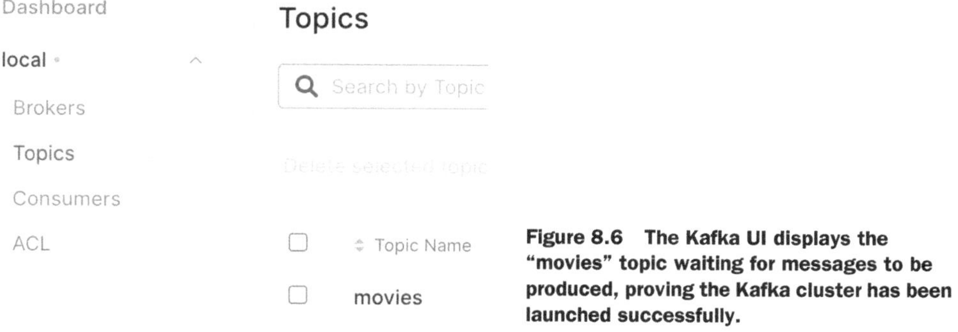

Figure 8.6 The Kafka UI displays the "movies" topic waiting for messages to be produced, proving the Kafka cluster has been launched successfully.

To consume an event on the Kafka cluster for the "movies" topic, you can run the following package script:

```
consume:kafka:message
```

The consuming server implementation, as shown in listing 8.6, shows how the service consumes the event by subscribing to the topic and listening to events published on the topic.

8.4 Event handler consumer test implementation

Now, we'll implement the contract tests for the consumer event. We'll show how the implementation of the message and movie event handler are directly connected in the contract tests. This means that any change to the event handler implementation within the service will automatically change the test implementation as well. The important thing to take from the movie messaging service is the fact that the message and handler implementation that is used within the test is the same that is used within the service. The only difference is the Kafka service has been replaced by the Pact mock server. The Pact consumer test has been added next to the movie.handler file (but can be added wherever your Jest tests are placed), shown in figure 8.7.

```
∨ movies
  JS movie.handler.js
  JS movie.handler.pact.test.js
```

Figure 8.7 Movie handler and pact movie handler tests next to each other in the movies folder structure

Once the test file has been created, the class needs imports with the Pact message function and asynchronous message handler, as shown in the following listing. In addition, the relative path to the movie handler function is referenced and imports any Pact matchers to be used.

Listing 8.8 Pact handler test imports

```
const {
  MatchersV3,
  MessageConsumerPact,
  asynchronousBodyHandler,
} = require("@pact-foundation/pact");
const movieEventHandler = require('./movie.handler');
const { like } = MatchersV3;
const path = require("path");
```

Before constructing the Pact interactions, the Pact consumer message configuration should be set up underneath the Jest `describe` section. The configuration includes the consumer and provider names, the folder to store the generated Pact files, and the log level for the test output, as shown in the following listing.

Listing 8.9 Pact message configuration

```
describe("Kafka handler", () => {
  const messagePact = new MessageConsumerPact({
    consumer: "ConsumerEvent",
    provider: "EventProducer",
    dir: path.resolve(process.cwd(), "pacts"),
    logLevel: "info",
  });
```

Once the message Pact has been configured, the next step is to build our Pact contract for the asynchronous body handler to verify, as shown in figure 8.8. To build the Pact contract, follow these steps:

1. Start with a description of the contract interaction.
2. Add message content.
3. Add event metadata.

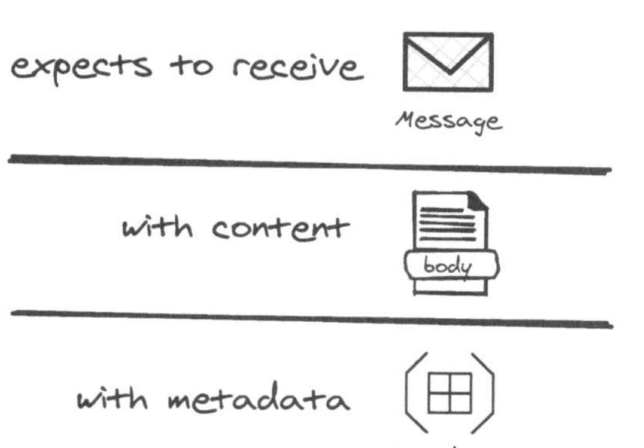

Figure 8.8 The Pact contract builder to be passed to the provider includes the following: expects to receive, with content, and with metadata.

The first step of the builder, Expects to Receive describes the specific interaction: in this example, adding a new movie, as shown in listing 8.10. This will be passed to the provider, who can set any data they require before the test starts and produce the `movie add event`, for example, if they need to delete any movie of the same name in the database to make the movie name a unique value.

Listing 8.10 Expects to receive

```
.expectsToReceive("a movie add event")
```

The second step of the builder, With Content, states the expected message content, including the JSON key-value pairs and type matchers. In this example, as shown in listing 8.11, the `like` matcher is used, which just requires the actual value to be something like that type of value.

Listing 8.11 With content

```
.withContent({
  name: like("The World's End"),
  year: like("2013")
})
```

The third step of the builder, With Metadata, sets any header style values needed. In this Kafka example, as shown in listing 8.12, the Kafka topic is sent alongside the content type of the content.

Listing 8.12 With metadata

```
.withMetadata({
  "contentType": "application/json",
  "kafka_topic": "movies",
})
```

Once the builder components have been set to define the expectations of the event message, then the event handler must be verified to check that the expectations match the actual event handler code, as shown in figure 8.9. We do this by using Pact's `asynchronousBodyHandler` function and passing the `movieEventHandler` as an argument, as follows.

Listing 8.13 Verify `event handler`

```
.verify(asynchronousBodyHandler(movieEventHandler));
```

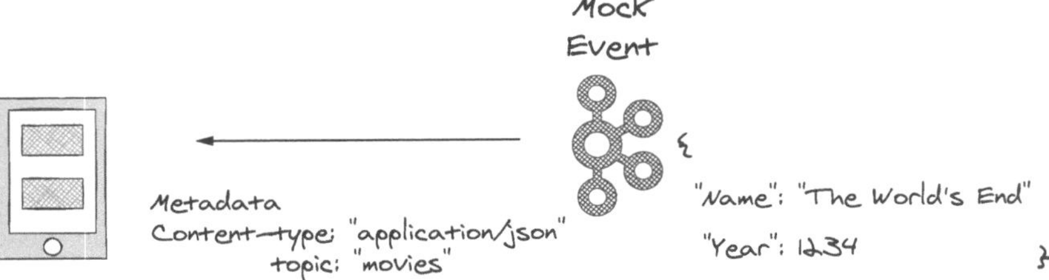

Figure 8.9 Pact response where the mock event becomes the actual response content with metadata within the test

Listing 8.14 shows show how the test looks all together. All the builder components connect with the `messagePact` object, which was set up previously in listing 8.9. The verification step will generate the pact contract if it's successful.

Listing 8.14 Movie event handler test

```
it("accepts a movie event", () => {
  return messagePact
  .expectsToReceive("a movie add event")
  .withContent({
    name: like("The World's End"),
    year: like("2013")
  })
  .withMetadata({
    "contentType": "application/json",
```

```
    "kafka_topic": "movies",
  })
  .verify(asynchronousBodyHandler(movieEventHandler));
});
```

The next section will look at running the consumer test to generate the Pact contract.

8.5 Event consumer contract generation

Running the test in the console with the script command `npm run test:event:consumer`, you should see the word PASS in green on your screen, as shown in figure 8.10.

```
PASS events/consumer-event/src/movies/movie.handler.pact.test.js
  Kafka handler
    receive a add movie event
      ✓ accepts a movie event (9 ms)

Test Suites: 1 passed, 1 total
Tests:       1 passed, 1 total
```

Figure 8.10 Console output showing the Pact Kafka handler test has passed

On completion of the test, if you get the PASS word next to the test, then the Pact file should have been written to the pacts folder at the root of the project, as shown in figure 8.11.

```
> events
> graphql
> node_modules
∨ pacts
  {} ConsumerEvent-EventProducer.js...
```

Figure 8.11 Pacts folder showing the generated ConsumerEvent-EventProducer.json file ready to be published to the Pact Broker

The Pact JSON file that we built maps all sections to JSON objects. Listing 8.15 shows the consumer and provider names. This creates the link in the Pact Broker for the interactions within the Pact file.

Listing 8.15 Event movie Pact, part 1

```
"consumer": {
  "name": "ConsumerEvent"
},
"provider": {
  "name": "EventProducer"
}
```

Then, in the penultimate section, the messages array appears between the consumer and provider. First, the `contents` object, which was generated from the `withContent` method, contains the message values provided within the test. As shown in listing 8.16, the next field, `description`, was generated from the `expectsToReceive` method. The next section, `matchingRules`, references the matchers used within the `withContent` method, for example, `like("2013")`, as shown in figure 8.11. Finally, the metadata object contains the values defined within the `"with metadata"` method, as shown in figure 8.12.

Listing 8.16 Event movie Pact, part 2

```
"messages": [
    {
      "contents": {
        "name": "The World's End",
        "year": "2013"
      },
      "description": "a movie add event",
      "matchingRules": {
        "body": {
          "$.name": {
            "combine": "AND",
            "matchers": [
              {
                "match": "type"
              }
            ]
          },
          "$.year": {
            "combine": "AND",
            "matchers": [
              {
                "match": "type"
              }
            ]
          }
        }
      },
      "metadata": {
        "contentType": "application/json",
        "kafka_topic": "movies"
      }
    }
  ]
```

Finally, Pact metadata, as shown in listing 8.17, is added to the Pact JSON file, which is taken from the package used and the Pact specification file format we defined.

Listing 8.17 Event movie Pact, part 3

```
"metadata": {
  "pact-js": {
    "version": "12.1.0"
  },
```

```
    "pactRust": {
      "ffi": "0.4.9",
      "models": "1.1.11"
    },
    "pactSpecification": {
      "version": "3.0.0"
    }
  }
```

Once the contract has been generated, publish the contract to the Pact Broker, as shown in figure 8.12.

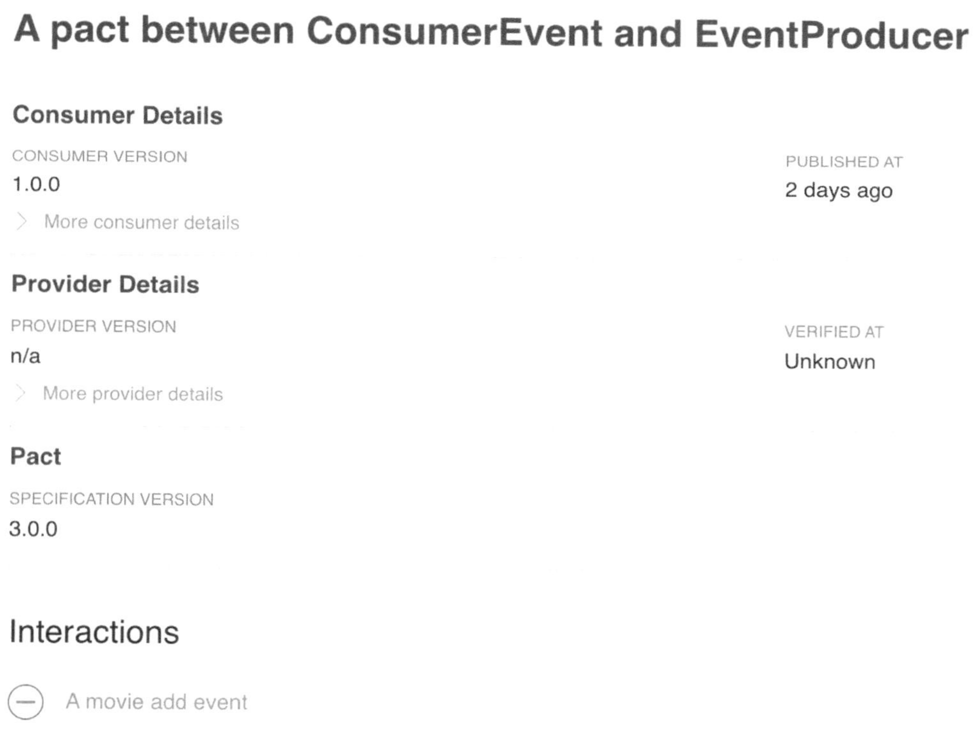

Figure 8.12 The Pact Broker version of the consumer event contract with an event producer, ready for verification with the provider

At this point, the producer of the message can verify the message contract.

8.6 Kafka producer implementation

Now, we'll explain the implementation of the event provider in our example. To provide some context for the implementation, let's look at the event producer within our service. This function handles the Kafka connection, as shown in listing 8.18, constructing the event and sending the message to Kafka. The kafkajs package is imported to create the connection to the Kafka broker. The Kafka configuration takes the client ID and a list of brokers; the client ID must be unique to identify the specific producer. After configuring the Kafka connection, the producer function is then called on the Kafka object.

Listing 8.18 Movie event producer setup

```
const { Kafka } = require("kafkajs")
const { createMovie } = require("./movie.event")

const clientId = "movie-event"
const brokers = ["localhost:29092"]
const topic = "movies"

const kafka = new Kafka({ clientId, brokers })
const producer = kafka.producer()
```

Once the Kafka configuration has been set up, the event can be sent to the connected Kafka instance, as shown in listing 8.19. First, make the connection to the Kafka instance. Then, construct the message content using the `createMovie` function, as shown in listing 8.18. Finally, send the message to the Kafka topic, which takes the topic name and messages array. The message object must include a key and value that contain the movie message content.

Listing 8.19 Movie event producer message

```
const produce = async (name, year) => {
    await producer.connect()
    const message = createMovie(name, year)
    await producer.send({
        topic,
        messages: [
          {
            key: "1",
            value: JSON.stringify(message)
          }
        ],
    })
}

module.exports = produce
```

The message content was set up using method `createMovie`. This function simply returns the added movie object, setting the values of `name` and `year` passed into the function. It's important to separate out the creation of the message content. So, however your project and code are set up, consider the fact that the Pact message framework is independent of any message broker. Therefore, the message content should be abstracted for the Pact test, as follows.

Listing 8.20 Create movie

```
function createMovie(name, year) {
    return {
        name: name,
        year: year,
    }
}

module.exports = {
    createMovie
}
```

Once the producer function has been implemented, the test can be added. To produce an event on the Kafka cluster for the "movies" topic, you can run the following package script:

```
npm run produce:kafka:message
```

The produce Kafka message script runs the index.js file, generating a message with key "1" and contents defined within the index file:

```
const produce = require("./src/movie.producer");

produce("test", "2023")
```

As shown in figure 8.13, the movie producer performs the following actions:

1. Connects to the local Kafka instance
2. Creates the movie event message
3. Publishes the message to the Kafka topic

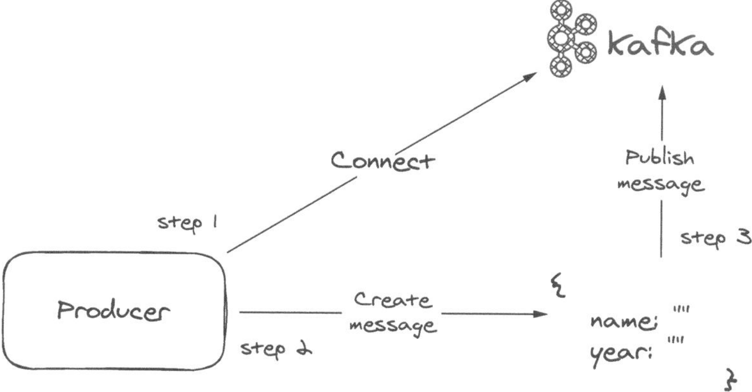

Figure 8.13 Event producer connecting to Kafka service and publishing the created message, ready for testing

8.7 Event producer test implementation

We'll be setting up the test alongside the movie.event code (see figure 8.14). This enables any changes to the event message to automatically be picked up by the provider test implementation.

```
∨ event-producer
  ∨ src
    JS movie.event.js
    JS movie.event.pact.test.js
    JS movie.producer.js
```

Figure 8.14 Event producer folder structure, including movie.event.pact.test under the source folder alongside movie.event and movie.producer, similar to unit test location

When starting to write the producer test, first perform the imports from Pact and the `createMovie` function from movie.event, as follows.

Listing 8.21 Movie producer test setup

```
const {
    MessageProviderPact,
    providerWithMetadata,
  } = require('@pact-foundation/pact');
  const { createMovie } = require('./movie.event');
```

The main part of the message provider test is the constructor of the `MessageProviderPact` method. This sets the message provider's contents and metadata, as well as the Pact Broker and provider details. The message providers section takes an object, with the Pact interaction description as the key—`"a movie add event"` in this example. Then, the value of the message provider is the provider with the metadata function. The `providerWithMetadata` function constructs the body content as the first argument and the metadata of the event as the second argument. In this example, as shown in listing 8.22, we're passing the `createMovie` function we set up earlier in listing 8.20.

Listing 8.22 Message provider constructor

```
const provider = new MessageProviderPact({
  messageProviders: {
    'a movie add event': providerWithMetadata(() =>
      createMovie("The World's End", "2013"), {
        kafka_topic: 'movies'
    }),
  },
  logLevel: 'info',
  provider: 'EventProducer',
  providerVersion: '1.0.0',
  providerVersionBranch: 'main',
```

```
    pactBrokerUrl: process.env.PACT_BROKER_URL,
    pactBrokerToken: process.env.PACT_BROKER_TOKEN,
  });
```

Finally, the actual test block for the movie event provider is shown in listing 8.23. The test simply verifies the message provider set up within the message provider Pact constructor. The constructor defines the Pact Broker details, meaning that all contracts associated with the provider name `'EventProducer'` will be pulled down from the broker and verified, as shown in figure 8.15.

Listing 8.23 Movie event provider test

```
it('sends a valid movie', () => {
    return provider.verify();
});
```

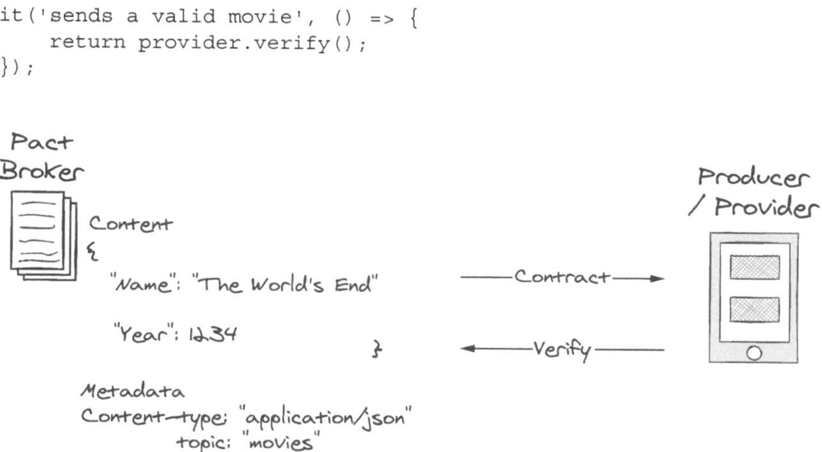

Figure 8.15 Producer/Provider pulling down the Pact contract from the Pact Broker to verify the content and metadata of the message

On running the test from the console, if the test is successful, the output should display the word PASS along with the word OK next to the specific content and metadata verified, as shown in figure 8.16.

```
Verifying a pact between ConsumerEvent and EventProducer

  a movie add event (4s 544ms loading, 162ms verification)
    generates a message which
      includes metadata
        "topic" with value "movies" (OK)
        "contentType" with value "application/json" (OK)
      has a matching body (OK)

PASS events/event-producer/src/movie.event.pact.test.js
  Event producer tests
    send a movie add event
      ✓ sends a valid movie (10600 ms)
```

Figure 8.16 Movies event producer test run output, showing successful verification of the contract, including the metadata and body content

Summary

- In an event-driven setting, the subscriber to the event topic is the consumer, and the producer of the event is the provider, forming the contract testing relationship.
- Pact supports event messages as part of the core pact-js package to be used alongside JavaScript test frameworks.
- The Pact builder constructs the contents data and metadata expectations, creating the contract test messages for the producer.
- Pact message tests generate contracts on completing a successful test run, represented within the messages array in the Pact specification.
- The Pact message producer test implementation concentrates on the message body method only, meaning it's independent of any specific event tools.

9 Storing, hosting, and securing the contracts

This chapter covers

- Why we need Pact Broker
- Pact Broker core features
- Pact Broker options
- Software as a service Pact Broker (PactFlow)
- Self-hosted Pact Broker
- Software as a service versus self-hosted Pact Broker

Throughout the previous chapters, we generated and published a few contracts to Pact Broker. As defined previously in section 3.4, the broker's purpose isn't to arrange but to organize and facilitate the contract life cycle, wherever the contracts are being stored. We also stated that the broker holds the information about the different consumers and providers, such as when the latest contract was published, the contract version, and when the provider last verified the contract. This chapter explores the different Pact Broker options and where it's best to store contracts for different scenarios. Pact Broker offers much more than just storing contracts; we explore some of these features, including the network diagram and stub URL. In addition, you need to consider not only the features but also whether to pay for a hosted version of the broker or self-host on your own. We often get asked whether investing in PactFlow or maintaining their open source Pact Broker is worth it.

This chapter will be of interest to those individuals or teams performing a tool analysis, decision-makers on tool spending, and those in charge of maintaining self-hosted tooling. We share our opinions based on our experiences and conversations with Pact users in the testing community. However, it's important to have conversations internally with your team to consider what the right option is for your team. By the end of this chapter, you should be confident about deciding on the right Pact Broker option.

In previous chapters, we've touched on publishing contracts to and verifying contracts with Pact Broker. Figure 9.1 shows a simplified view of the Pact Broker role. Pact Broker is part of the contract testing flow in the following steps:

1. The consumer pushes the consumer contracts to Pact Broker.
2. The provider pulls the contracts from Pact Broker.
3. The provider publishes the verification status of the contract to Pact Broker.
4. The consumer pulls the verification status from Pact Broker to check if they can deploy their app.

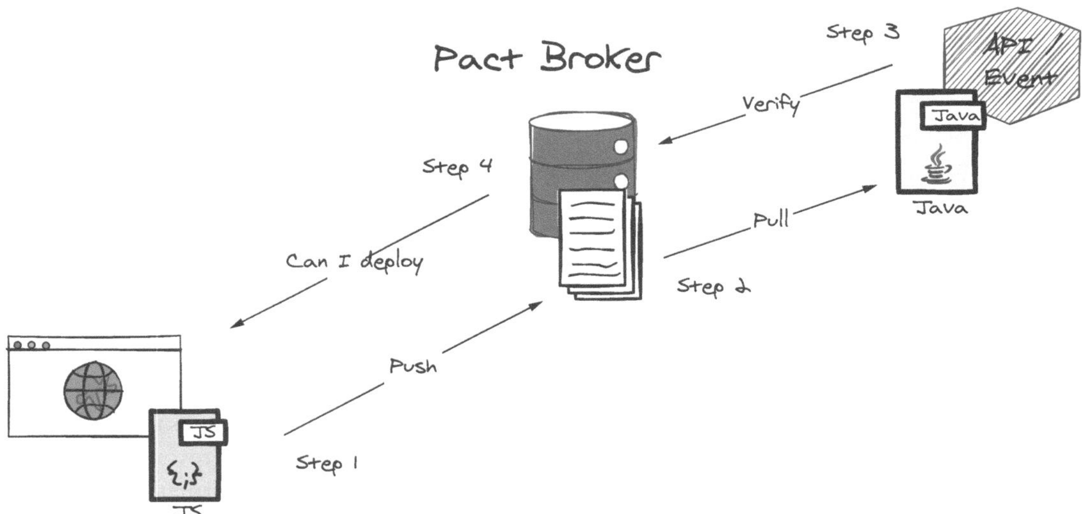

Figure 9.1 Contract testing flow, showing Pact Broker interactions with consumers and providers

The Pact Broker's role within the software development life cycle needs some explanation. When working in distributed teams building microservices, there are many moving parts.

9.1 Why we need Pact Broker

Why do we need Pact Broker for the contract testing process? There are several ways that Pact Broker supports the process:

- Sharing contracts across repositories
- Changing contracts between branches and environments
- Coordinating releases across teams
- Integrating into continuous integration/continuous deployment (CI/CD) processes and pipelines

Often, repositories are split by application, service, or team, for example, frontend and backend. However, both teams need contracts, so the conversation starts to decide where the contracts should be stored. Contracts can be stored within the provider service repository or in an independent repository shared between teams. The contracts then need a custom implementation to share them between repositories within the testing phase. Pact Broker provides an easy way to share contracts. Another way that Pact Broker supports the contract testing process is by tracking contract changes between branches and environments. Throughout the development process, contracts will change, and different teams will make changes at different times.

Imagine the provider service has a bug in one of their endpoints. They fixed the bug in version 2.1.1 and want to deploy it as soon as possible. Therefore, the change to the API must be compatible with all consumer interactions. At the same time as the provider is making their change, consumers are also updating the UI with additional data from the API endpoint, changing their interactions in the contract. However, the consumers won't be deploying the changes until next week. In this situation, the provider service needs to verify the contract version in production and in the new contracts. As shown in figure 9.2, Pact Broker shows all the different contract versions and where the provider verifications point to, which makes the scenario described much easier to test.

One way to ensure contract changes that doesn't break anything within the applications is to run regression tests across the risk areas. The contracts within Pact Broker can facilitate the release process and provide more confidence that specific contract differences don't cause problems. Finally, the contract-sharing process can be integrated into CI solutions. Pact Broker provides a command-line interface (CLI) that offers easy access to provider verification statuses and webhooks to trigger dependent CI pipelines.

9.1.1 Pact Broker core features

When using a monolith application, keeping track of versions and changes in dependencies is easy. However, with microservices, there are many moving parts and code changes to align. Pact Broker offers some core features that help keep track of all the dependencies.

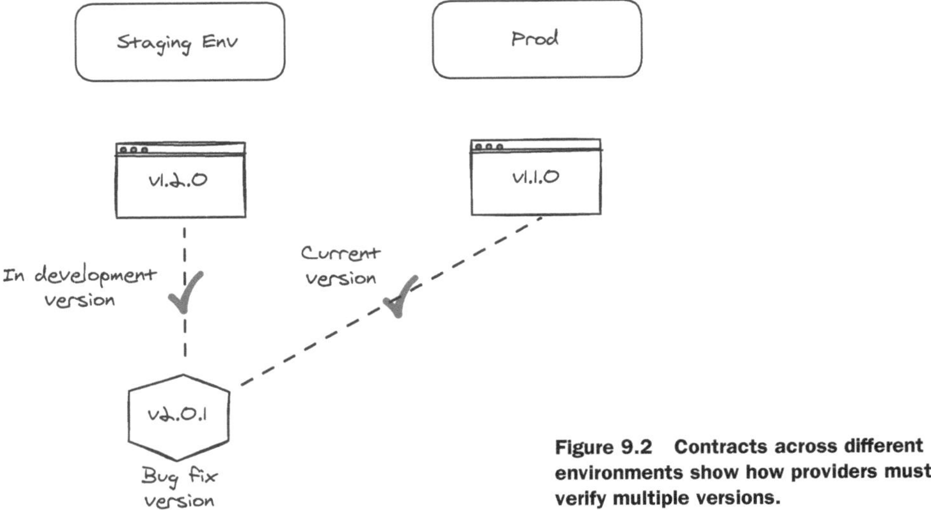

Figure 9.2 Contracts across different environments show how providers must verify multiple versions.

First, a key reason why contract testing gets introduced from a provider's perspective is to account for all the consumers who interact with their service. This understanding of consumers can be difficult to achieve when working in a large-scale microservices environment. Visualizing who all the consumers are can be achieved by distributed tracing and monitoring how services are connected. Pact Broker offers an excellent visualization of how services are connected, known as the network diagram. When consumers publish their contracts to Pact Broker, they provide the provider name as part of the contract. The consumer and provider names then become the points on the network diagram, as shown in figure 9.3. Visualizing the consumers in one place provides an easy way for provider teams to communicate changes to consumer teams.

Versioning APIs can be very challenging if versioning is a strategy within the project's API development process. With Pact, the consumer and provider have a version associated with a contract. Specific Pact contracts get verified. Pact Broker pairs the consumer and provider versions to form the verification status. Figure 9.4 shows that provider version 2.0.1 can successfully interact with the consumer but not version 3.0.1.

Best practices from Pact documentation (https://mng.bz/r14D) suggest the following:

- The consumer version updates anytime the Pact contract changes.
- App version numbers should be unique.

Pact is very clever regarding multiple consumer contract versions; if the contract file hasn't changed in content, Pact Broker can infer verification status. Verifications don't need to be repeated when the contract file hasn't changed.

OVERVIEW NETWORK DIAGRAM MATRIX

Diagram Style

Chord

MoviesAndroidApp

WebConsumer

MoviesAPI

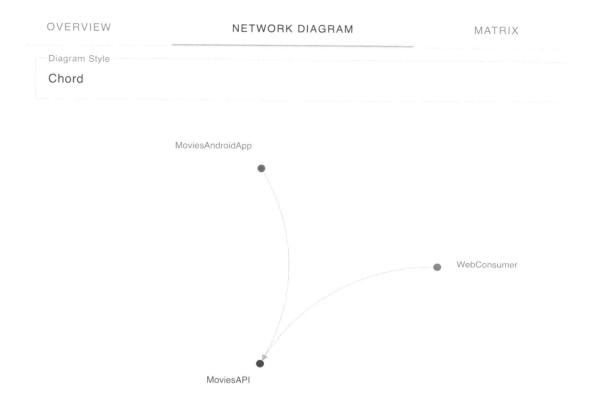

Figure 9.3 Pact Broker network diagram, showing the consumers making requests to the API service provider

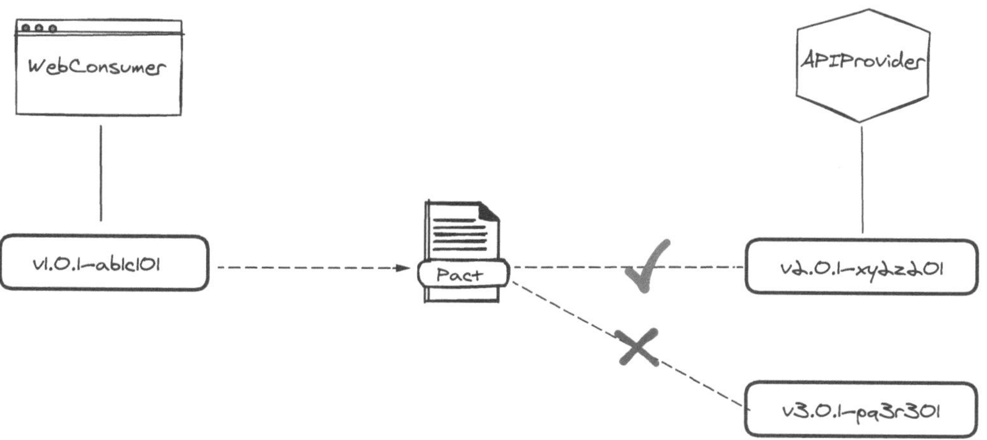

Figure 9.4 Consumer and provider versions associated with the Pact contract form the verification status.

Pact Broker provides a simple view of the different versions and verification statuses. The matrix, which is a table of each consumer contract and provider version, is shown in figure 9.5. The matrix shows that both consumer versions 1.0.0 and 1.02 have been verified successfully by provider version 1.0.0. However, consumer version 1.0.1 still needs verification by the provider. The UI team can deploy consumer versions 1.0.0 and 1.0.2, whereas 1.0.1 wouldn't be safe to deploy currently.

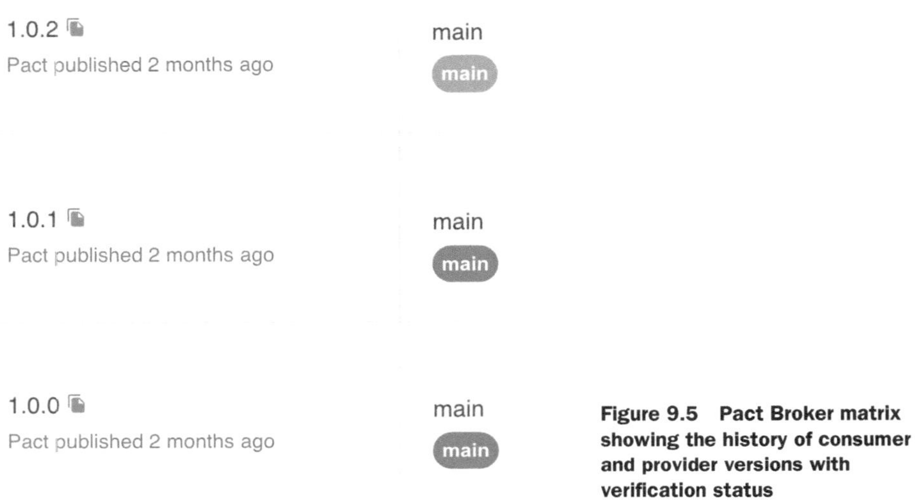

Figure 9.5 Pact Broker matrix showing the history of consumer and provider versions with verification status

The verification status of the contract can be in the following states:

- The contract has been successfully verified.
- The most recent verification of the contract isn't compatible.
- The contract hasn't been verified yet.
- A new version of the pact has been published since the last verification result was received.

The can-i-deploy command in the Pact Broker CLI uses the matrix to ensure that the consumer application can be deployed without risk. The query's output to the matrix determines whether the changes are backward compatible. The matrix also displays information regarding branch, tags, and environments. The Branch & Tags column and the Envs column are important for contract testing within the CI pipeline, which will be explained in more detail in chapter 10.

9.2 Pact Broker options

Before you start publishing contracts, there needs to be a solution available to receive them. As you already know from previous chapters, there needs to be an independent source of the contracts because consumers and providers code is usually kept separate. The first decision to make is whether you want to go down the open source, software as a service (SaaS), or no Pact Broker route:

- *Option 1*—Own contract storage solution, no Pact Broker (e.g., cloud storage, Amazon Simple Storage Solution [Amazon S3])
- *Option 2*—Purchase hosted Pact Broker using SmartBear's PactFlow
- *Option 3*—Self-hosted open source Pact Broker

Each solution has pros and cons, and a detailed version of the comparison table is provided in appendix A. For now, a summary of the key points is given in table 9.1.

Table 9.1 Pros (+) and cons (–) for each form of Pact Broker.

SaaS (PactFlow)	Own Storage Solution	Open Source
– Higher running costs	+ Low setup costs	+ Low setup costs
+ Easy setup and free account	+ No barrier to getting started	– Infrastructure needs to be provisioned and configured
+ Secure authentication	+ Slots into existing secure infrastructure	– Only username and password authentication method
+ Additional features including (OpenAPI specification support)	– Lack of out-of-the-box contract testing features	+ Simple UI and core consumer contract testing features

Option 1 is crafting your own contract storage solution, which removes the barriers to getting started with contracting testing. Using your existing storage solutions, such as Amazon S3 in Amazon Web Services (AWS) or a Git repository in GitHub, reduces the overhead of maintaining more infrastructure. However, storing the contracts in a storage location doesn't provide the benefits of a tailored contract testing solution. We aren't going to elaborate on this option further within this chapter, but it was mentioned before in chapter 3, and a replica of figure 3.9 is provided in figure 9.6. This example showed how the message contracts are published to a GitHub repository and then downloaded from the repository to test the contract.

Option 2, the third-party hosted Pact Broker, provides assurances around stability and removing the burden of maintaining the infrastructure. However, the third-party hosted option comes at a cost, dependent on the size of the team and the number of integrations. In section 9.3, we'll show how to register and set up a PactFlow account.

Option 3, the open source Pact Broker, offers flexibility and is free initially before factoring in maintenance and hosting costs. Pact Broker has a few deployment options for deploying within your infrastructure. Deploying within your infrastructure provides confidence around security and a sense of control. Section 9.4 of this chapter will explore the different deployment options in more detail.

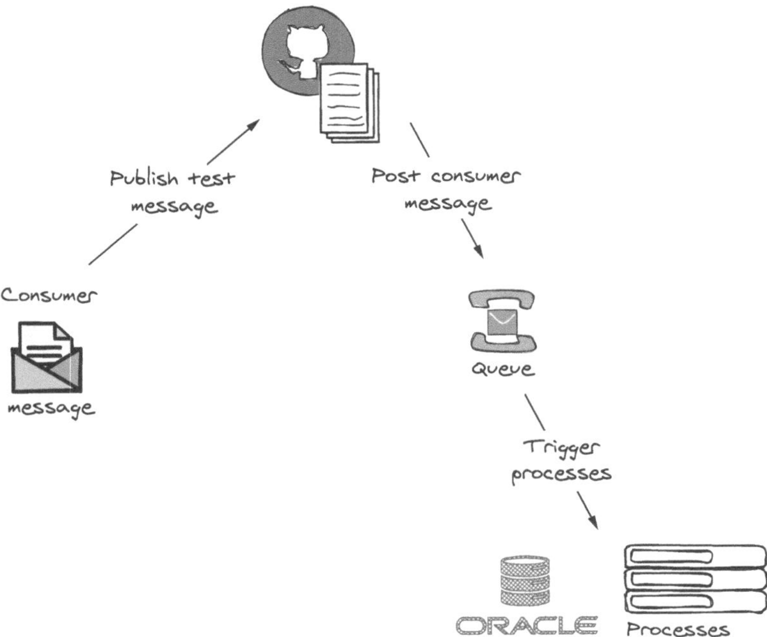

Figure 9.6 The contract storage solution is GitHub repository in this contract testing example without Pact Broker.

To make a calculated decision on which option fits with the requirements for your project, you'll likely want to see it in action. In the next section, we'll look at option 2, as this is a great starting point for initiating a contract testing proof of concept. Option 1 is also great for those without experience with a broker or those who don't have the time to set up the infrastructure for option 3.

9.3 SaaS Pact Broker (PactFlow)

PactFlow is the chosen SaaS Pact Broker provider, as this is the original tool from the team that created Pact. PactFlow MVP was launched in 2016 (https://pactFlow.io/about/) by Matt Fellows, Beth Skurrie, and Ron Holshausen. PactFlow has evolved a lot over the years by incorporating features to support its users, from single sign-on (SSO) to Pact plugins. To publish the contracts in the other chapters, we simply set up a free version from the PactFlow website, enabling us to demo the end-to-end process of contract testing, which is exactly what people should do when running a proof of concept. However, committing to the contract testing journey isn't that simple. Using Pact Broker will probably involve others in the decision-making process, especially those who control the budget.

The Pact Broker overview provides key information to simplify the API or event interactions. Contracts published to PactFlow are shown in figure 9.7; the homepage shows the contract pairings and an overview of the contract details.

Applications

My Favorites
Applications By Team
All Applications

WebConsumer

Bi Web Consumer
BiWebConsumer

Web Consumer
WebConsumer

Figure 9.7 The Pact Broker homepage displays a simple API contract overview.

9.3.1 Setting up PactFlow

To start with PactFlow, visit https://pactFlow.io/try-for-free/, and sign up for a free plan, as shown in figure 9.8. Follow the instructions and user verification.

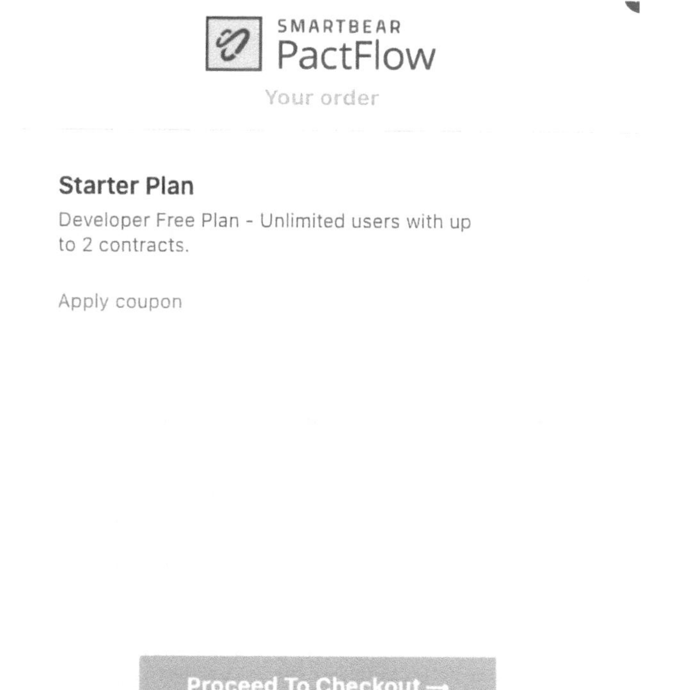

Figure 9.8 PactFlow order form for a free starter plan to set up a hosted Pact Broker

Once the account has been created, you should see an example contract on the homepage. The contract was between MyConsumer and MyProvider. Once the account has been set up, it's ready to receive contracts from the consumers.

9.3.2 PactFlow API token

To publish contracts to Pact Broker, you'll need the following:

- Broker URL
- Broker API token

The Pact Broker base URL can be seen in the browser address bar (e.g., https://mariecruz.pactFlow.io/) or copied from the API tokens page. The Pact Broker API token can be found in the settings (<URL>/settings/api-tokens) as shown in figure 9.9; then, copy the Read/Write Token when publishing or verifying contracts. The token with write permissions is reserved to be used within the CI pipeline, whereas the Read Only Token is only for the provider to test locally.

API Tokens

Base URL

https://mariecruz.pactflow.io Copy base URL

All API Tokens

My API Tokens System Account Tokens

Read only token

Read only
Last used 2024-01-28 23:22:40 GMT
Never expires

Copy Token Value

Read/write token

Read/write
Last used 2024-05-05 22:13:46 GMT+1
Never expires

Copy Token Value

Figure 9.9 The Pact Broker settings page contains API tokens for publishing and verifying contracts.

Communicating with Pact Broker is done via a CLI tool that provides a wrapper around the API. The publishing endpoint is a `PUT` method, which takes a Pact contract as the body. The URL subdirectory comprises the provider and consumer names, followed by the contract version. Here's an example:

```
https://mariecruz.pactFlow.io
/pacts/provider/MyProvider/consumer/MyConsumer/version/latest
```

The `version` part of the URL can be substituted with a specific version number. In the scenario depicted earlier in figure 9.2, you're developing a web app in parallel with changes being made to an API provider. The web app team backlog has different priorities compared with the API provider; therefore, changes are made out of sync. The implications of this in terms of the contract are that the API provider may be a couple of versions ahead in production. In this scenario, the API provider makes a breaking change to their API, requiring a new major version. Therefore, two versions of the API are supported during this time. The consumer web app is still pointing to the old API version, so we'll need to update the version in the URL, for example, /version/1.0.0. In chapter 6, we touched on a scenario with a breaking change, as shown in figure 9.10. The old version, the V1.0.0 `"year"` field, has been changed to `"date"`. Therefore, while the consumer web app is still displaying Year only on the UI, they will point to /pacts/provider/APIProvider/consumer/WebConsumer/1.0.0 in Pact Broker.

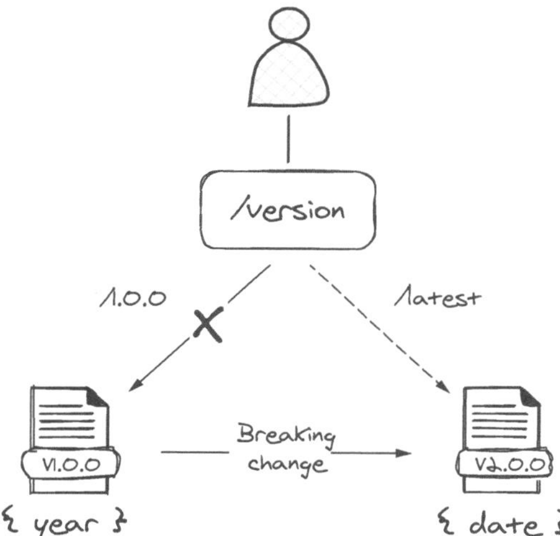

Figure 9.10 Pact Broker shows consumers updating their version after a breaking change to the contract.

Now we're all set up with PactFlow, so we'll move on to user management.

9.3.3 PactFlow user management

Once Pact Broker receives contracts, more teams will want to join the action. Therefore, new users will want to be added to PactFlow (unlimited users are included on the free plan). Many engineers using PactFlow probably won't interact with Pact Broker regularly, as they will use Pact through their CI pipeline via the Pact Broker CLI. For the CI pipeline, a system account should be set up to interact with Pact Broker, as shown in figure 9.11.

1 users

☐	Name	Status	Roles
☐	CI	Enabled	CI/CD

Figure 9.11 PactFlow system account set up for CI to interact with Pact Broker

Users can be set up for tech leads or developers involved in the release process. Another option PactFlow offers is SSO—including GitHub, Google, and Microsoft—which can provide users with on-demand access to Pact Broker. To invite users by email, navigate to the settings, and choose the Users option from the left menu. Select Invite New Users, and enter their name and email, as shown in figure 9.12.

Users

← Back to Users List

Invite User

NAME*

EMAIL*

More

Invite users

Figure 9.12 Invite new users to PactFlow to view Pact contracts.

Users can have different roles, as mentioned regarding the CI user. Types of roles include the following:

- Viewer
- CI/CD
- Administrator

Most users only need viewer permissions to help debug contract problems or see different contract versions. The CI/CD role will allow actions such as publishing and verifying contracts. Finally, the administrator role will be in charge of actions such as user management and API token rotation.

9.3.4 Other PactFlow features

PactFlow's core feature is sharing and verifying contracts, but there are a couple of other things that add value to the contract testing process. Following are some features we'll mention due to their effect on projects we've been involved with:

- Stubs
- Provider verification badges

A great feature in PactFlow is the stub functionality, which enables contracts to be used as a stub via a direct URL, as shown in figure 9.13. Within PactFlow, all contracts are automatically allocated a hosted API stub URL. The functionality is also available within open source by spinning up a stub server locally.

There are a couple of different scenarios where we see this being used in a software development project. When developing frontend and backend services in parallel, a

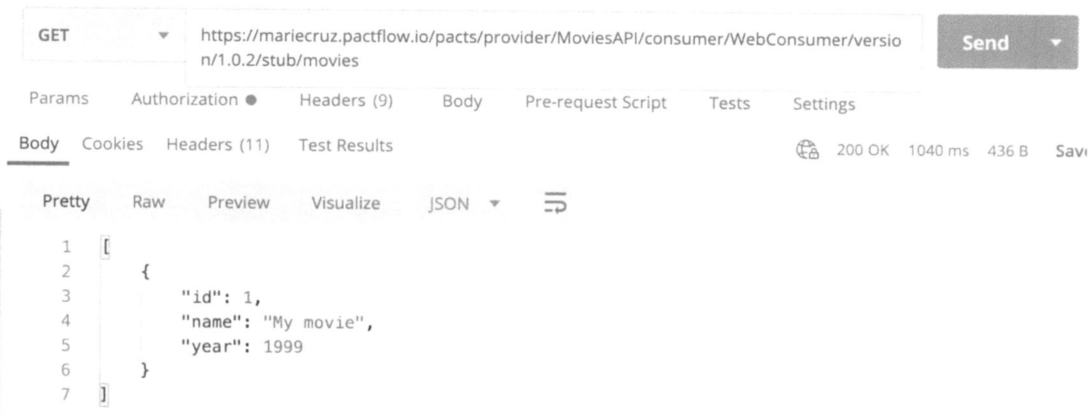

Figure 9.13 Postman request to the `MoviesAPI` provider stub, which returns a response based on the consumer contract

consumer-driven contract stub can be used. While developing the frontend part, the stub can be used, and as soon as the backend service is available, they can verify the contract, which also verifies the stub. Within the unit tests for the frontend, the stub could be used where a mock response would usually be. Another suite of tests that could benefit from contract stubs is the end-to-end test suite. When end-to-end tests mock out external services to check the frontend application in isolation, static mocks are created. End-to-end tests with contract stubs offer more confidence that the frontend changes can be deployed without integration problems. For example, we can use the Cypress framework to demonstrate how this could be engineered by substituting a Cypress fixture with a PactFlow stub, as shown in listing 9.1. Within the `before` statement of the test, a task is run to get the stub response data. The API request is intercepted, and the response is substituted with the stubbed response.

Listing 9.1 Cypress test with intercept

```
describe('Web consumer', () => {
    const endpoint = '/movies'
    before(() => {
        cy.task('getStub', endpoint).then((data) => {      <- getStub function shown in listing 9.2
            cy.intercept(
            `http://localhost:4000${endpoint}`,           <- API service running on port 4000
              (req) => {
                req.reply(data)
            }).as('movies')
        })
    })

    it('List movies', () => {
        cy.visit(endpoint)
        cy.wait('@movies')
```

```
        cy.get('[data-cy="name"]').should('have.text', 'My movie')
    })
})
```

The `getStub` task makes a request to Pact Broker with the API token header and returns the contract's expected response data as a stub.

Listing 9.2 Cypress plugin task

```
getStub(endpoint) {
      const result = axios.get(
`${PACTFLOW_BROKER_URL}/pacts/provider/MoviesAPI/consumer/WebConsumer/version
     /latest/stub/${endpoint}`,
        {
          headers: {
            Authorization: 'Bearer <PACTFLOW_API_TOKEN>',
            Accept: 'application/json'
          }
        }).then(response => { return response.data })
      return result
    }
```

Axios HTTP client

PactFlow settings

If the developers work collaboratively with testers writing end-to-end tests inside their project, then consumer contracts will be generated within the frontend project and can be used as mocks in the Cypress tests directly from Pact's output folder. The Cypress example in listing 9.1 and 9.2 isn't the most optimal way to use contract mocks; however, it's a nice solution if the end-to-end tests currently use static mocks.

Another feature we're going to touch on in this chapter is provider verification badges. As we mentioned earlier in section 9.3.3 regarding user management, some users will solely interact with Pact Broker through the CLI within their CI pipelines. Within the CI pipeline, a great way to visualize the status of the tests is through a status badge. PactFlow provides status badges for each contract between services, as shown in 9.14. Display the provider verification status badge within a README so those running the CI pipeline can see the information they need.

Figure 9.14 Provider verification status badge to display Pact Broker contract status within the CI pipeline

9.4 Self-hosted Pact Broker

There are a few different options for spinning up the open source version of Pact Broker, depending on your existing infrastructure and potential security requirements or maintenance strategy. In this section, we'll set up Pact Broker using the following:

- Docker
- Kubernetes

It's possible to set up Pact Broker from scratch with nginx, PostgreSQL, and Ruby, where instructions are available on the Pact foundations GitHub (https://mng.bz/V240).

9.4.1 Pact Broker with Docker

The Docker images offer the core functionality for Pact Broker just by running a single command. A prerequisite to running the image is having Docker (https://docs.docker.com/get-docker/) installed on the server. There are a couple of options for images to consider for Pact Broker:

- pactfoundation/pact-broker
- dius/pact-broker

We've chosen to use the DiUS version of Pact Broker, as it offers some resiliency by restarting processes if the broker were to crash. The dockerized Pact Broker has a dependency on a PostgreSQL database. Therefore, we've chosen to use Docker Compose (docker-compose file) to run the service. The docker-compose file contains the DiUS Pact Broker and PostgreSQL database services, as follows.

Listing 9.3 Pact Broker docker-compose.yml

```
version: "3"

services:
  postgres:
    image: postgres
    healthcheck:
      test: psql postgres --command "select 1" -U postgres
    environment:
      POSTGRES_USER: postgres
      POSTGRES_PASSWORD: password
      POSTGRES_DB: postgres

  pact-broker:
    image: dius/pact-broker
    depends_on:
      - postgres
    environment:
      PACT_BROKER_DATABASE_USERNAME: postgres
      PACT_BROKER_DATABASE_PASSWORD: ${DB_PASSWORD}
      PACT_BROKER_DATABASE_HOST: postgres
      PACT_BROKER_DATABASE_NAME: postgres
      PACT_BROKER_BASIC_AUTH_USERNAME: prescott
      PACT_BROKER_BASIC_AUTH_PASSWORD: ${BROKER_PASSWORD}
      PACT_BROKER_BASIC_AUTH_READ_ONLY_USERNAME: cruz
      PACT_BROKER_BASIC_AUTH_READ_ONLY_PASSWORD:
      ${BROKER_READ_PASSWORD}
      PACT_BROKER_LOG_LEVEL: INFO
      PACT_BROKER_DATABASE_CONNECT_MAX_RETRIES: "10"
    ports:
      - "92:80"
```

The environment variable needs to be set for the database.

The environment variable needs to be set for the Pact Broker credentials.

Once the docker-compose.yml has been created in the root of the project, the `up` command can be run to start the services shown in the following listing.

Listing 9.4 Docker compose command

```
docker compose up -d
```

When the images have been pulled and downloaded from Docker Hub, then the processes will run to start the PostgreSQL service. When the health check for the service is successful, then the Pact Broker service will start up. Once both have been started successfully, Pact Broker will be available at localhost on port 92 (`http://localhost:92`). Navigating to the URL should show the Pact Broker home screen with an example contract. As shown in figure 9.15, the docker version provides the core functionality of Pact Broker only.

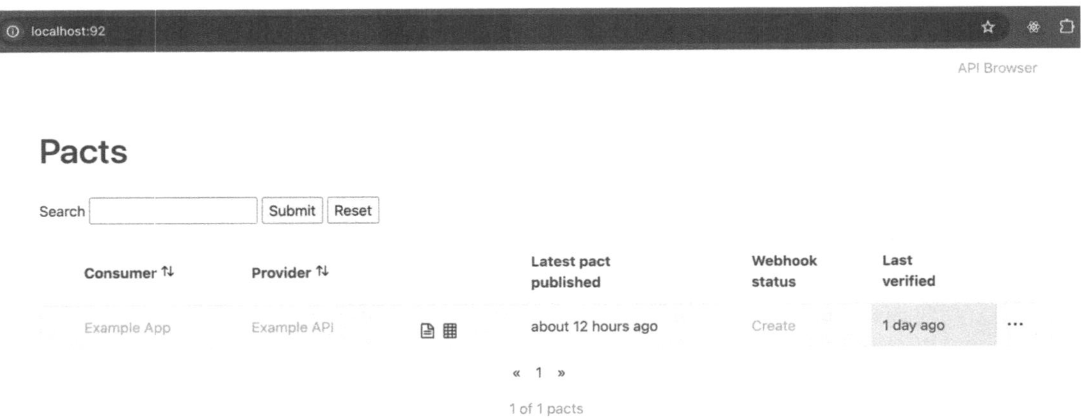

Figure 9.15 Dockerized Pact Broker service running on localhost, ready to accept new contracts

Compared with the PactFlow version in the previous part of the chapter, the UI is more basic, and there are minimal settings and additional features configured. Authentication with a username and password was added to the Pact Broker instance as well.

To communicate with the broker, use the Pact CLI, as shown in section 4.4 or also provided as a Docker image. As an example, let's publish the Pact files within the pacts folder of the book GitHub project (https://github.com/mdcruz/pact-js-example). Simply run the command from the root of the pact-js-example project, shown in listing 9.5. The command mounts the local folders to be accessible in the Docker container and sets the Pact Broker base URL to publish the contracts with the app version.

Listing 9.5 Pact CLI publish contracts

```
docker run --rm \
--network=host \          ◁— Network access to localhost
 -w ${PWD} \
 -v ${PWD}:${PWD} \
 -e PACT_BROKER_BASE_URL=http://localhost:92 \
  pactfoundation/pact-cli:latest \
  publish \
  ${PWD}/pacts \
  --consumer-app-version 0.0.0
```

If the command is successful, then the URL of the published pacts will be output to the terminal, as shown in figure 9.16.

```
$ docker run --rm --network=host -w ${PWD} -v ${PWD}:${PWD} -e PACT_BROKER_BASE_URL=h
/pact-cli:latest publish ${PWD}/pacts --consumer-app-version 0.0.0

Publishing GraphQLConsumer/GraphQLProvider pact to pact broker at http://localhost:92
```

Figure 9.16 Contracts were published to a local Pact Broker with Pact CLI without any authentication.

Publishing the contracts is done; now it's time to share the contracts with the provider service team and sell them the dream of contract testing.

9.4.2 Kubernetes Pact Broker

If we're looking to add a more robust solution for the Pact Broker service, then the container can be deployed via Kubernetes. The self-healing element could be helpful in terms of maintenance and, therefore, save time, which could be spent on writing more contract tests. There are a couple of prerequisites required:

- Kubernetes
- Helm

After the dependencies have been installed, the Helm chart can be installed from ArtifactHUB (https://mng.bz/ZVMO). We're using an existing Helm chart to simplify the Kubernetes setup and configuration. First, we need to add the Helm chart repository with the `helm` command shown in listing 9.6. The first argument after the `repo add` command is the name given to the charts, followed by the URL where the charts are stored.

Listing 9.6 The `helm repo add` command

```
helm repo add kube https://almorgv.github.io/helm-charts/charts
```

Then, install the pact-broker Helm chart from the repository that was added by using the `install` command shown in listing 9.7. The first argument after `install` states the name of the Kubernetes cluster, followed by the location of the Pact Broker Helm charts.

Listing 9.7 The `helm install` command

```
helm install pact-broker kube/pact-broker
```

If the command runs successfully, the terminal output should be similar to figure 9.17.

```
NOTES:
1. Get the application URL by running these commands:
  export POD_NAME=$(kubectl get pods --namespace default -l "app.kubernet
ance=pact-broker" -o jsonpath="{.items[0].metadata.name}")
  export CONTAINER_PORT=$(kubectl get pod --namespace default $POD_NAME -
tainerPort}")
  echo "Visit http://127.0.0.1:8080 to use your application"
  kubectl --namespace default port-forward $POD_NAME 8080:$CONTAINER_PORT
```

Figure 9.17 Helm install terminal output, showing the Kubernetes run commands

Copy and paste both `exports` and `kubectl` commands in the terminal from the output of the `helm install` command. Once the commands have been run, the code shown in figure 9.18 should be output to the terminal.

```
$   echo "Visit http://127.0.0.1:8080 to use your application"
Visit http://127.0.0.1:8080 to use your application
~/book/pact-js-example on main*
$   kubectl --namespace default port-forward $POD_NAME 8080:$CONTAINER_PORT
Forwarding from 127.0.0.1:8080 -> 80
Forwarding from [::1]:8080 -> 80
```

Figure 9.18 Kubernetes output, showing the Pact Broker URL

Navigating to `http://localhost:8080/` should display the Pact Broker homepage, as shown earlier in figure 9.15.

9.5 SaaS vs. self-hosted Pact Broker

Now, we've been through the setup for both the SaaS version of Pact Broker in PactFlow and the open source version of Pact Broker. Reflecting on each Pact Broker implementation, we'll look at the pros and cons. Some key considerations include security, maintenance, and exclusive features.

As we saw in section 9.3.2, PactFlow users can authenticate using an API bearer token. The token can be easily rotated and revoked if required. However, the open source version of Pact Broker shown earlier in listing 9.3 supports username and password as credentials only. The credentials for Pact Broker were set up upon launching Pact Broker.

Another important factor that teams often weigh up is the possible maintenance effort. As shown in section 9.4.2, deploying the open source Pact Broker with Kubernetes could help stabilize it, but it still requires some maintenance. Pact Broker will require security patches and dependency updates. Support is well represented by the open source community. However, paying for a hosted version comes with the peace of mind that dependencies are kept up-to-date. In addition, support is provided by the PactFlow team to help when needed. Weighing up the maintenance costs against the costs of the SaaS is another important factor to consider.

In addition, the PactFlow team has built some features on top of the core offering, which may boost the pros list:

- UI enhancements
- Additional contract types
- Third-party integrations

PactFlow's UI enhancements include the can-i-deploy functionality, as shown in figure 9.19, which provides an easy way to check the verification status of the app's contract dependencies manually.

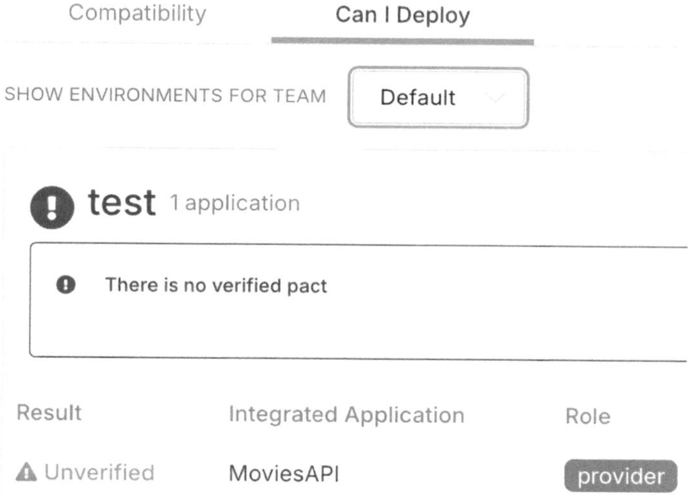

Figure 9.19 Can I Deploy UI within PactFlow, showing additional benefits of PactFlow

Another feature PactFlow offers that could help sell contract testing to teams is the support for the additional contract type of OpenAPI specification. Teams with existing OpenAPI specifications can therefore use existing tools and frameworks. We'll elaborate on this more in chapter 11 on bi-directional contract testing (another feature only supported by PactFlow).

Summary

- The purpose of Pact Broker is to share contracts, monitor contract changes, help coordinate releases, and integrate into CI/CD pipelines.
- Pact Broker core features, such as the matrix and network diagram, help visualize contract changes in a simple way.
- PactFlow provides additional features on Pact Broker, such as API tokens and user management to improve security.
- PactFlow contract stub feature means it can be used within an end-to-end test framework to improve validity.
- Contracts are published to the broker using the Pact Broker CLI, providing an easy way to integrate with CI/CD solutions.
- Pact Broker can be dockerized and deployed with Kubernetes, offering an easy way to self-host the broker.
- SaaS provides stability and features that seamlessly integrate with developer tools, whereas self-hosting Pact Broker provides flexibility and low costs for the core functionality.

10 Setting up contract testing in a CI/CD pipeline

This chapter covers

- Basic continuous integration/continuous delivery setup
- Advanced features to improve the continuous integration/continuous delivery setup
- Webhooks configuration and setup

In previous chapters, we showed you how to get started with consumer-driven contract testing (CDCT) using different types of consumers and providers. The examples we shared run from your local machines, and contract version numbers were changed manually.

To get the full benefit of contract testing, the consumer and provider tests need to be integrated into a continuous integration/continuous deployment (CI/CD) pipeline and triggered automatically when different teams push changes, especially if the changes concern the contract itself, to get a continuous feedback loop. In this chapter, we guide you on how to add your contract tests to a CI/CD pipeline step-by-step. We break it down so you know which steps concern the consumer and which steps concern the provider. We use GitHub Actions to demonstrate the integration of contract tests. However, the workflow should be similar if using other

CI/CD platforms such as CircleCI, Jenkins, or GitLab. We also discuss advanced features such as versioning, branches, environments, deployments or releases, can-i-deploy tool, and webhooks to ensure you and your teams have a seamless workflow once contract tests are added to respective pipelines.

10.1 Basic CI/CD setup for the consumer and provider

As mentioned, we use GitHub Actions to demonstrate how you can set up your contract tests as part of a pipeline. GitHub Actions is a CI/CD platform that you can use to automate your build, test, and deployment pipeline. If you're more familiar with other CI/CD platforms, getting started with GitHub Actions is fairly easy and quick. All you need is a GitHub repository! We only show the basics here, but if you want to know more about GitHub Actions in detail, check out https://docs.github.com/en/actions.

Because the example project found in https://github.com/mdcruz/pact-js-example contains both the consumer and provider code for simplicity, we show only one workflow. In real-world projects, there will be at least two workflows: one for the consumer project and one for the provider project. The basic workflow will be similar regardless and is shown in figure 10.1.

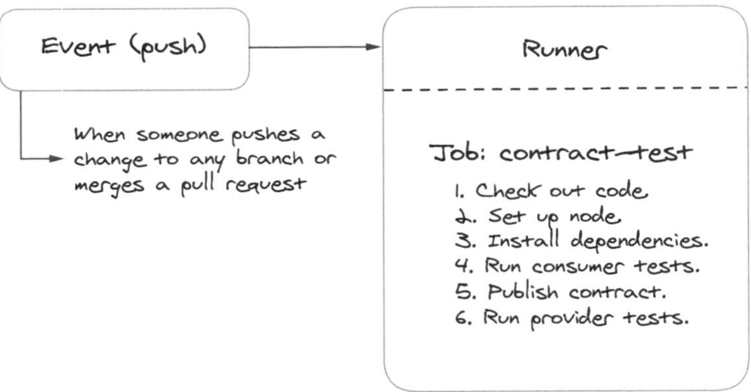

Figure 10.1 A simple visualization of the contract testing workflow via GitHub Actions. This runs the web consumer tests, publishes the contract, and runs the provider verification test.

The workflow is triggered whenever someone pushes changes to any branch or merges a pull request to the main branch. This trigger can also be customized depending on your project needs. For the basic workflow, we define only one job, which is to run the contract testing workflow, but this job can be run sequentially or in parallel with other jobs. The steps in our `contract-test` job include the following:

1. Checking out the GitHub project so the workflow can access it
2. Setting up the Node action so dependencies can be cached

3 Installing the project dependencies added to your package.json file
4 Running the web consumer tests
5 Publishing the contract to PactFlow
6 Running the provider tests

The npm commands for steps 3-6 in the preceding list were introduced in previous chapters already, so there is nothing new here. Steps 1 and 2 are standard actions provided by GitHub.

10.1.1 Setting up GitHub Actions

To set up GitHub Actions in your own GitHub projects, you just need to create a workflow file of type YAML in a directory called .github/workflows. If you check out the basic-ci-setup branch of the example GitHub project, you should see a file named contract-test-sample.yaml inside the .github/workflows directory, and it should contain the following content:

```
name: Run contract tests          <- The workflow's name

on: push          <- The event that will trigger the workflow

env:                              <- The environment variables needed for the workflow
  PACT_BROKER_BASE_URL:
${{ secrets.PACT_BROKER_BASE_URL }}
  PACT_BROKER_TOKEN: ${{ secrets.PACT_BROKER_TOKEN }}

jobs:
  contract-test:          <- The job's name
    runs-on: ubuntu-latest
    steps:                        The series of steps to run the workflow
      - uses: actions/checkout@v4
      - uses: actions/setup-node@v4
        with:
          node-version: 18
      - name: Install dependencies
        run: npm i
      - name: Run web consumer contract tests
        run: npm run test:web:consumer
      - name: Publish contract to PactFlow
        run: npm run publish:pact
      - name: Run provider contract tests
        run: npm run test:provider
```

When integrating your contract tests to a CI/CD platform, make sure that any environment variables are stored securely as a secret. In our case, we need to store the `PACT_BROKER_BASE_URL` and `PACT_BROKER_TOKEN`. To understand how secrets are stored in GitHub Actions, check out https://mng.bz/RN60.

To see the workflow in action, run the workflow in GitHub Actions. You should end up on screen similar to figure 10.2.

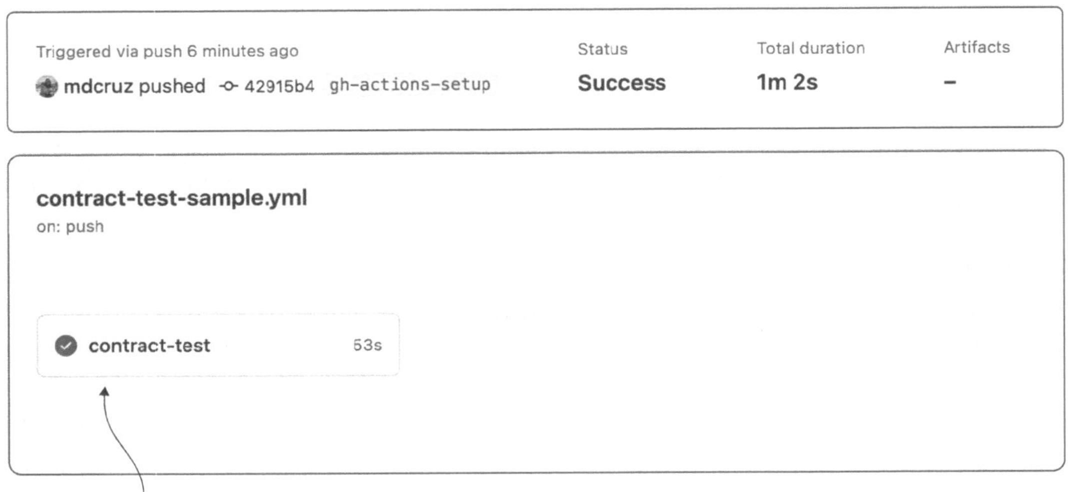

Figure 10.2 An example workflow run for our contract testing project. The workflow has one job that passed successfully.

10.1.2 Example configuration for other CI/CD platforms

If you're using other CI/CD platforms such as CircleCI (https://circleci.com), the configuration steps will be similar. Here is an example configuration snippet that you can use:

```
version: 2.1
jobs:
  build:
    docker:
      - image: circleci/node:latest
    steps:
      - checkout
      - run:
          name: Setup environment variables
          command: |
            echo "export PACT_BROKER_TOKEN=$PACT_BROKER_TOKEN"
>> $BASH_ENV
            echo "export PACT_BROKER_BASE_URL=
$PACT_BROKER_BASE_URL" >> $BASH_ENV
      - run:
          name: Install project dependencies
          command: npm install
      - run:
          name: Run consumer contract tests
          command: npm run test:consumer
      - run:
```

Uses the docker image for the latest node version

The environment variables needed for the workflow

The series of steps to run the workflow

```
      name: Publish contract to PactFlow
      command: npm run publish:pact
  - run:
      name: Run provider contract tests
      command: npm run start:and:test:provider
```

The series of steps to run the workflow

For other CI/CD platforms, it's best to check their respective documentation. However, the npm commands should remain similar, unless you change the name of the commands itself.

Now that you've had a quick overview of what a basic contract testing workflow looks like when integrated to a CI/CD pipeline, let's look at how we can improve the workflow by introducing concepts such as automated versioning, branches, can-i-deploy tool, Pact deployments, and webhooks.

10.2 Advanced features to improve the CI/CD setup

As mentioned in chapter 9, Pact has a lot of features to help you with your contract testing experience such as the *pacticipant* (a party that participates in a contract, e.g., a consumer and provider) versions, using branches, recording deployments and releases, and using the can-i-deploy tool, to name a few. In this section, we show how to integrate these features.

10.2.1 Configuring consumer and provider versions

If you remember from chapter 4, we were updating the consumer contract version, especially if there were changes to the contract. For a more automated approach, the versions need to be configured in a way that's unique on the release branch or merge to the main branch. One way to do this is using the GitHub commit ID, which is called a Secure Hash Algorithm (SHA) or a hash. Using the GitHub SHA ensures that the contract changes can be easily traced to the relevant code changes.

To follow along in the following hands-on guide, make sure you have a copy of the example GitHub project (https://github.com/mdcruz/pact-js-example), and switch to a new branch called setup-advanced-pact-features. Once you're in the setup-advanced-pact-features branch, the first thing you need to update is the contract-test-sample.yaml file and introduce a new environment variable called `GITHUB_SHA`, which should contain the value of the GitHub SHA. To do this in GitHub Actions, add the following code snippet:

```
env:
  PACT_BROKER_BASE_URL: ${{ secrets.PACT_BROKER_BASE_URL }}
  PACT_BROKER_TOKEN: ${{ secrets.PACT_BROKER_TOKEN }}
  GITHUB_SHA: ${{ github.sha }}
```

Next, let's update command `publish:pact` in the package.json file to use the `GITHUB_SHA` environment variable instead of the manual version:

```
"scripts": {
     "publish:pact": "pact-broker publish ./pacts
```

```
--consumer-app-version=$GITHUB_SHA --tag=main
--broker-base-url=$PACT_BROKER_BASE_URL
--broker-token=$PACT_BROKER_TOKEN"
}
```

This ensures that when the contract is published, the version will point to the commit ID that introduces the change. To test the change, feel free to commit the changes to your local GitHub branch, push the changes remotely to your own fork, and create a pull request.

When the workflow completes, log in to your PactFlow account, select the WebConsumer and MoviesAPI integration, and click Matrix to view the matrix table. You should see a screen similar to figure 10.3 where the consumer version is now a unique identifier instead, which we can link to a specific GitHub commit.

Figure 10.3 Matrix table for WebConsumer and MoviesAPI integration. The consumer version is now set to the GitHub SHA instead of a manual version.

Let's update the MoviesAPI provider versions to use the GitHub SHA by updating the provider/provider-contract-spec.js file. Within the provider options of this file, update the value of `providerVersion` to use the `GITHUB_SHA` environment variable:

```
const options = {
  …
  pactBrokerUrl: process.env.PACT_BROKER_BASE_URL,
  pactBrokerToken: process.env.PACT_BROKER_TOKEN,
  providerVersion: process.env.GITHUB_SHA,
  …
}
```

Go ahead and save all the changes. Once you push the changes to your remote branch and the workflow completes, head back to your PactFlow account, and you should now see a screen similar to figure 10.4.

Both the consumer and provider now contain the GitHub SHA as unique versions. Pact also automatically verifies all the relevant versions that are compatible. As an

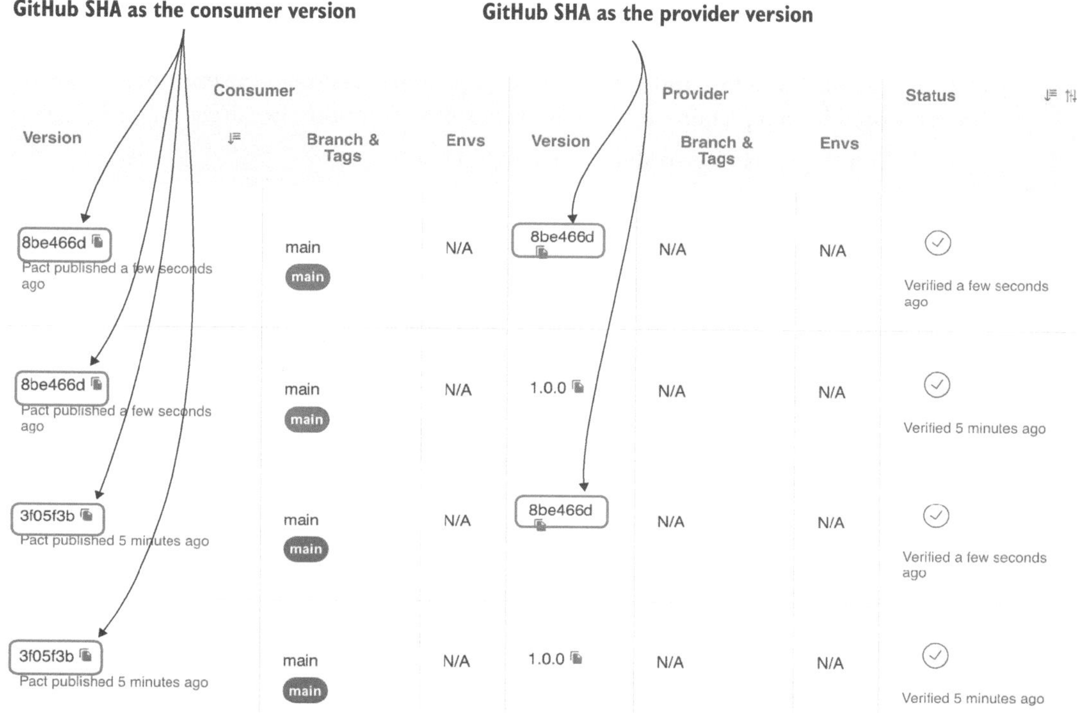

Figure 10.4 Matrix table for WebConsumer and MoviesAPI integration. The provider version now also has the GitHub SHA as its version instead of a manual version.

example, the consumer team can look at the matrix table and can confidently say that commits `8be466d` and `3f05f3b` can be deployed to production because these versions have been verified successfully.

10.2.2 Configuring branches

When introducing contract testing as part of a pull request or feature branch workflow, a problem that we've faced in the past was that the providers can sometimes verify the incorrect contract due to consumers uploading contracts that are still works in progress. For example, let's say the consumer is working on a feature that involves changing the contract. Because this is an early feature that is still a work in progress, a few changes still need to be iterated. However, because the changes are being committed to the pipeline, the contract testing workflow has started. The consumer pipeline fails, as expected, because the work is still in progress. On the provider pipeline, let's say that one of the developers is introducing some minor code changes too. The developer is confident it won't break the contract because the code change isn't a breaking change. The developer is surprised to find that their pull request is also failing because the provider verification has verified the incorrect contract.

To avoid situations where the verification process isn't accurate, branches in Pact were introduced to ensure providers verify the correct contracts. Branches represent your typical Git branches and often contain different versions, representing numerous commits on a branch. There are two situations in which branches are created in Pact:

- When the consumer publishes a contract
- When the provider verifies the contract

To configure a branch, you need to update the contract-test-sample.yaml file and introduce a new environment variable called `GITHUB_BRANCH`, which will contain the value of the GitHub branch. To do this in GitHub Actions, add the following code snippet:

```
env:
  PACT_BROKER_BASE_URL: ${{ secrets.PACT_BROKER_BASE_URL }}
  PACT_BROKER_TOKEN: ${{ secrets.PACT_BROKER_TOKEN }}
  GITHUB_SHA: ${{ github.sha }}
  GITHUB_BRANCH: ${{ github.ref_name }}
```

To use this branch when publishing a contract from the consumer side, you need to update command `publish:pact` again in the package.json file and replace the `tag` option with `branch`:

```
"scripts": {
     "publish:pact": "pact-broker publish ./pacts
--consumer-app-version=$GITHUB_SHA
--branch=$GITHUB_BRANCH
--broker-base-url=$PACT_BROKER_BASE_URL
--broker-token=$PACT_BROKER_TOKEN"
}
```

To test the workflow as part of the pipeline, commit the changes again to your local GitHub branch, and push the changes remotely to your own fork. When the workflow completes, go back to your PactFlow account, select the WebConsumer and MoviesAPI integration, and on the Overview tab, you should see a screen similar to figure 10.5, where there are now two contracts verified successfully: one for the pull request branch and one for the main branch. In your case, the branch name should be setup-advanced-pact-features. You can also test the new workflow locally by replacing `--branch=$GITHUB_BRANCH` with `--branch=setup-advanced-pact-features`, and then, on your terminal, run command `npm run publish:pact` to publish the contract.

Now that we've configured branches in the consumer pipeline, we do the same for the provider pipeline. To configure a branch when the provider verifies the contract, we add additional options to the provider setup. For now, just update provider/provider-contract-spec.js.

Within the provider options, remove `consumerVersionTags` and add two new options: `providerVersionBranch` and `consumerVersionSelectors`.

The `providerVersionBranch` will have the `GITHUB_BRANCH` environment variable to represent the branch to which it belongs. The `consumerVersionSelectors` is a

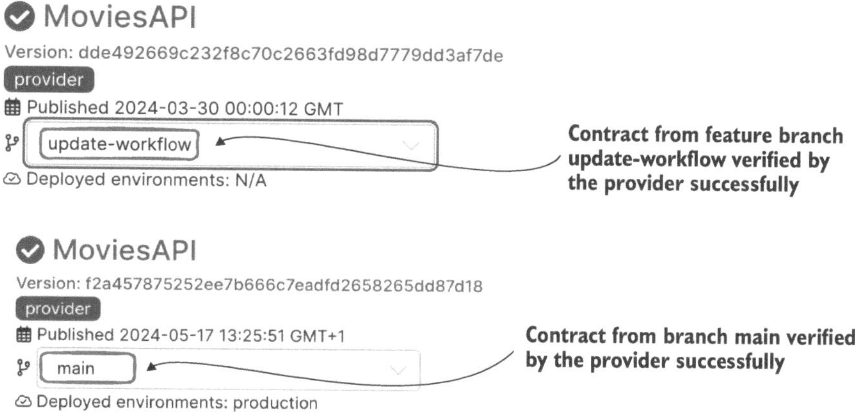

Figure 10.5 Two contracts from the WebConsumer to represent a contract generated from a feature branch and the main contract that has been merged to the main branch. Branches allow providers to verify the correct contracts.

mechanism introduced by Pact to represent which contracts the provider should verify and contain different properties. In our example, we want to ensure that the provider verifies the contract from the consumer's main branch to catch any contract problems before the provider merges their changes, so we need to set the `mainBranch` property to `true`. Because we now use `consumerVersionSelectors`, we don't need `consumerVersionTags` anymore.

If both consumer and provider teams work on the same feature, a recommended practice is to have the provider branch name match the branch name the consumer used. This means if the developer on the consumer side created a new branch called test-pact-features, the developer from the provider side should also create the same branch name. To enable the matching branch rule, we must set the `matchingBranch` property to `true` by adding the following code snippet:

```
const options = {
  ...
  providerVersion: process.env.GITHUB_SHA,
  providerVersionBranch: process.env.GITHUB_BRANCH,
  consumerVersionSelectors: [
    { mainBranch: true },
    { matchingBranch: true },
  ]
  ...
}
```

There are other properties for `consumerVersionSelectors`, so make sure to check out https://mng.bz/2gdd to see the full list.

To test the new workflow, commit the changes again to your local GitHub branch, and push the changes remotely to your own fork. If you go back to your PactFlow account, you should see a screen similar to figure 10.6 where the branch name is also configured on the provider side, and the provider is verifying two contracts: one from the matching branch name and one from the main branch. In your case, the branch name should be setup-advanced-pact-features. Similarly, you can also test

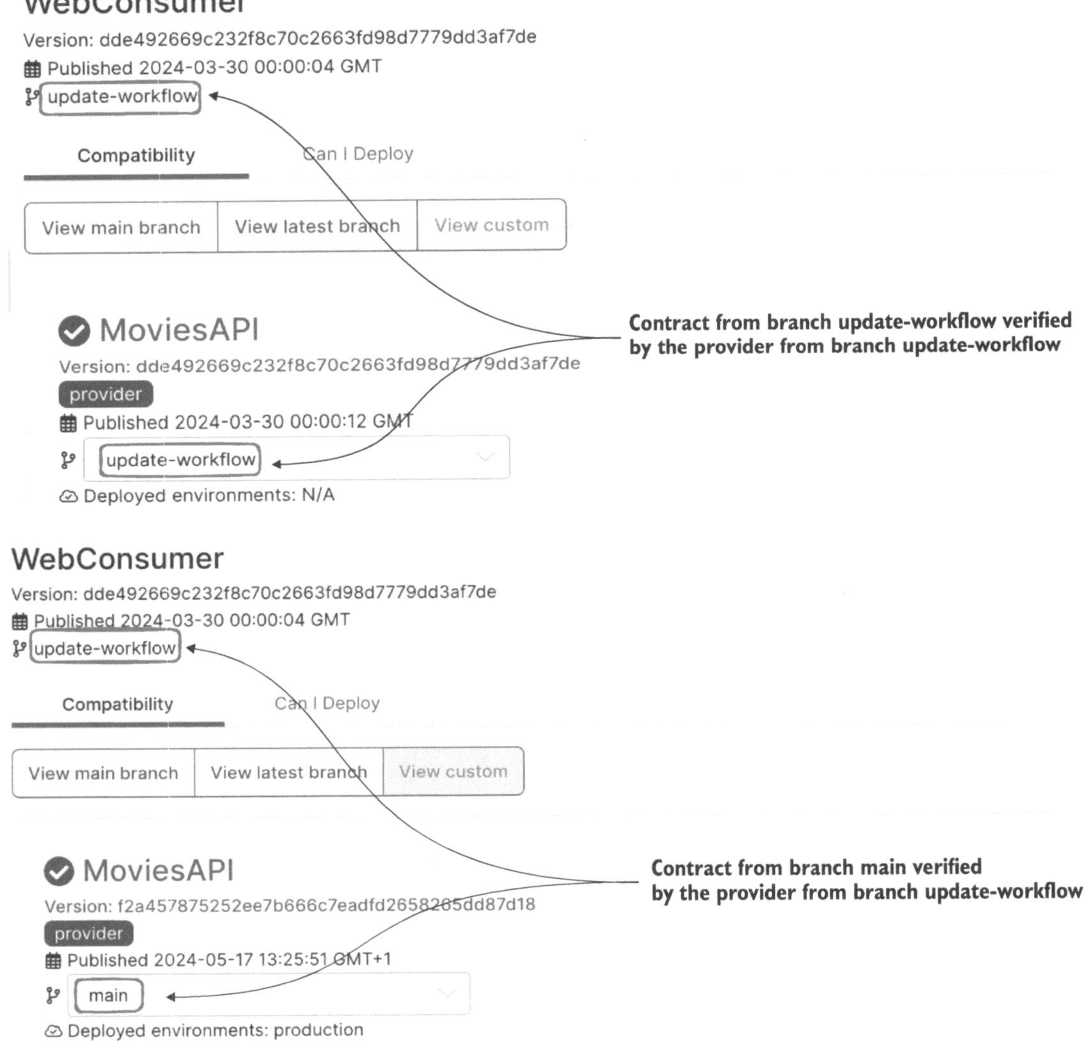

Figure 10.6 Two contracts from the WebConsumer verified successfully by the MoviesAPI provider. One of the contracts is from the same branch, test-pact-features, and the other is from the main branch.

the changes locally by replacing `providerVersionBranch: process.env.GITHUB_BRANCH` with `providerVersionBranch: setup-advanced-pact-features`, and then, on your terminal, run command `npm run test:provider` to run the provider verification.

At this stage, you should have an improved contract testing workflow where both consumers and providers record versions based on the GitHub commits and also record the GitHub branch from where the commits are made. The CI/CD setup that we have now is illustrated in figure 10.7.

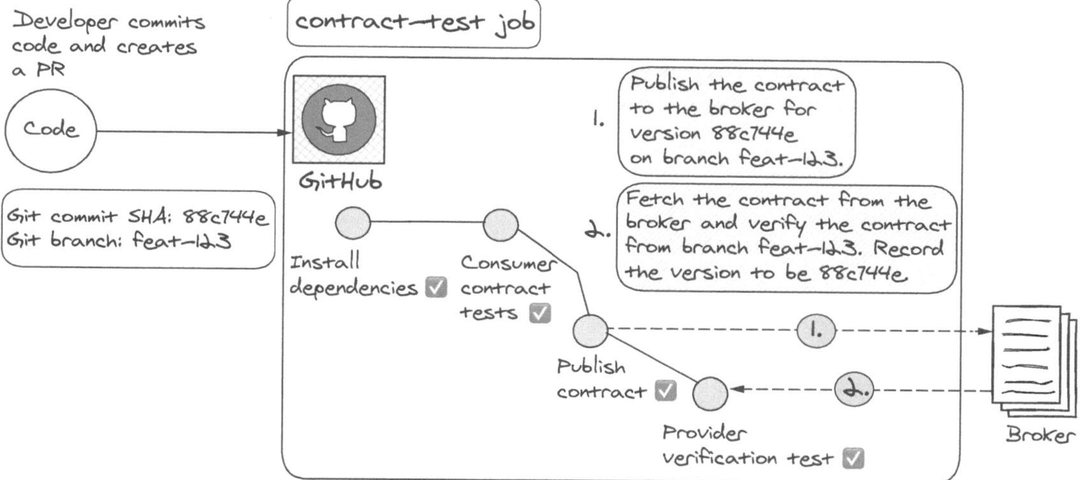

Figure 10.7 CI/CD setup for our contract testing job with versions and branches configured to allow providers to verify the correct contracts

10.2.3 Creating environments

Apart from recording the versions and branches, it's also a good idea to record the environment in which a version and a branch are deployed or released. This allows Pact to check if a specific version can be safely deployed.

Using figure 10.7 as a reference, let's say that branch feat-123 is good to go and ready to be deployed to production. Before merging this branch, it's a good idea to make sure that the environment structure you have is also recorded in Pact. For example, if your build pipeline includes deploying to three different environments (e.g., test, staging, and production), these three environments should also be created in Pact.

It's worth noting that Pact already prerecords default environments test and production. However, if you want to create a new environment to reflect your process better, this can also be done in a couple of ways:

- Using the `pact-broker` command, which comes built-in after installing Pact
- Using PactFlow's UI

As an example, if you want to create a new environment called staging using the `pact-broker` command, go back to your terminal and use the following command:

```
pact-broker create-environment --name staging --display-name staging
```

After running the command, you should see an output similar to:

```
Created staging environment in PactFlow
with UUID 88d7bce9-e5b0-49b8-827f-1d16a5621f4b
```

To see the newly created environment, go back to your PactFlow account, click the Settings button, and then select the Environments tab. You should land on the environments screen shown in figure 10.8.

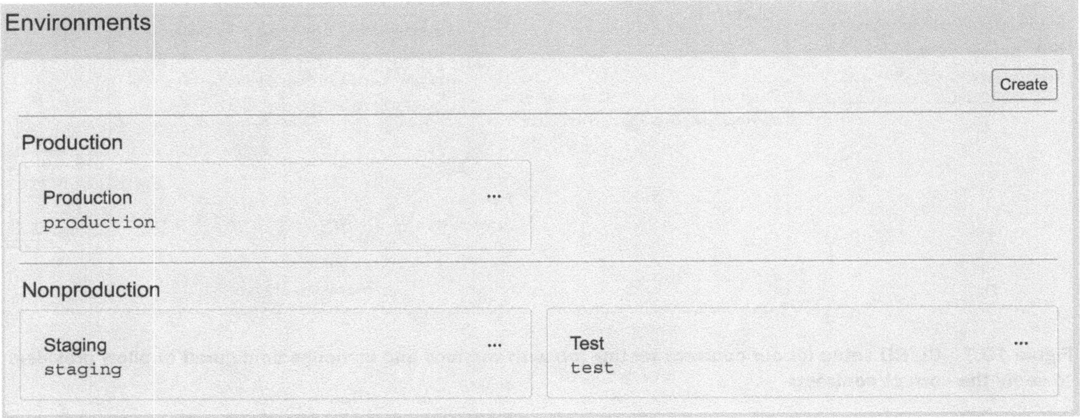

Figure 10.8 The list of environments that PactFlow knows now includes the newly created staging environment.

If you prefer to use PactFlow's UI, you can also edit or delete any of the environments created. To add a new environment using the UI, you can click the Create button, as shown in figure 10.8, and you should see a popup screen appear (see figure 10.9). You can provide the Name, Display Name, and whether it's a production environment from this screen.

Now that we have versions, branches, and environments configured, let's say that your team has deployed the current version to a production environment. How do we record that this version is the one being used by our users? Let's look at how to record deployments and releases with Pact.

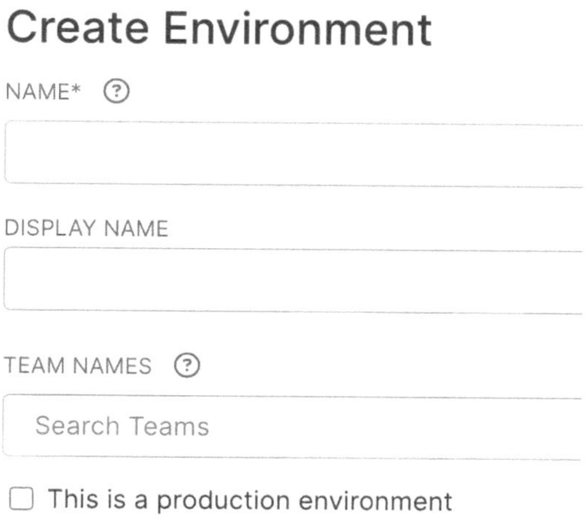

Figure 10.9 Create Environment screen from PactFlow where a new environment can be added

10.2.4 *Recording deployments and/or releases*

When changes are deployed to production or any other environment, it's also a good idea to record which version is in which environment in Pact to signify that there has been a deployment or release made. The concepts of *deployment* and *release* are similar in Pact, but there are some slight differences. If a version is said to be deployed in Pact, this means that previous versions will be marked as not deployed. This also means that there will only be one version recorded as deployed. Recording deployments are useful for APIs and web applications where only one version of the code can be used. On the other hand, if a version is said to be released in Pact, previous versions will remain unaffected and will still be marked as released. Recording releases are useful for mobile apps where users can use different versions.

RECORDING A DEPLOYMENT

To record a deployment, we'll use the `pact-broker` command again but use the `record-deployment` option this time. Add the following scripts to your package.json file:

```
"scripts": {
   …
   "record:web:consumer:deployment":
"pact-broker record-deployment
--pacticipant WebConsumer --version $GITHUB_SHA
--environment production",
   "record:provider:deployment":
"pact-broker record-deployment --pacticipant MoviesAPI
--version $GITHUB_SHA --environment production"
   …
}
```

`record:web:consumer:deployment` records the WebConsumer's current version as the version that is deployed to production, while `record:provider:deployment` takes care of recording the provider version deployed to production. Next, let's add these two new commands as additional steps to our contract testing workflow by updating the contract-test-sample.yml file:

```
jobs:
  contract-test:
    runs-on: ubuntu-latest
    steps:
      ...
      - name: Run provider contract tests
        run: npm run test:provider
      - name: Record web consumer deployment
        if: github.ref == 'refs/heads/main'
        run: npm run record:web:consumer:deployment
      - name: Record provider deployment
        if: github.ref == 'refs/heads/main'
        run: npm run record:provider:deployment
```

To test the new workflow, commit the changes again to your local GitHub branch, and push the changes remotely to your own fork. You might notice that the new steps will be skipped because of the conditional statement added, so to test that it's working, merge the pull request to your main branch. Once the workflow has finished running, go back to your PactFlow account, and on the WebConsumer and MoviesAPI integration overview, you should see an output similar to figure 10.10.

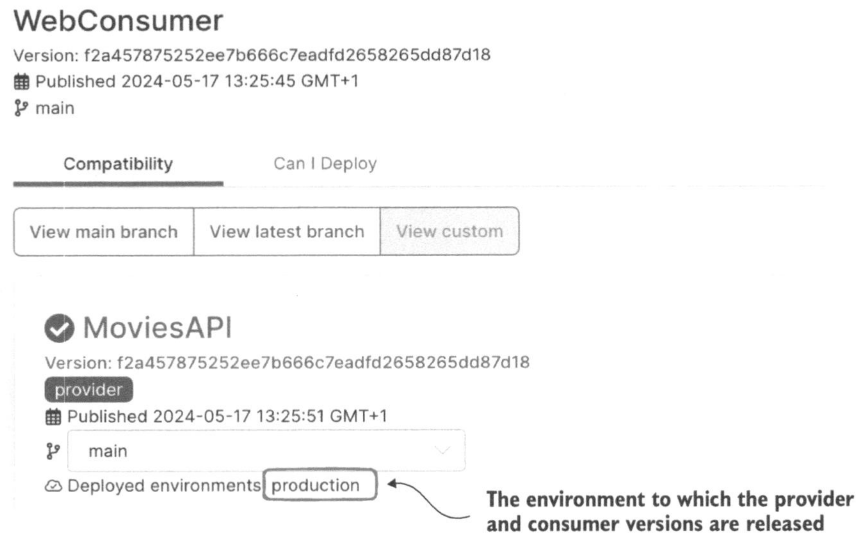

Figure 10.10 WebConsumer and MoviesAPI integration with deployments recorded to the production environment. This indicates that these two versions are available in production.

Similarly, you can also test the changes locally by replacing `$GITHUB_SHA` with your version value. On your terminal, run commands `npm run record:web:consumer:deployment` and `npm run record:web:provider:deployment`.

Recording a release

The steps for recording a release are very similar to how we've recorded a deployment. We'll still use the `pact-broker` command but will use the `record-release` option this time. As an example, if you want to record a release for the mobile consumer that we introduced in chapter 5, you can use the following command instead:

```
pact-broker record-release
--pacticipant MoviesAndroidApp
--version $GITHUB_SHA
--environment production
```

When you log in to PactFlow, the release will be recorded under a different field called Release Environment, as shown in figure 10.11.

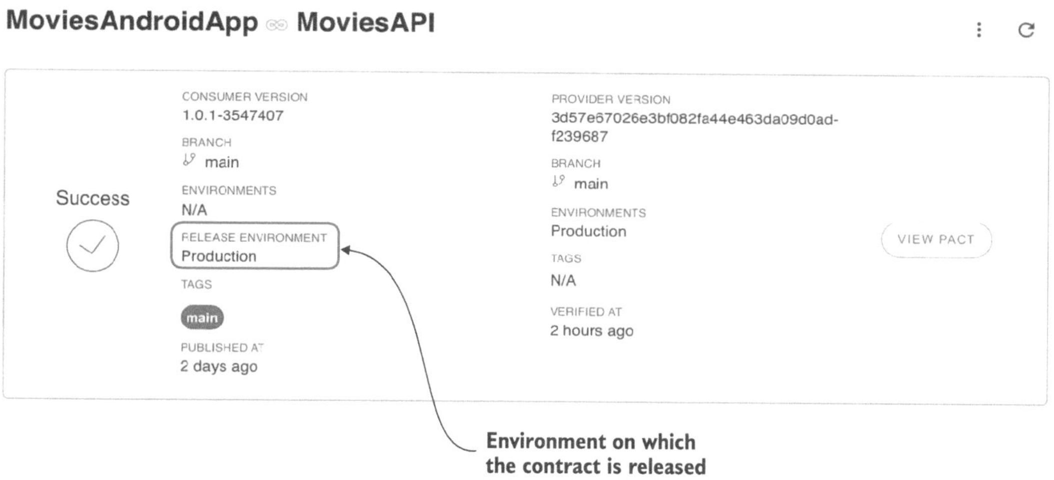

Figure 10.11 MoviesAndroidApp and MoviesAPI integration with the consumer release recorded to the production environment

At this stage, the contract testing workflow should now have versions, branches, and deployments or releases configured. The CI/CD setup that we have now is illustrated in figure 10.12.

Now that we've recorded a specific version to be deployed in an environment, another recommended setup is to update the provider configuration to verify contracts currently deployed in an environment to ensure that changes in the provider

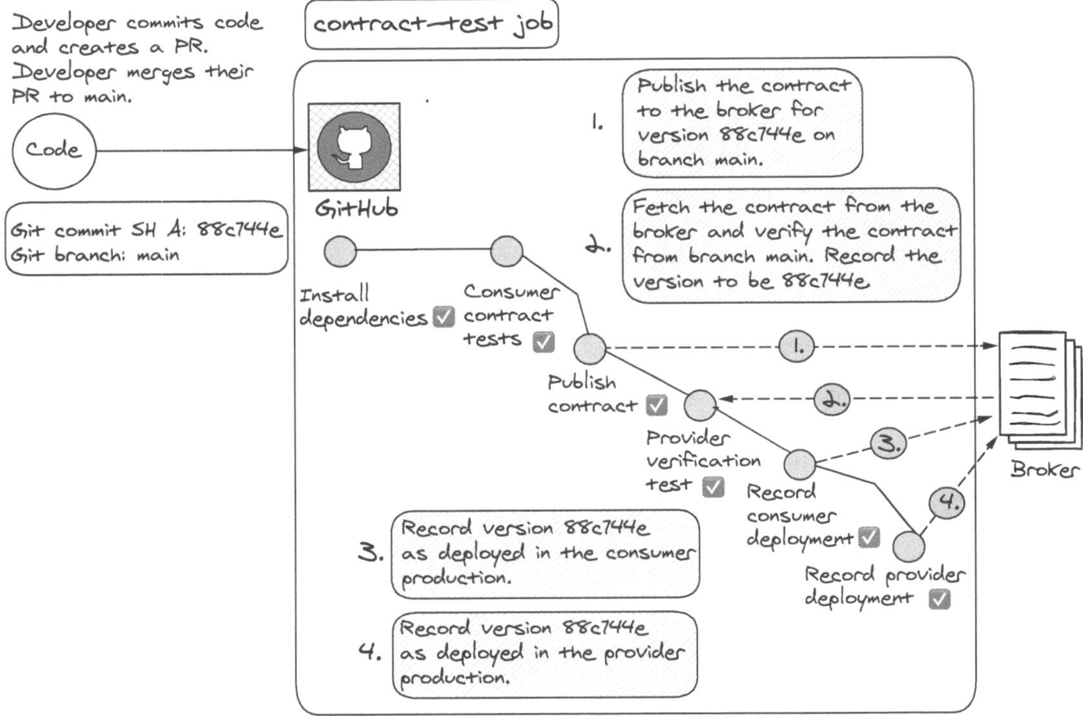

Figure 10.12 CI/CD setup for our contract testing job with deployments or releases configured to signify which versions are deployed to an environment, such as production

are verified against the deployed consumer version. Currently, we've set the `mainBranch` and `matchingBranch` properties to `true`. Another property that we can set is the `deployedOrReleased` property. To do that, let's update the provider/provider-contract-spec.js file:

```
const options = {
  ...
  consumerVersionSelectors: [
    { mainBranch: true },
    { matchingBranch: true },
    { deployedOrReleased: true }
  ],
  ...
};
```

Once the provider verification runs, it will verify contracts from the consumer from the main branch, contracts from any matching branch names, and contracts that have been deployed or released to an environment. When code changes are being merged by multiple developers and deployed to production, how can we ask Pact to ensure that the versions we're about to deploy to production are compatible with the ones already in production? You can look at the broker manually and check if the versions are compatible, but this could be time-consuming, especially as your contract testing efforts scale up. To check this automatically, let's use the cool Pact feature called can-i-deploy that we've mentioned a few times earlier in this book.

10.2.5 Using the can-i-deploy tool

The can-i-deploy tool is a feature introduced by Pact that lets you query the matrix table to verify if certain versions ready to be deployed to an environment have a successful verification result with the version already deployed in the same environment. This is useful when your team wants that extra safety net to ensure they can confidently deploy their changes to production. In addition, this can also help the team move to a CD model where a code is automatically deployed to production when all the jobs pass.

You might work in an organization where teams deploy different changes to a main branch, but the changes aren't frequently deployed to production. In such cases, there could be scenarios where the code deployed to production differs from the latest code deployed to a main branch, so you still need to verify if the code you currently have is compatible with the changes deployed to production. The can-i-deploy tool works by checking the individual entries from the matrix table and checking if the consumer or provider version you're about to deploy is compatible with the other versions deployed to an environment, as listed in table 10.1.

Table 10.1 How can-i-deploy works

Consumer Version	Provider Version	Verification Status
12	40	Failed
13	41	Failed
13	42 (production)	Passed
14	42 (production)	Failed

Looking at table 10.1, we can easily visualize which consumer and provider versions are compatible. If provider version 42 has been deployed to production, we know that consumer version 13 can be deployed too, but not version 14 because it's not compatible with the version being used in production. To implement can-i-deploy in our contract testing workflow, we'll add two new scripts in our package.json file:

```
"scripts": {
   ...
   "can:i:deploy:consumer": "pact-broker
can-i-deploy --pacticipant WebConsumer
--version=$GITHUB_SHA --to-environment production",
   "can:i:deploy:provider": "pact-broker
```

```
can-i-deploy --pacticipant MoviesAPI
--version=$GITHUB_SHA --to-environment production"
    ...
}
```

The `can:i:deploy:consumer` verifies if the WebConsumer's current version is safe to be deployed to production, while the `can:i:deploy:provider` verifies if the provider version can be deployed to production. Next, let's add these two new commands as additional steps to our contract testing workflow by updating the contract-test-sample.yml file:

```
jobs:
  contract-test:
    runs-on: ubuntu-latest
    steps:
     ...
      - name: Run provider contract tests
        run: npm run test:provider
      - name: Can I deploy provider?
        run: npm run can:i:deploy:provider
      - name: Record provider deployment
        run: npm run record:provider:deployment
      - name: Can I deploy web consumer?
        run: npm run can:i:deploy:consumer
      - name: Record web consumer deployment
        run: npm run record:web:consumer:deployment
```

In real-world projects, these steps must be added before merging changes to a main branch or deploying to any environment. If you have test and production as your environments, it's recommended to have two can-i-deploy scripts for each environment just in case the versions deployed in each environment differ.

Testing the workflow is similar to how we've tested the deployments and/or releases feature. Once the GitHub workflow has finished running, click the workflow, view the workflow details, and expand the steps we just added to integrate can-i-deploy. You should see an output similar to figure 10.13.

```
Computer says yes \o/

CONSUMER     | C.VERSION   | PROVIDER  | P.VERSION   | SUCCESS? | RESULT#
-------------|-------------|-----------|-------------|----------|--------
WebConsumer  | 6f06517...  | MoviesAPI | 6f06517...  | true     | 1

VERIFICATION RESULTS
--------------------
1. https://mariecruz.pactflow.io/pacts/provider/MoviesAPI/consumer/WebConsumer/pact-version/b3
29af91bc759753563c8707c5beb4795fe85865/metadata/Y3ZuPTZmMDY1MTdlYzNiMTdmODg1NGI4MmZlNjAxMjBiNz
dhMmQ0Y2I0NmM/verification-results/341 (success)

All required verification results are published and successful
```

Figure 10.13 Test output of running the `can:i:deploy:consumer` command

Similarly, you can also test the changes locally by replacing `$GITHUB_SHA` with your consumer version value and running command `npm run can:i:deploy:consumer` on your terminal. If the version you provide doesn't exist, Pact will complain that there are no contracts or verification published. On the other hand, if the version you provided fails the can-i-deploy check, Pact will complain that the verification provided for the version was unsuccessful, and the step will fail.

At this stage, the contract testing workflow has been further improved and provides additional confidence that any changes merged are ready to be deployed without any contract problems. The CI/CD setup that we have now is illustrated in figure 10.14.

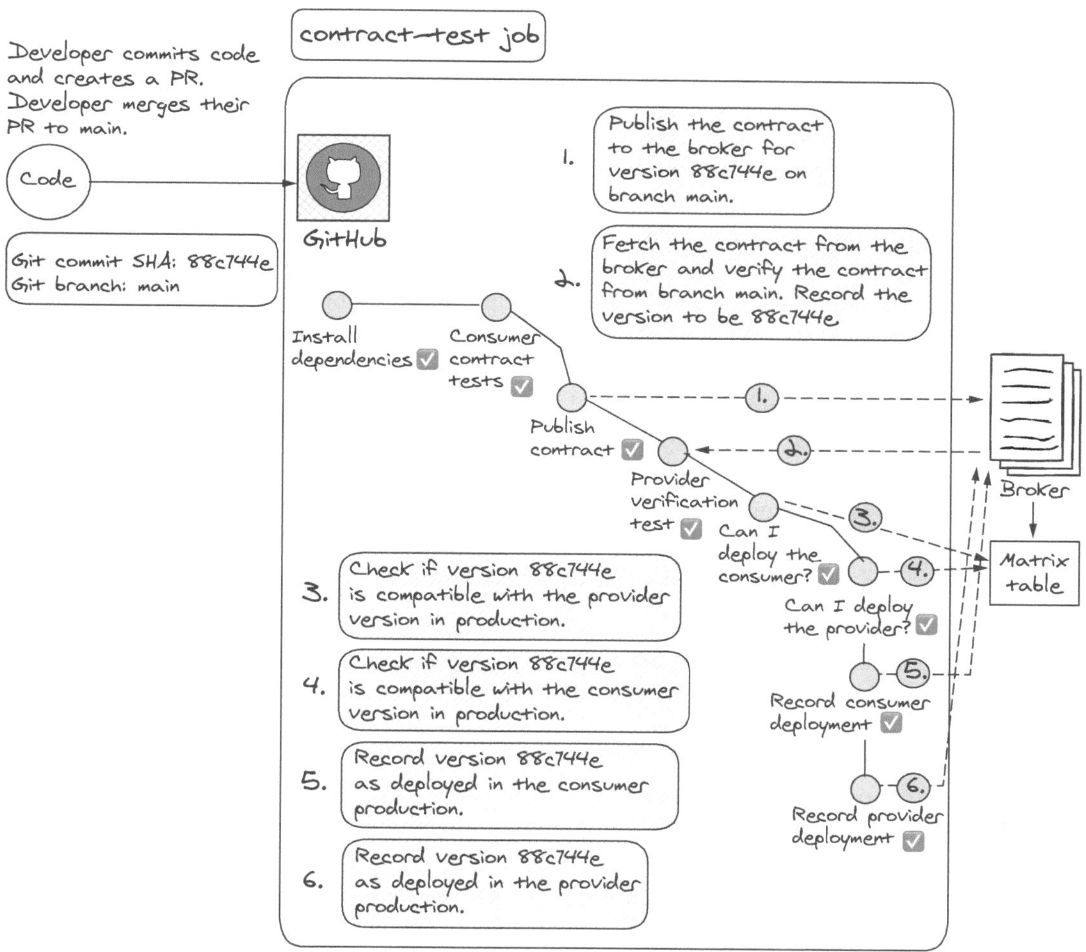

Figure 10.14 CI/CD setup for our contract testing job with versions, branches, and can-i-deploy integration

10.3 Chapter exercises

To apply what you learned in sections 10.1 and 10.2, we want you to add the GraphQL contract tests introduced in chapter 7 as part of the GitHub workflow. The following exercises will test your knowledge about the advanced concepts of contract testing, such as versioning, branches, environments, deployments or releases, and can-i-deploy:

- *Exercise 10.1*—Add the GraphQL consumer and provider tests as separate steps in contract-test-sample.yml.
- *Exercise 10.2*—Update the graphql/provider/graphql-server-contract.spec.js file, and configure the provider version to use the `GITHUB_SHA` environment variable for automated versioning.
- *Exercise 10.3*—Update the graphql/provider/graphql-server-contract.spec.js file, configure the provider version branch to use the `GITHUB_BRANCH` environment variable for automated branching, and set up the `consumerVersionSelectors` to have the `mainBranch` and `matchingBranch` properties set to `true`.
- *Exercise 10.4*—Create two new scripts in your package.json file to record a production deployment to mimic the latest versions of GraphQL consumer and provider being deployed to production.
- *Exercise 10.5*—Add the record deployment scripts for GraphQL consumer and provider tests as separate steps in contract-test-sample.yml.
- *Exercise 10.6*—Update the graphql/provider/graphql-server-contract.spec.js file, and update `consumerVersionSelectors` to have the `deployedOrReleased` property set to `true`.
- *Exercise 10.7*—Create two new scripts in your package.json file to use the can-i-deploy tool to ask Pact if subsequent GraphQL consumer and provider versions are safe to deploy to production.
- *Exercise 10.8*—Add the can-i-deploy scripts for GraphQL consumer and provider tests as separate steps in contract-test-sample.yml.

Feel free to test each step as you go along before proceeding to the subsequent step. If you get stuck at any point, refer to the main branch of https://github.com/mdcruz/pact-js-example or check out appendix C for the answers.

10.4 Webhooks

The final concept that we want to cover in this chapter is the use of webhooks in Pact. Until now, we've been working on a single GitHub project containing both the consumer and provider workflows, so every change in our contract triggers the provider verification because it was running in a single workflow. However, consumer code isn't co-located with the provider code in real-world projects.

If the consumer and provider are in separate GitHub projects and separate workflows, when the consumer makes changes to the contract, the relevant provider verification job won't be triggered automatically, which can cause the consumer workflow to fail on the can-i-deploy job. This happens because Pact can't pre-verify the contract because the contract has changed. To work around this problem, you can ask a team member from the provider team to manually trigger the provider verification job, and when the job passes, you can rerun the can-i-deploy job on the consumer pipeline. However, this workaround is clearly not ideal!

Instead, we'd like the provider verification job to be triggered automatically when the consumer has changed something in the contract. We don't need to rerun the entire provider pipeline; we want to run just the provider verification job and publish the results to our Pact Broker. Pact webhooks can help us achieve this setup as visualized in figure 10.15. According to the Pact documentation (https://docs.pact.io/pact_broker/webhooks):

> *Webhooks allow you to trigger an HTTP request when a pact is changed, a pact is published, or a verification is published. The most common use case for webhooks is to trigger a provider build every time a pact changes, and to trigger a consumer build every time a verification is published.*

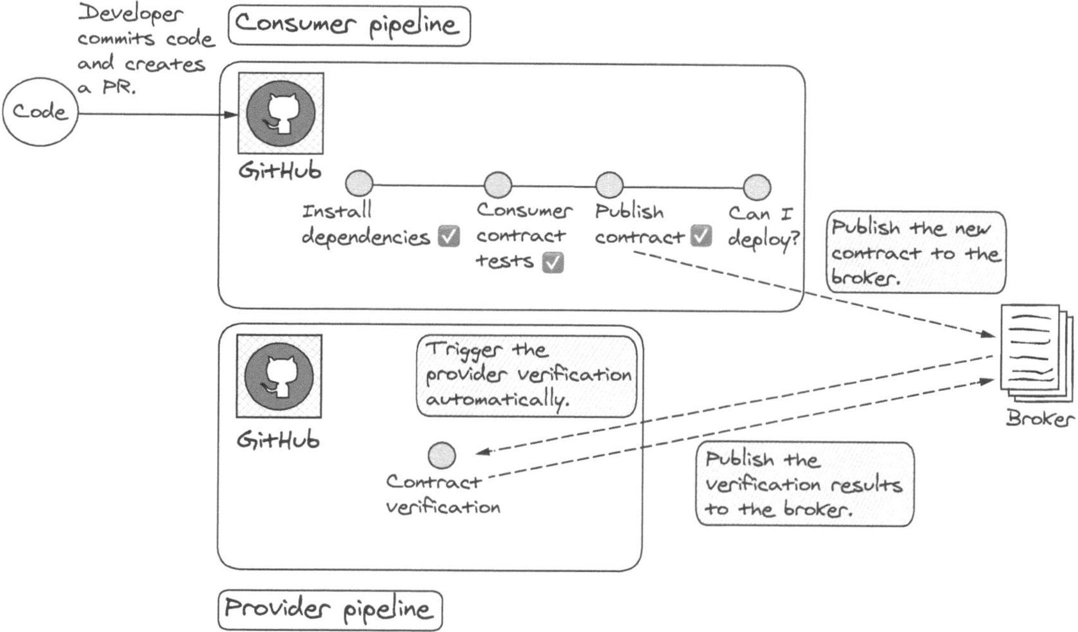

Figure 10.15 Consumer and provider pipeline in different GitHub projects. When a consumer publishes a contract that has changed, this should trigger the provider verification job from the provider pipeline.

For the webhook to be triggered, Pact needs to listen to some events. In this chapter, we only focus on the event type triggered when a new contract is published with changed expectations, which is the "contract requiring verification published" event. If you want to know what other event types Pact supports, check out https://docs.pact.io/pact_broker/webhooks#events.

To demonstrate how webhooks work, we've created a separate GitHub project containing only the web consumer code, which you can access here: https://github.com/mdcruz/consumer-example. The provider code still remains in the existing GitHub project at https://github.com/mdcruz/pact-js-example. In the following sections, we guide you through how to set up a Pact webhook so you can also apply it to your work projects.

10.4.1 Creating the Pact webhook

A Pact webhook can be created via the PactFlow UI or via the `pact-broker` command. Creating a webhook consists of the following steps:

1. Creating a GitHub personal access token with the `public_repo` access granted
2. Adding the GitHub token to PactFlow
3. Creating the Pact webhook

We won't cover how to create a GitHub personal access token, but if you want a detailed explanation of how to do this, go to https://mng.bz/1adV.

ADD THE GITHUB TOKEN TO PACTFLOW

To add the GitHub token to PactFlow, go back to your PactFlow account, click the Settings button, select the Secrets tab, and then click the Create Secret button. You should see the page shown in figure 10.16. Enter a name such as `githubToken`, and then paste the personal access token you created from GitHub.

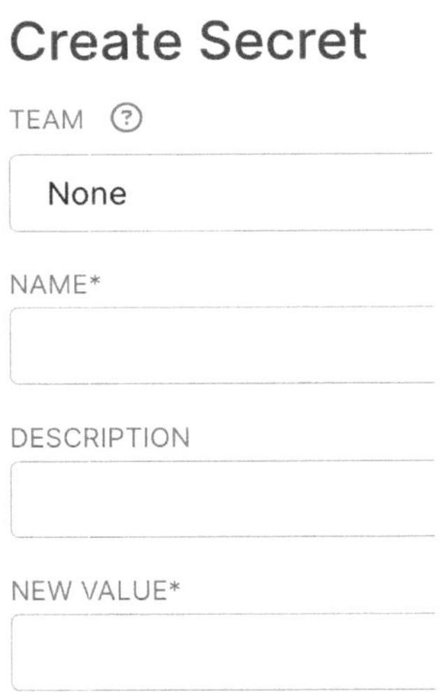

Figure 10.16 PactFlow creates a secret to store the GitHub token.

When you click the Create Secret button, you should see the new token secret created under the name `githubToken`.

Create the Pact webhook via the PactFlow UI

To create a webhook in the PactFlow UI, go back to your PactFlow account, click the Settings button, select the Webhooks tab, and then click the Add Webhook button. You must fill in a few fields when you're on the webhook screen. Let's walk through each field and the details you must provide.

- *Description*—The webhook description, for example, "Webhook for MoviesAPI provider".
- *Consumer dropdown*—The consumer that triggers the webhook. For now, set this to WebConsumer.
- *Provider dropdown*—The provider that is triggered by the webhook. For now, set this to MoviesAPI.
- *Events*—The event(s) that Pact needs to listen for to trigger the webhook. For now, select the Contract Published That Requires Verification checkbox.
- *URL*—The URL to send the webhook request to. For GitHub, this will follow the https://api.github.com/repos/<YOUR_GITHUB_ACCOUNT>/<REPO>/dispatches format, for example, https://api.github.com/repos/mdcruz/pact-js-example/dispatches. If you cloned the GitHub project, make sure to use your own GitHub account instead of mdcruz.
- *Headers*—The headers to be added as part of the webhook request. This will be in a key:value pair and should have the following:

```
Content-Type: application/json
Accept: application/vnd.github.everest-preview+json
Authorization: Bearer ${user.githubToken}
```

The GitHub token that we added as a secret to PactFlow

- *Body*—The request body to be added as part of the webhook request. This will be in a JSON object format and should have the following:

```
{
  "event_type":
"contract_requiring_verification_published",
  "client_payload": {
    "pact_url": "${pactbroker.pactUrl}",
    "sha": "${pactbroker.providerVersionNumber}",
    "branch": "${pactbroker.providerVersionBranch}"
  }
}
```

The name of the event

An HTTP-based URL containing the newly published contract

The provider version number

The branch associated with the provider version number

Once all the information is added, you should have a screen similar to figure 10.17.

You can test the webhook by clicking the Test button. You should see logs similar to figure 10.18 if everything has been configured correctly.

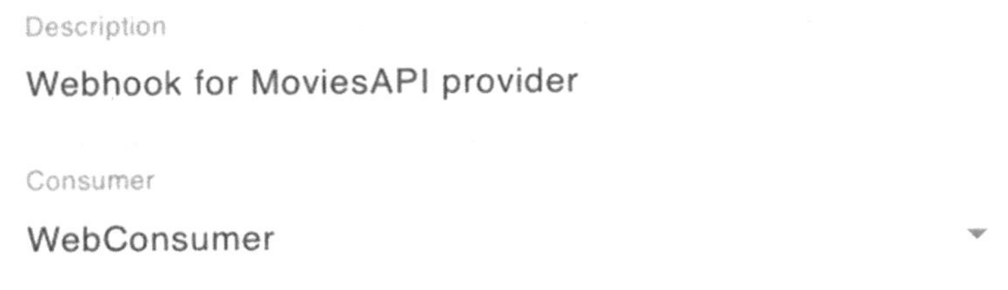

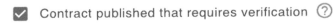

Figure 10.17 Edit the webhook screen in PactFlow with all the relevant information fields to create a webhook successfully.

```
[2024-03-01T21:36:41Z] DEBUG: Webhook context {"base_url":"https://mariecruz.pactflow.io","event_name":"test"}
[2024-03-01T21:36:41Z] INFO: HTTP/1.1 POST https://api.github.com/repos/mdcruz/pact-js-example/dispatches
[2024-03-01T21:36:41Z] INFO: accept: application/vnd.github.everest-preview+json
[2024-03-01T21:36:41Z] INFO: user-agent: Pact Broker v2.109.1
```

Figure 10.18 Logs for testing the Pact webhook showing that the webhook request has succeeded

CREATE THE PACT WEBHOOK VIA THE PACT-BROKER COMMAND

Alternatively, you can also use the `pact-broker` command to create a webhook via the command line and use the `create-webhook` option. The following command will create the same webhook example:

```
pact-broker create-webhook \
https://api.github.com
[CA] /repos/mdcruz/pact-js-example/dispatches \
    --request=POST \
    --header 'Content-Type: application/json' \
'Accept: application/vnd.github.everest-preview+json' \
'Authorization: Bearer ${user.githubToken}' \
      --data '{ "event_type": \ "contract_requiring_verification_published",
     \
"client_payload": { "pact_url": "${pactbroker.pactUrl}", \
"sha": "${pactbroker.providerVersionNumber}", \
"branch": "${pactbroker.providerVersionBranch}" } }'  \
    --broker-base-url=$PACT_BROKER_BASE_URL \
    --broker-token=$PACT_BROKER_TOKEN \
    --consumer=WebConsumer \
    --provider=MoviesAPI \
```

The URL containing the newly published contract

The headers to be added as part of the POST request

The request body to be added as part of the POST request

The URL for the Pact Broker

The token for the Pact Broker

The consumer who will trigger the webhook

The provider to be triggered by the webhook

```
--description 'Webhook for MoviesAPI provider' \    <-- The webhook description
--contract-requiring-verification-published         <-- The name of the event
```

10.4.2 Creating a different GitHub workflow for provider verification

Now that we've created the webhook, we also need to create a separate GitHub workflow for the provider verification that will be triggered whenever the "contract requiring verification published" event is observed.

If you check out the main branch of the example GitHub project at https://github.com/mdcruz/pact-js-example, you should see another file named webhook-sample.yaml inside the .github/workflows directory, and it should contain the following content:

```
name: contract_requiring_verification_published     <-- The workflow's name

on:
  repository_dispatch:
    types:
      - contract_requiring_verification_published   <-- The event that will trigger the workflow

env:
  PACT_BROKER_TOKEN: ${{ secrets.PACT_BROKER_TOKEN }}
  PACT_PAYLOAD_URL:
${{ github.event.client_payload.pact_url }}
  GITHUB_SHA: ${{ github.event.client_payload.sha }}
  GITHUB_BRANCH: ${{ github.event.client_payload.branch }}   <-- The environment variables needed for the workflow

jobs:
  contract-verification-via-webhook:     <-- The job's name
    runs-on: ubuntu-latest
    steps:                               <-- The series of steps to run the workflow
      - name: checkout specific SHA if
webhook providers pact URL
        uses: actions/checkout@v4
        if: ${{env.PACT_PAYLOAD_URL}}
        with:
          ref: ${{env.GITHUB_SHA}}
      - uses: actions/setup-node@v4
        with:
          node-version: 18
      - name: Install dependencies
        run: npm i
      - name: Run provider contract tests
        run: npm run test:provider
```

This workflow is triggered when there is a `repository_dispatch`. A `repository_dispatch` in GitHub is basically an HTTP request to your GitHub project instructing GitHub to start any action or webhook. In our example, a `repository_dispatch` with the event type `contract_requiring_verification_published` will trigger the workflow.

Looking at the environment variables, `PACT_BROKER_BASE_URL` is missing and replaced with `PACT_PAYLOAD_URL`. This is because we want to verify the newly published contract from the consumer that caused the `contract_requiring_verification_published` event to be triggered. The steps in our `contract-verification-via-webhook` are as follows:

1. Checking out the specific GitHub SHA if the Pact URL is from the webhook
2. Setting up a Node action so dependencies can be cached
3. Installing the project dependencies added to your package.json file
4. Running the MoviesAPI provider tests

10.4.3 Updating provider options

To use the `PACT_PAYLOAD_URL`, we need to update the provider options to use this URL instead if this is provided. Looking at the provider/provider-contract.spec.js file, the provider options should look similar to the following code snippet:

```
const options = {
  provider: 'MoviesAPI',
  providerBaseUrl: `http://localhost:${port}`,
  pactBrokerToken: process.env.PACT_BROKER_TOKEN,
  providerVersion: process.env.GITHUB_SHA,
  providerVersionBranch: process.env.GITHUB_BRANCH,
  publishVerificationResult: true,
  ...
}

if (process.env.PACT_PAYLOAD_URL) {
  console.log(`Pact payload URL specified: ${process.env.PACT_PAYLOAD_URL}`)
  options.pactUrls = [process.env.PACT_PAYLOAD_URL]
} else {
  console.log(
    `Using Pact Broker Base URL:
    ${process.env.PACT_BROKER_BASE_URL}`
  )
  options.pactBrokerUrl = process.env.PACT_BROKER_BASE_URL,
  ...
};
```

Sets the options.pactUrls if PACT_PAYLOAD_URL is present

Sets the options.pactBrokerURL if PACT_BROKER_BASE_URL is present

10.4.4 Retries for can-i-deploy

Now that we've created a workflow that will automatically trigger the provider verification, we might end up in situations where the provider verification result is unknown because the provider build is still running and may still need to finish running before the can-i-deploy consumer job. In this situation, the result of can-i-deploy will be unknown. To address this, you can add the `--retry-while-unknown=<NUM>` as part of the can-i-deploy command, as shown in the following code snippet, where `<NUM>` corresponds to the number of times to retry the can-i-deploy tool while the provider verification is still running and the result is still unknown:

```
"scripts": {
    "can:i:deploy:consumer": "pact-broker can-i-deploy
--pacticipant WebConsumer --version=$GITHUB_SHA
--to-environment production --retry-while-unknown=10"
  }
```

10.4.5 Testing the webhook

To test the webhook, create a fork of https://github.com/mdcruz/consumer-example, and clone the project locally. Once you have a copy of the project, switch to a new branch, and update the consumer expectation of any of the consumer tests from the consumer-contract.spec.js file. For example, you can update the WebConsumer expectations that they are now expecting a status code of 201 instead of 200, for demonstration purposes, as shown in the following code snippet:

```
provider
  .uponReceiving('a request to all movies')
  .withRequest({
    method: 'GET',
    path: '/movies',
   })
   .willRespondWith({
     status: 201,
     body: eachLike(EXPECTED_BODY),
   });
```

Commit the changes to your new branch, and push it to your forked project. You should see the contract-test job running and eventually failing on the can-i-deploy step because the verification between the WebConsumer and the version of MoviesAPI that is currently in production failed.

On the provider pipeline, workflow `contract_requiring_verification_published` was triggered automatically, as shown in figure 10.19. However, it failed because the provider sent a status code of 200 instead of 201.

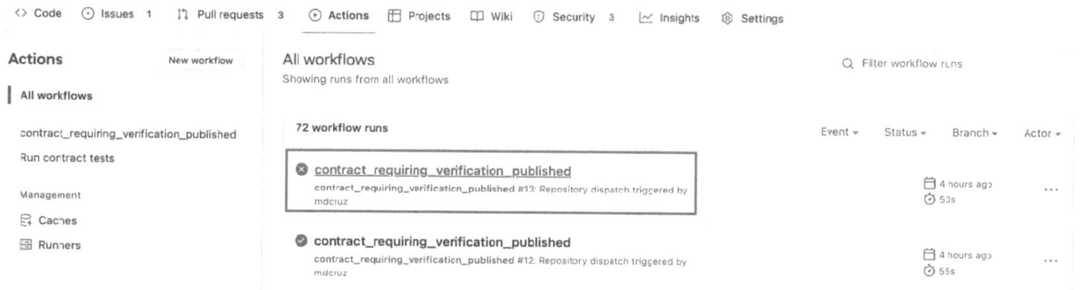

Figure 10.19 Failed workflow from the provider side due to a mismatch in consumer expectations

And there you have it! At this stage, you should now be familiar with how to integrate your contract tests into a CI/CD pipeline. An excellent resource worth mentioning that can also help with further learning on this topic is a curated CI/CD workshop from the Pact team at https://docs.pactflow.io/docs/workshops/ci-cd.

Summary

- To get the full benefit of contract testing, the consumer and provider tests must be integrated into a CI/CD pipeline and be triggered automatically when different teams push changes.
- Using a unique identifier such as a GitHub commit ID or SHA ensures that contract versions can be identified from code changes.
- Pact provides a way to configure branches to ensure that providers verify the correct contract. The branches are typically repository branches from which the code is committed.
- If consumer and provider teams are working on the same feature, it's a recommended practice to use the same branch name.
- Pact recommends creating environments similar to your deployment structure to make sure that Pact can track which versions will be deployed to which environments.
- After changes are deployed to an environment, it's recommended to record the deployment or release so Pact knows which versions are deployed.
- Deployed versions in Pact work slightly different than released versions. If a version is said to be deployed in Pact, this means that previous versions will be marked as not deployed. If a version is said to be released in Pact, previous versions will still be marked as released.
- The can-i-deploy tool is a feature introduced by Pact that lets you query the matrix table to verify if certain versions ready to be deployed to an environment have a successful verification result with the version already deployed in the same environment.
- Pact webhooks need to be created and configured automatically to trigger the provider verification job when there are contract changes from the consumer.
- For a webhook to be triggered, Pact listens to specific events. The "contract requiring verification published" event is triggered when the consumer has published a contract with amendments.
- When using Pact webhooks, you need to set the `pactUrls` options instead of `pactBrokerUrl` to ensure the provider verifies the newly amended contract sent by the webhook request.
- To ensure that the can-i-deploy step retries while the provider verification is still running and the result is still unknown, you can add --retry-while-unknown=<NUM> as part of the can-i-deploy command.

Part 3

Provider-driven contract testing

While consumer-driven contract testing (CDCT) remains the most popular approach, it might not suit how your teams work. PactFlow introduced the concept of provider-driven contract testing (PDCT) or bi-directional contract testing to address the limitations of CDCT. With this knowledge, you can use existing tests and generate contracts from them.

This part of the book explores the concept of PDCT in more detail. Chapter 11 delves into the theory behind PDCT, why it was introduced, and how it's different from CDCT. You also learn how to implement popular contract test adapters such as Cypress consumer adapter, WireMock consumer adapter, Postman provider adapter, and Dredd provider adapter. Finally, chapter 12 looks at converting your existing integration or end-to-end tests into contract tests. By the end of this section of the book, you'll have gained confidence in implementing PDCT in your work projects if this approach suits your team better.

11 Implementing provider-driven contract testing

This chapter covers

- Introduction to provider-driven contract testing
- Implementing consumer test adapters
- Implementing provider tests with API testing tools

As mentioned in chapter 1, section 1.4, consumer-driven contract testing (CDCT) is when the consumer creates the contract and shares it with the data providers, essentially driving the requirements. The consumer-driven approach aims to avoid over-engineering from the provider side by only providing the data the consumer needs. Throughout chapter 2, we provide the benefits of adopting CDCT, and, in chapter 6, we talk about provider tests that verify consumer contracts. However, we also mentioned that the CDCT approach only works with good team communication and buy-in, and there could be scenarios where teams can't adopt this approach.

For instance, imagine that in the web consumer example used in chapter 1, the consumer has decided to use a third-party data provider who provides random images of dogs, as shown in figure 11.1.

In this scenario, the consumer team already has an established contract testing process, having implemented a CDCT approach with the internal data provider team maintaining the User API. The consumer team wants to extend their contract testing process to the third-party data provider because of the benefits it provides.

However, the consumer team lacks visibility of the third-party provider's pipeline setup or testing strategies. Another possible additional challenge is delayed communication because the data provider isn't an internal team. While we have the consumer championing contract testing already, the third-party data provider isn't in the exact alignment. In these scenarios, adopting CDCT can become more problematic.

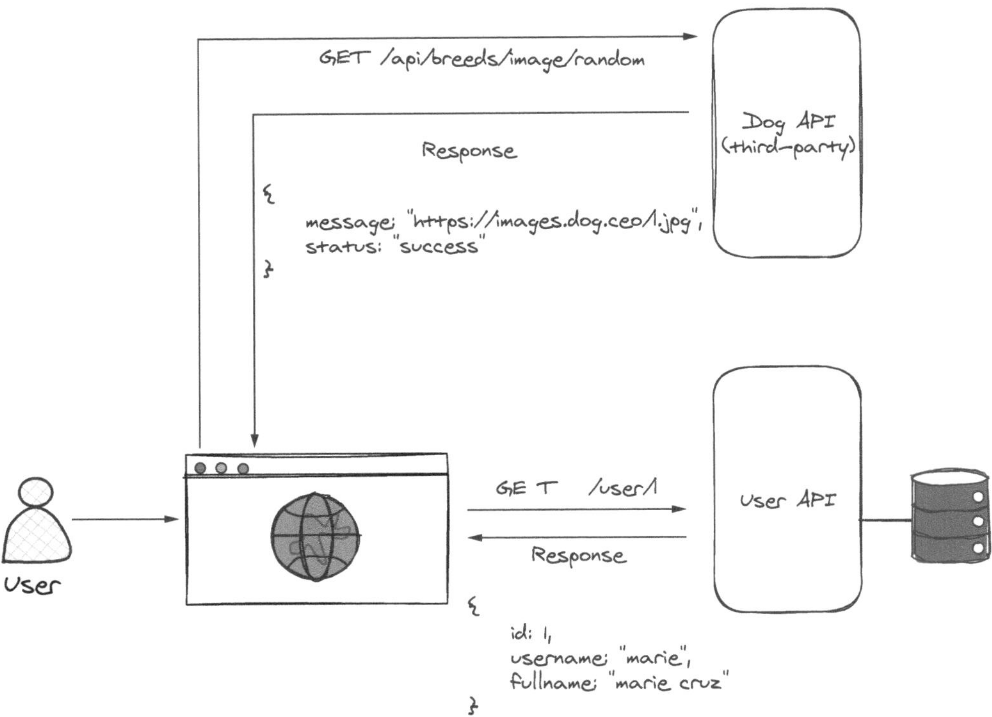

Figure 11.1 An interaction between a web consumer and User API, who are both internal teams. The web consumer also gets data from a third-party API.

Another example, but from a data provider perspective, is that you might have a public API that doesn't know who its consumers are. In this scenario, it makes more sense for the public API to drive the requirements and force the consumers to propagate API changes rather than the other way around.

With these challenges in mind, the alternative approach to CDCT is the provider-driven contract testing (PDCT) approach, also known as bi-directional, which is unique to PactFlow and not available in the open source Pact tool. In this penultimate chapter, we discuss in more detail why PDCT was introduced and how it differs from the CDCT approach we've been discussing so far in this book. We also share an example of how PDCT works in action. Finally, we provide an overview of PactFlow adapters that you can use to support PDCT and also walk you through some technical examples.

11.1 Introduction to provider-driven contract testing

Bi-directional contract testing, as defined by PactFlow in https://mng.bz/PNq9, is a type of static contract testing where two contracts—one representing consumer expectations, and another representing the provider's capability—are compared to ensure they are compatible. We describe this as *provider-driven* in this chapter because this is most likely the scenario where the OpenAPI contracts already exist. The PDCT approach comprises the following steps:

1. The provider uploads their version of a contract, which could be generated from an existing OpenAPI specification.
2. The consumer uploads their version of a contract, which is generated from existing tests.
3. The two contracts are uploaded to a PactFlow. PactFlow compares the two contracts and checks if they are compatible, a process known as cross-contract validation. PactFlow compares the shape of the consumer's expected response to the shape of the provider's actual response.
4. The provider or consumer uses Pact's can-i-deploy tool to check if they are safe to deploy their changes to production.
5. The provider or consumer deploys their changes.

The steps are also visualized in figure 11.2, which you've seen already in chapter 3, section 3.7.2.

With the arrival of PDCT, both the consumer and provider use their current testing setup, use PactFlow adapters to generate contracts from their existing tools, and convert them into a contract testing solution easily, without the need for using a different testing framework such as Pact.

The thought of not using another different testing framework sounds amazing, right? However, one of the many reasons we chose Pact in this book is that it's currently the de facto standard framework for contract testing, especially for teams who want to adopt CDCT.

NOTE PDCT isn't a replacement for CDCT, but rather it helps teams to adopt contract testing easily, especially if they can't use CDCT.

Even with the numerous benefits, we're aware that there are still drawbacks with CDCT, especially when it comes to adoption. As first mentioned in chapter 2, section 2.5, CDCT has the following disadvantages:

- Takes time
- Requires a mindset shift
- Requires a lot of buy-in
- More technical than other testing activities
- Difficult to do when external teams are involved

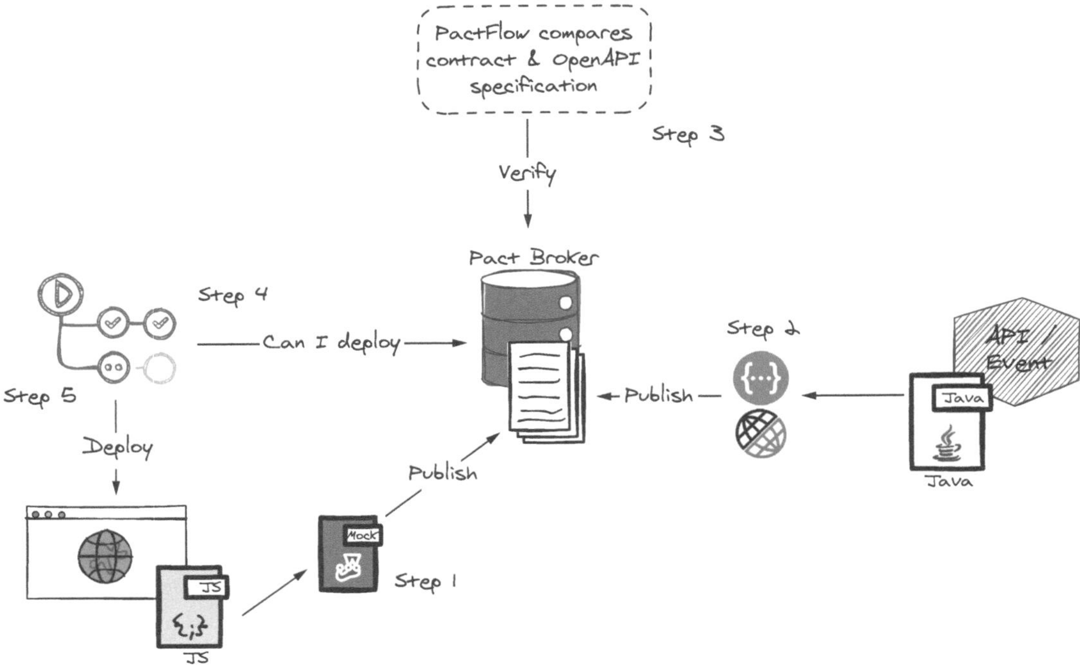

Figure 11.2 The PDCT life cycle, describing when the Pact broker compares consumer contract with the provider OpenAPI specification

There are also other drawbacks because the CDCT approach isn't suited for API-first design workflows. In a consumer-driven approach, the provider must wait for the consumer to publish the contract first. What if this approach doesn't suit your development and testing needs?

In the following subsections, we explain in more detail why PDCT was introduced, how PDCT addresses all the drawbacks of CDCT, and some tradeoffs to be aware of that also come with PDCT. By the end of this chapter, you really should have no excuse for not trying out contract testing!

11.1.1 Why was PDCT introduced?

Over time, there has been a big increase in how much CDCT is used, especially as more and more people starting using microservices. This way of testing is popular because it helps developers feel more confident about their work, makes deployments happen faster, cuts down on problems when things go live, and saves money on testing. Lots of companies, no matter how big or small, are swapping out their older, end-to-end tests for CDCT because they're becoming such a key part of how they do integration testing.

Even though many find CDCT helpful, it's not a perfect solution, and some people face difficulties when trying to make it work well at a larger scale. The PactFlow team recognized these challenges and looked for ways to address them. Some of the problems they wanted to solve included the following:

- The need for a lot of technical knowledge and effort
- Limitations in who can use it (mostly those who work directly with the code)
- Its compatibility with specific types of systems and workflows, such as those focused on designing APIs

These problems might result in certain organizations taking longer to realize the benefits, needing to consider different testing methods, or facing challenges when expanding to very big teams and systems. To address these problems, the PactFlow team expanded the breadth of contract testing capabilities beyond the popular Pact framework to enable new modes of contract capture and compliance, a broader set of use cases, and a simplified developer experience.

11.1.2 How PDCT addresses the drawbacks of CDCT

The core premise of PDCT is that more team members can get involved, using their favorite tools to implement a powerful contract-testing solution with the support of PactFlow. In the following subsections, we discuss how PDCT addresses the drawbacks of CDCT.

CDCT has a steep learning curve

It's no surprise that learning about CDCT has its own challenges. As we first mentioned in chapter 2, section 2.5, CDCT is more technical than other testing activities. The steep learning curve might deter team members from trying out tools such as Pact.

CDCT requires you to learn a new testing framework (Pact)

PDCT offers a simplified workflow and—unlike CDCT—it doesn't require you and your teams to learn a new testing framework. PactFlow has introduced the concept of adapters (https://mng.bz/JNq0), which allows you to generate contracts from existing tools.

To expand, if you and your teams are already using existing testing tools and you want to use these tools for contract testing, PDCT supports the bring your own (BYO) tools concept. From a provider perspective, providers can use their existing API tests or OpenAPI specification, rather than introduce new contract tests and Pact verification tasks into their pipeline. On the other hand, from a consumer perspective, consumers can use existing test frameworks that they already have in place and generate contracts as a by-product of these tests.

PactFlow has numerous adapters for both consumers and providers. Popular consumer adapters that are supported include Cypress, Mock Service Worker (MSW), mountebank, Nock, Playwright, and WireMock. On the other side, popular provider adapters that are supported include Postman, Dredd, REST Assured, ReadyAPI, and SoapUI. Because there are a lot of adapters, we're only going to cover how to get started with PDCT using Cypress and WireMock for the consumer adapter. For the provider adapters, we'll cover Postman and Dredd. To get the most up-to-date list of adapters, always refer to the PactFlow's documentation site (https:/ docs.pactflow .io/docs/examples/). You can also create custom adapters for your specific tooling (https://mng.bz/w5aq).

CDCT isn't suited for third-party APIs or public APIs

Because CDCT requires a lot of communication and coordination between consumers and data providers, it could be challenging to implement if there are third-party or public APIs. PDCT addresses this drawback by not requiring the same level of coordination.

As an example, teams maintaining third-party or public APIs can simply upload a copy of their OpenAPI specification to PactFlow, and this specification acts as their contract already. They just need to use Pact's can-i-deploy tool to have that safety net so that they can deploy their changes safely to production, especially after introducing big changes. In addition, if you follow a more API-first design workflow, data providers can upload their contract immediately without waiting for the consumer to upload their contract.

CDCT requires access to the codebase

Implementing CDCT requires you to co-locate the tests to the codebase itself. While this is one of the recommended practices when it comes to writing automated tests, we acknowledge that there are situations when some testers or other roles don't have access to the codebase. PDCT, on the other hand, allows team members who aren't confident with their programming skills to get started with contract testing. For example, if they have a copy of the OpenAPI specification, they just need to upload this to PactFlow, and PactFlow will verify on their behalf.

11.1.3 Drawbacks with PDCT

While PDCT addresses the problems found in a CDCT approach, there are still drawbacks that you need to be aware of. We recommend that you take the time to understand your project requirements and first consider if a CDCT approach fits your needs instead.

PactFlow exclusivity

As mentioned already, PDCT (bi-directional) is a feature exclusive to PactFlow. While PactFlow has a free starting plan, it's limited. If you and your team require more contracts to be uploaded, then an enhanced pricing plan is needed. Check out https:// pactflow.io/pricing/ for PactFlow's pricing information.

PDCT is still a new approach

As of writing this book, PDCT is still a fairly new approach, introduced to the public in 2022. This can be seen as a drawback because support and resources might not be as widespread as they are for CDCT. However, PactFlow's documentation is always a good start.

Risk of false confidence

In the PDCT approach, the consumer contract isn't tested against the provider code but against the contract that the provider uploads. PactFlow depends on the accuracy of these contracts to inform you if they are compatible. Because PDCT relies on two contracts being uploaded, there is a risk of false confidence if the contract uploaded by the consumer reflects only some of the expected consumer interactions or if the provider doesn't provide an up-to-date API specification. When this happens, you can run into scenarios where breaking changes might slip to production.

11.2 Implementing consumer test adapters

Generating contracts from consumer test mocks, Cypress and WireMock have been chosen to demonstrate the Pact adapters functionality. The adapter packages are installed as part of the test project and offer custom commands or functions to convert mocks to Pact contracts. Using existing mocks is a great way to get started with contract testing.

11.2.1 Cypress consumer adapter

In this example, we'll be using Cypress to generate our contracts from mock responses. We'll use the Cypress `intercept` command to return the mock response. Then, we'll use Pact's `wait` command to wait for the API request to be made and generate the contract from the intercepted mocked response.

Listing 11.1 Cypress `intercept` and `wait` commands

```
describe('Movies', () => {
    before(() => {
        cy.setupPact('BiWebConsumer', 'MoviesAPI');
        cy.intercept('http://localhost:3001/movie/1', {
            statusCode: 200,
            body: { id: 1, name: "finding nemo", year: 2003 }
        }).as('movies');
    });

    it('Movies list', () => {
        cy.visit('/');
        cy.usePactWait('movies').its('response.statusCode').should('eq', 200);
        cy.contains('finding nemo').should('be.visible');
    });
});
```

Before we run the Cypress test, we need to set up a couple of things to use the Pact command and generate the contract file. First, the `pact-cypress-adapter` package needs to be installed:

```
npm i -D @pactflow/pact-cypress-adapter
```

After installing the package, the Cypress project can use the support commands and plugin functions. Add the plugin to `setupNodeEvents` within the e2e Cypress configuration file (cypress.config.js).

Listing 11.2 Cypress plugin config

```
const pactCypressPlugin =
require('@pactflow/pact-cypress-adapter/dist/plugin');
const fs = require('fs');

module.exports = defineConfig({
  e2e: {
    setupNodeEvents(on, config) {
      pactCypressPlugin(on, config, fs)
      return (on, config)
    },
  },
});
```

Finally, import the Cypress Pact adapter commands within the e2e file in the support folder.

Listing 11.3 Cypress support import

```
import '@pactflow/pact-cypress-adapter';
```

Now that everything is set up, run the Cypress test. The contract is generated from the mocked response setup in listing 11.1 shown earlier. Make sure to open two terminal windows. First, run the web app in the background:

```
npm run start:bi:web
```

Launch the Cypress tests once the web app is running and available at localhost:8000, as shown in figure 11.3.

Figure 11.3 Movies web app running locally on port 8000, ready for testing

The movies API is called on this page, returning a list of movies. In this example, "The Shawshank Redemption" is returned from the local API instance. Run the Cypress tests with the mocked movie response, which will return "Finding Nemo". Run the Cypress `run` script in the second terminal window.

Listing 11.4 Cypress run command

```
bi:consumer:cy:run
```

After the test is completed, the contract will be generated at `cypress/pacts`, as shown in listing 11.5. The metadata object contains the client data, mentioning that the Pact Cypress adapter has generated the contract. The request data described in the `cy.intercept` mock setup, as shown in the `request` object, the path has the API URL. The body also has the mocked response JSON taken from the `cy.intercept` mock setup shown in the `response` object.

Listing 11.5 Cypress Pact adapter contract

```
{
    "consumer": {
        "name": "BiWebConsumer"
    },
    "provider": {
        "name": "MoviesAPI"
    },
    "interactions": [
        {
            "description": "Movies list",
            "providerState": "",
            "request": {
                "method": "GET",
                "path": "/movie/1",                    <-- Intercepted request URL path
                "headers": {
                    "accept": "*/*"
                },
                "body": "",
                "query": ""
            },
            "response": {
                "status": 200,
                "headers": {
                    "content-type": "application/json",
                    "access-control-allow-origin": "http://localhost:8000"
                },
                "body": {                        <-- Response body expectations
                    "id": 1,
                    "name": "finding nemo",
                    "year": 2003
                }
            }
        }
    ],
    "metadata": {
        "pactSpecification": {
            "version": "2.0.0"
        },
        "client": {                               <-- Pact consumer adapter reference
            "name": "pact-cypress-adapter",
            "version": "1.3.0"
        }
    }
}
```

11.2.2 WireMock consumer adapter

In this example, we'll use WireMock to generate our contracts from mock responses. The WireMock server will return the mock responses. Then, Atlassian's WireMock Pact Generator will convert the requests and responses from the WireMock server. Add the dependencies Kotlin WireMock and WireMock Pact Generator to the app's build Gradle file (found in the GitHub repository at consumer-mobile/app/build.gradle.kts), as follows.

Listing 11.6 Gradle build test dependencies

```
testImplementation("com.marcinziolo:kotlin-wiremock:0.0.0")
testImplementation("com.atlassian.ta:wiremock-pact-generator:0.0.0")
```

Before we run the JUnit test, we need to set up WireMock to listen to the requests and generate the contract file. First, the WireMock server needs to be started, as shown in listing 11.7. Within the test class, a port is found and assigned to the local URL for the WireMock server. Then, the WireMock server `start` method is called within the `BeforeEach` function. Remember to stop the WireMock server after the test finishes too.

Listing 11.7 JUnit test with WireMock

```
import com.github.tomakehurst.wiremock.WireMockServer
import com.github.tomakehurst.wiremock.common.ConsoleNotifier
import com.github.tomakehurst.wiremock.core.WireMockConfiguration.options
import java.net.ServerSocket

@TestInstance(TestInstance.Lifecycle.PER_CLASS)
class MoviesApiBiTest {
    private val port = ServerSocket(0)
      .use { socket -> return@use socket.localPort }
    private val url
        get() = "http://localhost:$port"
    private var wireMockServer: WireMockServer? =
    WireMockServer(options().port(port).notifier(ConsoleNotifier(true)))

    @BeforeEach
    fun setUp() {
        wireMockServer?.start()

    ...

    @AfterEach
    fun afterEach() {
        wireMockServer?.resetAll()
        wireMockServer?.stop()
    }
```

A request listener needs to be configured for the contract to be generated from the WireMock server, as shown in listing 11.8. The Pact generator is built with the Pact provider name set and added to the WireMock server as a listener.

Listing 11.8 Mock service request listener

```
val provider = System.getenv()
          .getOrDefault("PACT_PROVIDER", "BiWiremockMoviesAPI")
        wireMockServer!!.addMockServiceRequestListener(
            WireMockPactGenerator
                .builder("BiMoviesAndroidApp", provider)
                .build()
        )
```

With the server and listener setup, include the mock for the "movies" URL within the test, as shown in listing 11.9. Chain the `get` method to the instance of the WireMock server, which contains the request URL to intercept and respond to headers, status code, and body.

Listing 11.9 WireMock mock response

```
wireMockServer?.get {
            url equalTo "/movies"
        }!! returns {
            header = "Content-Type" to "application/json"
            statusCode = 200
            body = """{
            "data": [{
              "Id": 100,
              "Name": "Frozen",
              "Year": 2013
            }]
            }
            """
        }
```

Once the mock has been set up, the client request and response assertion can be made within the test, as follows.

Listing 11.10 JUnit test request and assertion

```
val movies = runBlocking { MovieClient(url).getMovies()};

assertThat(movies.data[0].Id, equalTo(100))
```

Running the test will generate the Pact contract when the test passes successfully (code in the GitHub repository can be found at consumer-mobile/app/src/test/java/com/example/movie/MoviesApiBiTest.kt). The Pact file can be found in the app/build/pacts folder, as follows.

Listing 11.11 WireMock generated Pact file

```
{
  "consumer": {
    "name": "BiMoviesAndroidApp"
  },
```

```
  "provider": {
    "name": "BiWiremockMoviesAPI"
  },
  "interactions": [
    {
      "description": "GET /movies -> 200",
      "request": {
        "method": "GET",
        "path": "/movies",
        "headers": {
          "connection": "keep-alive",
          "accept-encoding": "gzip",
          "user-agent": "okhttp/5.0.0-alpha.2"
        }
      },
      "response": {
        "status": 200,
        "headers": {
          "content-type": "application/json"
        },
        "body": {
          "data": [
            {
              "Id": 100,
              "Name": "Frozen",
              "Year": 2013
            }
          ]
        }
      }
    }
  ]
}
```

11.2.3 Publish consumer contracts

Creating consumer contracts from mocks generates a contract in the Pact specification format. Therefore, the generated Pact file can be published as described in chapter 4, section 4.4. For the Cypress and WireMock examples, update the folder location, if necessary, with the `publish:pact` script, as shown in the following listing.

Listing 11.12 The `publish:pact` script

```
"publish:pact": "pact-broker publish ./pacts --consumer-app-
version=1.0.0 --tag=main --broker-base-url=$PACT_BROKER_BASE_URL --broker-
token=$PACT_BROKER_TOKEN
```

11.3 Implementing provider tests with API testing tools

For verifying contracts from provider integration tests, Postman and Dredd have been chosen to demonstrate the PactFlow BYO API testing tool functionality. PactFlow supports OpenAPI specifications and test reports to verify contract interactions. Using existing integration tests is a great way to get started with contract testing.

11.3.1 Postman and OpenAPI example

In this example, we'll use Postman to verify the contracts via the OpenAPI specification. The Newman npm package tests the endpoints using the command-line collection runner. Then, the OpenAPI specification and Newman test results for PactFlow will be published to compare with the consumer contract. Running the test from the provider project, make sure to install the Newman npm package:

```
npm install --save-dev newman
```

The provider projects that the OpenAPI specification endpoint gets downloaded as part of the package script before publishing the contract to the broker, as follows.

Listing 11.13 OpenAPI download `curl` command

```
"bi:swagger":
"curl -X GET 'http://localhost:3001/swagger.json' >
./output/movies-api.json"
```

The API tests are created with Postman as a collection of requests. The collection contains each request detailed within the swagger API specification. Export the collection to run with the Newman command-line interface (CLI), as shown in figure 11.4.

Figure 11.4 Postman collections containing the API requests referenced within the provider OpenAPI specification

Add the exported collection to the provider/postman-tests/ project folder, and run the `newman run` command, as shown in listing 11.14. The script references the exported Postman collection file and defines the report type and report output path. It adds the following script to the package.json file.

Listing 11.14 The `newman run` script

```
"bi:provider:newman":
"newman run ./provider/postman-tests/chapter-11.postman_collection.json
-r cli,json --reporter-json-export ./output/newman-report.json"
```

On completion of running the script on the terminal as

```
npm run bi:provider:newman
```

you'll find the test output report at ./output/postman-report.md, containing output details as shown in the following listing. The output includes the run stats with details of the test results.

Listing 11.15 Postman report output JSON

```
"run": {
  "stats": {
    "requests": {
      "total": 2,
      "pending": 0,
      "failed": 0
    },
    "tests": {
      "total": 2,
      "pending": 0,
      "failed": 0
    },
  }
```

11.3.2 Dredd and OpenAPI example

In this example, we'll use Dredd to verify the contracts using the OpenAPI specification. The Dredd npm package tests the endpoints using default or example values described within the OpenAPI documentation. Then, the OpenAPI specification and Dredd test results for PactFlow will be published to compare with the consumer contract. Running the test from the provider project, make sure to install the Dredd npm package:

```
npm install --save-dev Dredd
```

The provider project generates an OpenAPI specification JSON file from the documented code, as shown in the following listing. We're documenting the Express server functions, which contain the request handlers.

Listing 11.16 OpenAPI specification generated from Express server

```
/**
 * @openapi
 * /movies:
 *   get:
 *     description: Get all movies
 *     responses:
 *       '200':
 *         description: A list of movie objects
 *         content:
 *           application/json; charset=utf-8:
 *             schema:
 *               type: array
 *               items:
 *                 type: object
 *                 properties:
 *                   id:
```

```
 *                     type: integer
 *                   name:
 *                     type: string
 *                   year:
 *                     type: integer
 *                 example:
 *                   id: 1
 *                   name: James Bond
 *                   year: 2021
 */
server.get('/movies', (req, res) => {
  res.send(movies.getMovies());
});
```

The generated OpenAPI JSON file is available from the local service running at `http://localhost:3001/swagger.json`. This URL is passed to the dredd.yml file, which defines the test run's configuration, as shown in listing 11.17. The YAML file also references the language used, report output, and test endpoint.

Listing 11.17 Dredd configuration file

```
color: true
dry-run: null
hookfiles: null
language: nodejs
require: null
server: null
server-wait: null
init: false
custom: {}
names: false
only: []
reporter: [markdown]
output: [./output/report.md]
header: []
sorted: false
user: null
inline-errors: false
details: false
method: []
loglevel: warning
path: []
hooks-worker-timeout: 5000
hooks-worker-connect-timeout: 1500
hooks-worker-connect-retry: 500
hooks-worker-after-connect-wait: 100
hooks-worker-term-timeout: 5000
hooks-worker-term-retry: 500
hooks-worker-handler-host: 127.0.0.1
hooks-worker-handler-port: 61321
config: ./dredd.yml
blueprint: http://localhost:3001/swagger.json
endpoint: 'http://127.0.0.1:3001'
```

Run the `dredd` command, as shown in the following listing, by adding the following script to the `package.json` file.

Listing 11.18 Dredd run command

```
"bi:provider:dredd": "dredd"
```

On completion of running the script on the terminal as

```
npm run bi:provider:dredd
```

you'll find the test output report at ./output/dredd-report.md, which should look like figure 11.5. Each scenario detailed within the OpenAPI specification should have a test result in the output report.

```
output > report.md > # Dredd Tests > ## Pass: GET (200) /movie/1
1  # Dredd Tests
2  ## Pass: GET (200) /movies
3  ## Pass: GET (200) /movie/1
```

Figure 11.5 Dredd test output results, stating the scenarios tested

11.3.3 Publish provider API specification and test results

With PDCT, the provider must publish the test results alongside their OpenAPI specification. PactFlow offers a provider `publish` command as part of the Pact CLI `publish-provider-contract`. The `publish` command takes the OpenAPI specification file and test verification results alongside the tool used to run the API tests, as shown in the following listing, which references the Dredd example.

Listing 11.19 Publish provider contract and test results

```
pactflow publish-provider-contract
 ./output/movies-api.json                                  <-- OpenAPI specification file location
 --provider BiDreddMoviesAPI
 --provider-app-version $(npx -y absolute-version)
 --branch $(git rev-parse --abbrev-ref HEAD)
 --content-type application/json
 --verification-exit-code=0
 --verification-results ./output/dredd-report.md
 --verification-results-content-type text/plain
 --verifier dredd
```

The downloaded OpenAPI specification is in the output folder. The script downloads the OpenAPI file from the API provider running locally at the URL `http://localhost:3001/swagger.json`. It then uses cURL to copy the contents of the response from this endpoint to a local file, as shown in listing 11.20. Finally, it makes the OpenAPI file available for reference in the `publish-provider-contract` command.

Listing 11.20 Download OpenAPI specification script

```
curl -X GET 'http://localhost:3001/swagger.json' > ./output/movies-api.json
```

11.3.4 Checking consumer contracts

The provider has now published its OpenAPI specification and test verification results to PactFlow. Because its API is already in production, it has been recorded as deployed to that environment (as shown in chapter 10, section 10.2.3). Then, the consumer can check whether they can deploy their changes safely from the contract generated by their mocks, as shown in figure 11.6.

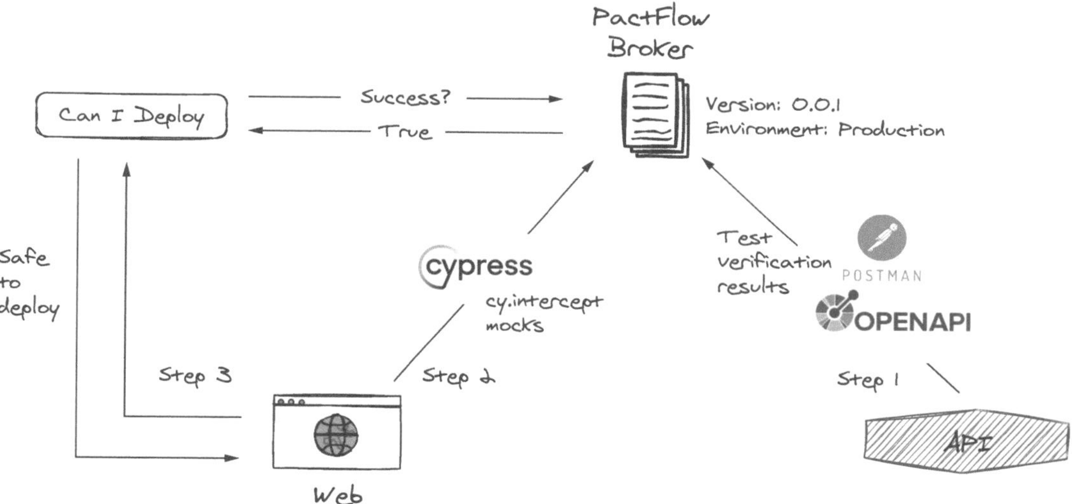

Figure 11.6 The can-i-deploy web app with Cypress mocks where the provider OpenAPI specification has been verified by Postman test results

Running the `can-i-deploy` command shows the verification was successful, as shown in figure 11.7.

```
> pact-broker can-i-deploy --pacticipant BiWebConsumer --version=0.0.1 --to-environment production

Computer says yes \o/
```

Figure 11.7 The can-i-deploy Cypress consumer and Postman provider output, showing SUCCESS as True if safe to deploy

From the output, there is a URL that takes you to the contract comparison screen with a detailed output of the compatibility checks that were performed between the consumer interactions and OpenAPI specification, as shown in figure 11.8.

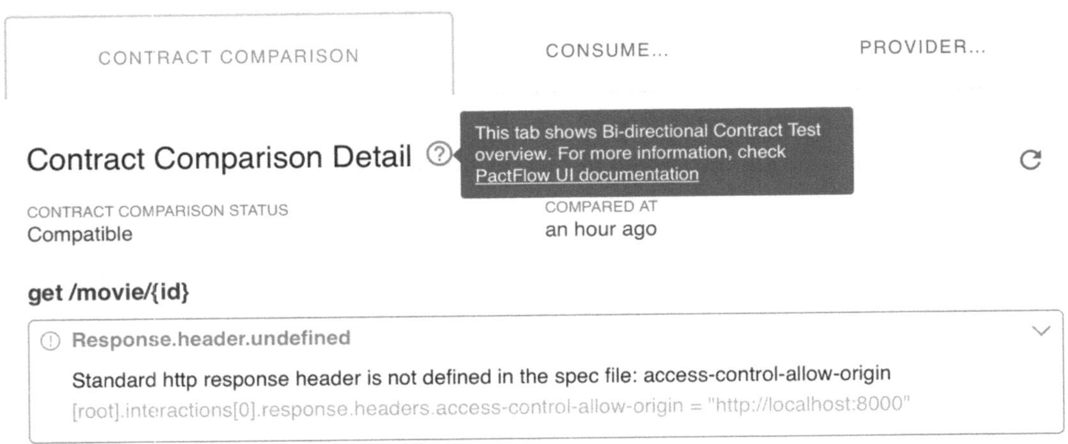

Figure 11.8 PactFlow Contract Comparison tab, showing provider-driven compatibility checks

Summary

- PDCT is a type of static contract testing where two contracts—one representing consumer expectations and another representing the provider's capability—are compared to ensure they are compatible.
- PDCT allows consumers to use their favorite tools such as Cypress and WireMock to generate contracts.
- PDCT allows providers to use their favorite tools such as Postman and Dredd to verify contracts.
- In a PDCT approach, the consumer contract isn't tested against the provider code but against the provider contract in the form of an OpenAPI specification.

12 Moving integration tests to contract tests

This chapter covers

- When to use integration tests over contract tests
- Identifying suitable integration tests to migrate into contract tests
- Refactoring integration tests to contract tests
- Refactoring end-to-end tests to contract tests

In chapter 2, section 2.2, we described how contract testing can replace other types of tests, in particular, integration tests. Contract testing sits above unit testing and below integration testing within the test pyramid, as shown in figure 12.1 (also referenced in chapter 2, figure 2.6). Think of contract testing like an asynchronous integration test. Even though it's still important to have integration tests, contract tests contribute to a more stable and scalable testing solution.

The list in figure 12.1 on the left side shows common reasons for migrating tests to contract tests:

- Slow
- High maintenance
- Expensive
- Breaks easily

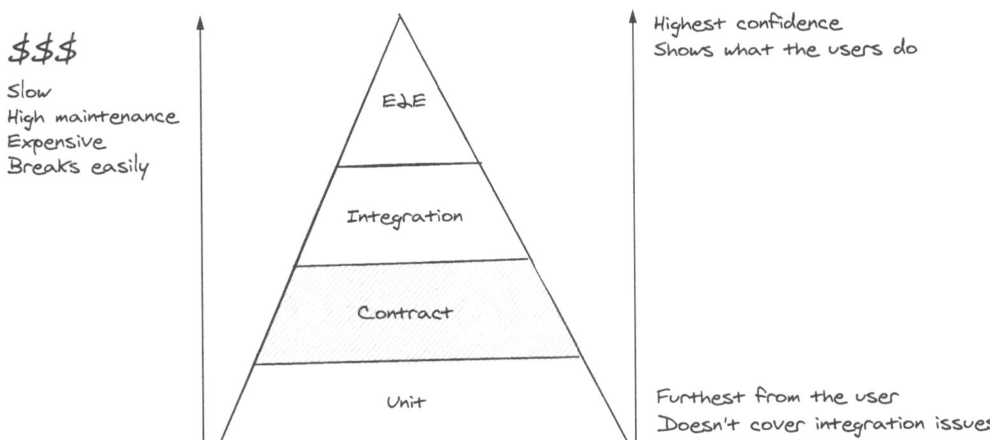

Figure 12.1 Test automation pyramid with contract testing, showing how tests higher up the pyramid are less scalable

During presentations introducing contract testing with Pact, we often ask attendees a couple of questions.

1. In your experience, how often do you find problems in an integration environment?
2. How often is your integration environment unstable?

In response to question 1, people rarely respond with *never* finding problems in the integration environment. However, most people respond by saying they *sometimes* find problems in the integration environment. In response to question 2, people rarely respond with *never* having stability problems in their integration environment. However, most people respond by *sometimes* having an unstable integration environment. The questions highlight both how important integration testing is and how inconsistent it is. Teams should also consider taking into account the time and cost of integration environments, as well as developer and tester time spent debugging.

12.1 When to use integration tests over contract tests

One of the most difficult parts of selling contract testing is persuading management and other people that contract tests add value beyond integration test coverage. We'll discuss identifying which integration tests to migrate in section 12.2. In many circumstances where legacy code exists, integration tests will already exist. In this scenario, there is an opportunity to consider which integration tests can be migrated to contract tests. We're not saying that all integration tests should be replaced by contract tests, and we'll look at refactoring legacy integration tests in section 12.3. There are other factors to consider when integrated environments are involved. For example, deployments are done via a build pipeline and infrastructure as code. Therefore, configuration is passed from build pipelines, and secrets are pulled from a secure vault.

Then, these configuration values and secrets are passed to the infrastructure code. What could go wrong? It's easy for integration values to get missed in an environment or for variables to be referenced incorrectly. Integration tests catch these types of deployment problems, whereas contract tests only test at the boundary of the service or application, as shown in figure 12.2.

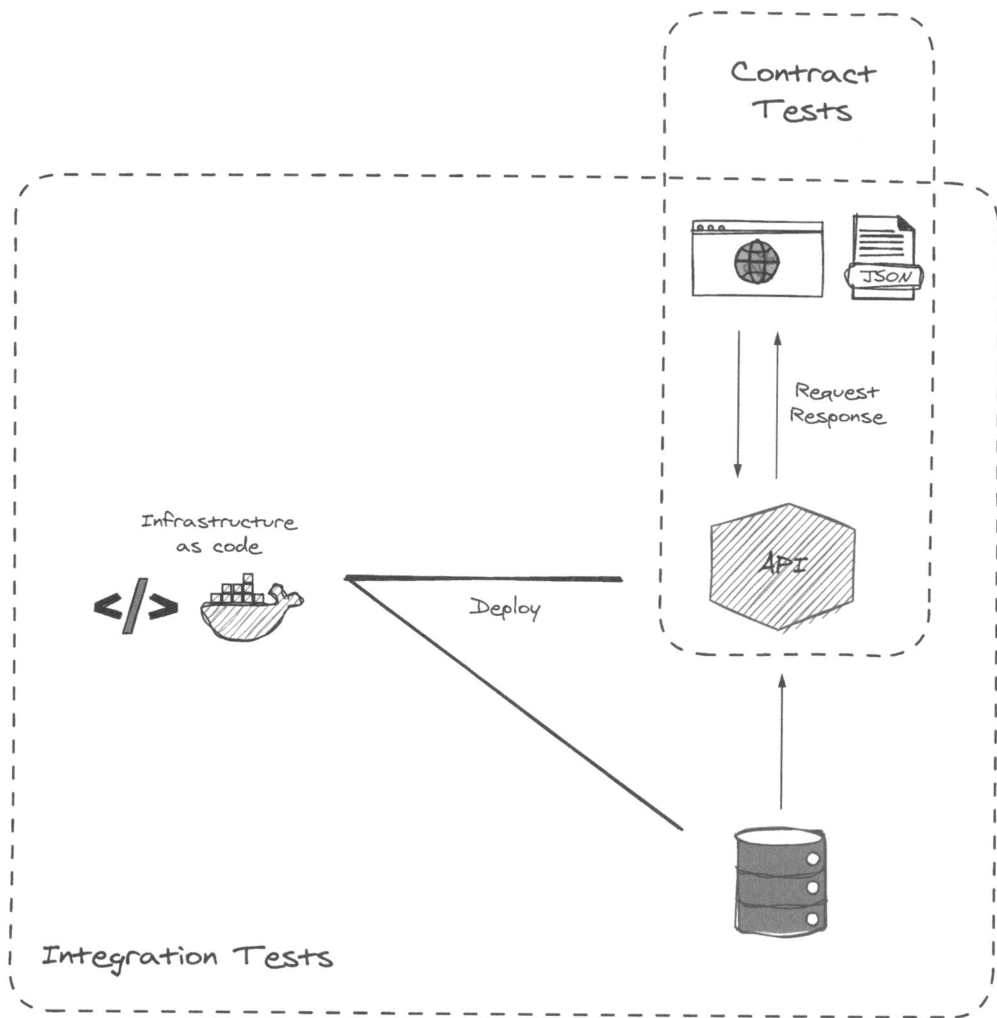

Figure 12.2 Contract and integration test responsibility boundary, showing how integration tests check for infrastructure and database problems as well as request and response errors

At the start of a software development project, an OpenAPI specification is often created. At this point, the frontend developer and backend developer or separate development teams can start working on the feature using the specification. The specification includes how to make a request to the endpoint and the expectations of the response, as shown in the following listing. At this point, it's static documentation, updated by a human as changes are made during the implementation of the feature.

Listing 12.1 OpenAPI specification example

```
---
openapi: 3.1.0
info:
  title: Provider Movies API
paths:
  "/movies":
    get:
      description: Get all movies
      responses:
        '200':
          description: A list of movie objects
          content:
            application/json:
              schema:
                type: array
                items:
                  type: object
                  properties:
                    id:
                      type: integer
                    name:
                      type: string
                    year:
                      type: integer
                  example:
                    id: 1
                    name: James Bond
                    year: 2021
  "/movie/{id}":
    get:
      description: Get a movie by Id
      parameters:
      - in: path
        name: id
        schema:
          type: integer
        required: true
      responses:
        '200':
          description: A movie object
          content:
            application/json:
              schema:
                type: object
                properties:
                  id:
                    type: integer
```

```
                name:
                  type: string
                year:
                  type: integer
              example:
                id: 1
                name: James Bond
                year: 2021
        '404':
          description: No movie exists
          content:
            text/plain:
              schema:
                type: string
                example: Movie not found
```

The expectations of the responses effectively become the mocks within frontend tests and become data used in backend test scenarios. As we've learned throughout the book so far, each part of the specification shown in listing 12.1 can be covered by a contract test. Implementing these scenarios as contract tests will catch any deviation from the implementation stated within the specification. In addition, contract tests provide earlier feedback before deploying changes to an environment. Getting early feedback saves teams a lot of time going back and forth. Once code has been committed and deployed to an environment, it's harder to debug, meaning it's slower to fix.

12.2 Identifying suitable integration tests to migrate

Lots of integration tests could be converted to contract tests. It's important to understand the separation of the purpose between the two types of tests. Suppose we look at the difference between unit tests and integration tests first. Unit tests run in isolation by mocking out any dependencies, whereas integration tests verify the actual dependencies. Now, if we compare unit tests with contract tests, we see that both use mocks. However, mocks created within contract tests are shared with provider services.

There are a few other distinctions to make when comparing integration and contract tests in relation to test capabilities. There will be some duplication between the tests around status codes and data structures. However, the level of detail and number of scenarios for each area will defer. Contract tests focus on verifying the specific details around the following:

- Data structure
- HTTP status codes
- Request and response headers
- API versions

The data structure of an API response, for example, will be referenced within integration tests to check for successful responses. Integration environments rely on a database with data for specific requests. Therefore, the assertions will be made against the specific data that was set up prior to the test running. However, contract tests focus on the structure of the data, providing matches for checking value types. Therefore, any data could be returned from the API response only to verify the structure of the data. The difference between the checks highlights that contract tests verify the structure of the data, and integration tests verify the actual data that is returned, as shown in figure 12.3.

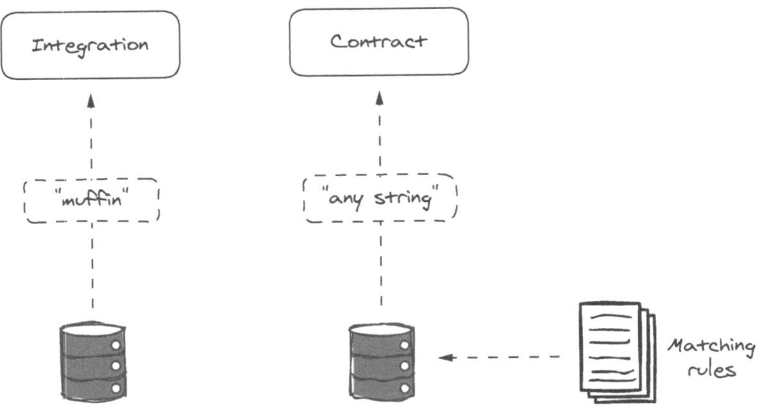

Figure 12.3 Integration tests return exact data, and contract tests return a version of the data type defined within the contract to make assertions more flexible.

The HTTP status codes associated with the request reflect the possible scenarios that occur from the response. For example, with integration tests and contract tests, scenarios need to be set to configure HTTP error conditions. The difference here is that consumers share their expectations of error conditions with the provider service. Usually, integration tests live alongside the provider code, therefore not fully understanding the consumer's expectations. With contract tests being run against local instances, it will be easier to set up error conditions. However, with integration tests being run within a deployed environment, it may be more difficult to set up error scenarios.

12.3 Refactoring integration tests to contract tests

Take an integration test like the one in listing 12.2, which has been implemented in Supertest (https://mng.bz/q0vw) to test the movies Express server. The test verifies the get movies response, including headers, status code, and body.

Listing 12.2 Supertest get movies

```
test("/movies", async () => {
    await request(server)
        .get("/movies")
        .expect("Content-Type", /json/)      ◁ Header
        .expect(200)                         ◁ Status code
        .expect((res) => {
```

```
            expect(res.body).toMatchObject([])          <-- Response body
        })
    })
```

The test in listing 12.2 has three `expect` statements, all of which could be verified within a contract test. The `Content-Type` header expects a JSON type, which would be a specific value in the contract. The `OK` status code represents an interaction from the movie's endpoint defining a successful contract interaction. The response body (`res.body`) expects the statement to match the object's properties and values. In this example, the response is an empty array, which could be represented as an array type within the contract. As outlined, all three `expect` statements could be replaced by a contract element. The contract equivalent is shown in listing 12.3. The `uponReceiving` method sets the state of the data required; no data exists in this example. The `withRequest` method sets the request method and path to get all movies. The `willRespondWith` method defines the expected headers, status code, and response body. After the provider expectations have been set, the request is executed with the mock provider URL.

Listing 12.3 Pact get movies

```
test('it should return an empty list', async () => {
  provider
    .uponReceiving('get movies when none exist in database')
    .withRequest({
      method: 'GET',
      path: '/movies',
    })
    .willRespondWith({
      headers: { 'Content-Type': 'application/json' },
      status: 200,
      body: like([]),
    });

  await provider.executeTest(async mockProvider => {
    const movies = await fetchMovies(mockProvider.url);
    expect(movies).toEqual([]);
  });
});
```

As listing 12.3 demonstrates, the test in listing 12.2 can easily be replicated as a consumer contract test. The benefit of converting this test is improved stability through passing the provider state. Integration environments often come with challenges of keeping the data in the right state between test runs. However, with the provider state in contract tests, the database can be set directly before the test run. Another reason the integration tests may be unstable is because the environment is down or a deployment is happening at the same time as the tests have been triggered. However, contract tests can be run against a local instance of the provider.

As shown in listing 12.4, the app is launched as part of the test file launching the Express server. Within the Pact verifier options, the provider name is referenced, which will pull down all consumer contracts related to the provider. The `uponReceiving` statement within the consumer test is referenced in the `stateHandlers` object as part of the Pact verifier options. The state handler performs actions before the provider tests run, such as deleting all movies within the database. Within the test, the `verifyProvider` function is called, verifying that the local implementation of the API is compatible with the consumer contract.

Listing 12.4 Pact provider for the movies API

```
const port = '3001';
const app = server.listen(port, () =>
  console.log(`Listening on port ${port}...`));

const options = {
  provider: 'MoviesAPI',
  providerBaseUrl: `http://localhost:${port}`,
  pactBrokerToken: process.env.PACT_BROKER_TOKEN,
  providerVersion: process.env.GITHUB_SHA,
  providerVersionBranch: process.env.GITHUB_BRANCH,
  publishVerificationResult: true,
  stateHandlers: {
    'get movies when none exist in database': () => {
      movies.deleteAll();
      return Promise.resolve({ description: 'Movies deleted' });
    }
  }
}

const verifier = new Verifier(options);

describe('Pact Verification', () => {
  test('should validate the expectations of movie-consumer', () => {
    return verifier
      .verifyProvider()
      .then(output => {
        console.log('Pact Verification Complete!');
          app.close();
      });
    });
});
```

Let's take a look at another example, this time in Postman, as shown in figure 12.4. Take the get movie by ID endpoint (`/movie/1`), which returns a JSON response, including ID, name, and year.

The Postman application can add tests from within the interface, and it also provides the option for JavaScript tests. As shown in figure 12.4, the tests verify the headers, status, and body of the response. As with the previous Supertest example, we can translate this test into a contract test, as shown in listing 12.5. The `uponReceiving`

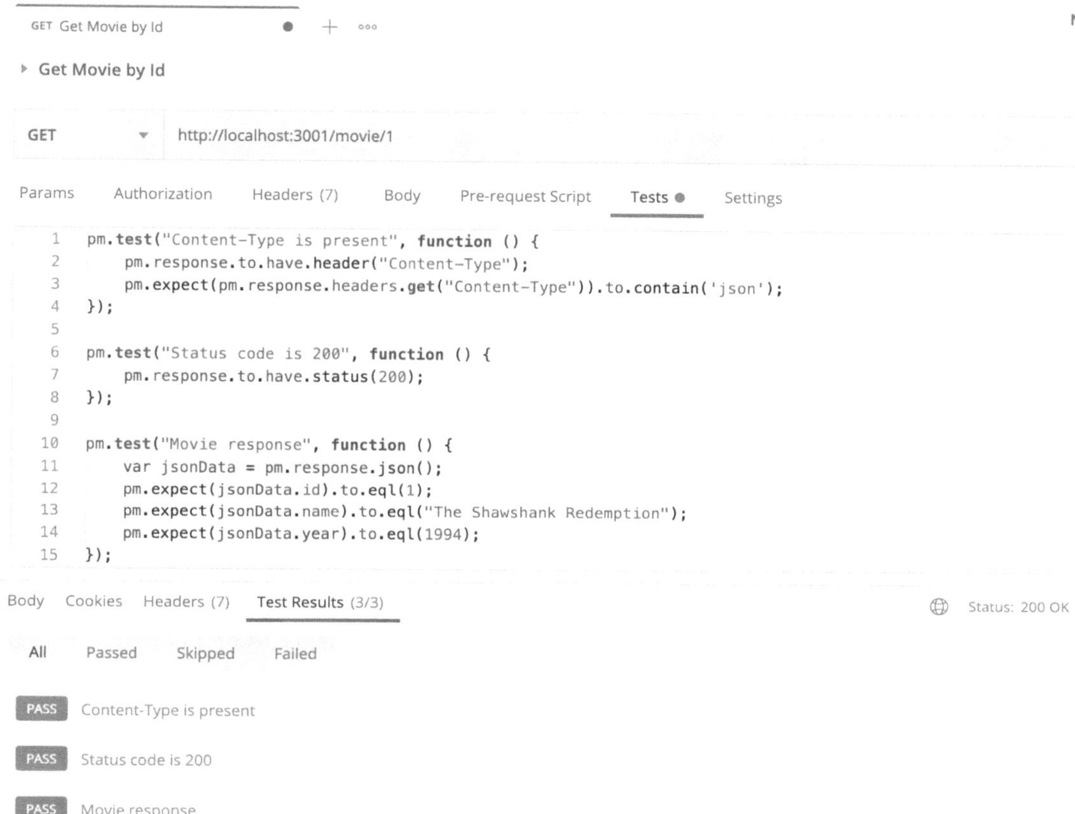

Figure 12.4 Get movie by ID request, showing the test results from within Postman

method sets the state of the data required; a movie with ID 1 will need to be in the database in this example. The `withRequest` method sets the request method and path to get a movie by ID. The `willRespondWith` method defines the expected headers, status code, and response body. The `body` contains matches of type integer and string to verify values against their type only. After the provider expectations have been set up, then the request to get the movie is executed with the mock provider URL and ID 1. The `expect` statement verifies that the response object isn't null.

Listing 12.5 Pact get movie by ID

```
test('it should return a movie object', async () => {
  provider
    .uponReceiving('get movie by id 1')
    .withRequest({
      method: 'GET',
      path: '/movie/1',
```

```
    })
    .willRespondWith({
      status: 200,
      headers: { 'Content-Type': 'application/json' },
      body: {
        id: integer(1),
        name: string("Barbie"),
        year: integer(2023)
      },
    });

  await provider.executeTest(async mockProvider => {
    const movie = await fetchSingleMovie(mockProvider.url, 1);
    expect(movie).not.toBeNull();
  });
});
```

Once the test has been run, the contract is generated with the interaction setup in figure 12.5. The contract shown in listing 12.6 can now be published to Pact Broker and be shared with the provider. The provider can then set up the data required and run against the local instance of the service to verify the contract. The benefit of converting this test is that the tests can be run in isolation. Another benefit is being able to set up the data easily, bypassing the provider state, which can be intercepted with middleware. Postman offers pre-request scripts where a request could be made to set up the data, but it wouldn't have the same flexibility as the native provider code.

Listing 12.6 Pact get movie by ID contract

```
{
  "consumer": {
    "name": "WebConsumer"
  },
  "interactions": [
    {
      "description": "get movie by id 1",
      "request": {
        "method": "GET",
        "path": "/movie/1"
      },
      "response": {
        "body": {
          "id": 1,
          "name": "Barbie",
          "year": 2023
        },
        "headers": {
          "Content-Type": "application/json"
        },
        "matchingRules": {
          "body": {
            "$.id": {
              "combine": "AND",
```

```
                "matchers": [
                  {
                    "match": "integer"
                  }
                ]
              },
              "$.name": {
                "combine": "AND",
                "matchers": [
                  {
                    "match": "type"
                  }
                ]
              },
              "$.year": {
                "combine": "AND",
                "matchers": [
                  {
                    "match": "integer"
                  }
                ]
              }
            },
            "header": {}
          },
          "status": 200
        }
      }
    ],
    "metadata": {
      "pact-js": {
        "version": "12.1.0"
      },
      "pactRust": {
        "ffi": "0.4.9",
        "models": "1.1.11"
      },
      "pactSpecification": {
        "version": "3.0.0"
      }
    },
    "provider": {
      "name": "MoviesAPI"
    }
  }
```


12.4 Refactoring end-to-end tests to contract tests

Another question we often get asked is which end-to-end (E2E) tests can be converted to contract tests. E2E tests have a different purpose and cover many different parts of the application. We did touch on a use case for contract testing within an E2E testing framework in chapter 9, as shown in listing 9.1. One use case is using contracts to replace mocks within E2E tests, as shown in figure 12.5.

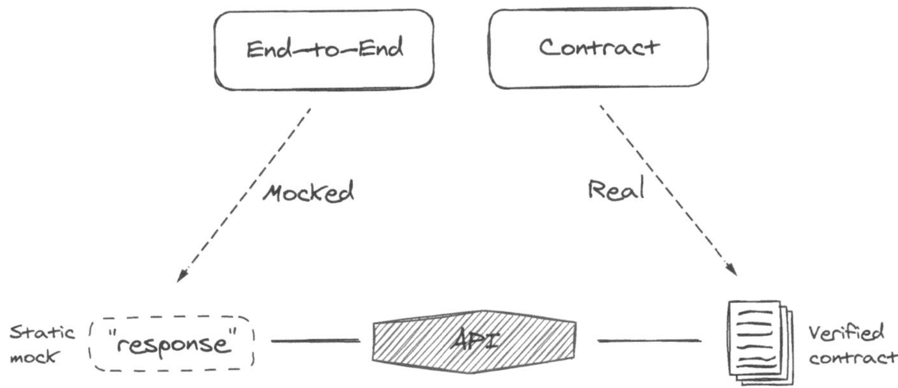

Figure 12.5 E2E tests are mocked, whereas contract tests use the real API provider to retain test coverage and increase reliability.

Contract tests support E2E tests to reduce flakiness and running time to execute the tests. If an E2E test checked an error scenario with an actual integrated endpoint, that would sometimes be unavailable due to a service outage. Ideally, this test would be moved down the test pyramid to a lower-level test using a mocked response. Introducing a mocked response as part of the E2E test will improve the test's stability but reduce its validity. Then, adding a contract test to check the isolated integration error scenario will enhance the validity with no risk of flakiness. Say we have a Cypress scenario that checks GitHub's search results website (www.github.com), as shown in listing 12.7. The Cypress test navigates to the GitHub website, where the web app sends a request to the `"/search/suggestions"` API endpoint while typing into the search box. The assertion for this test checks the relative URL `href` attribute.

Listing 12.7 E2E Cypress search result test

```
describe('GitHub website', () => {
    it('search query', () => {
        cy.visit('https://github.com/')
        cy.get('[aria-label="Search or jump to…"]').click()
        cy.get('#query-builder-test').type('pact')
        cy.get('[role="listbox"]').within(() => {
            cy.get('[data-type="url-result"]').children(() => {
                cy.get('a').should('have.attr', 'href', '/pact-
    foundation/pact_broker')
            })
        })
    })
})
```

In this example, the `href` attribute would come from the suggestion's response. The response to provide suggestions is sent to the GitHub user while searching. For the E2E test, a mock could replace the API response. The API response could be replaced within the Cypress test, and the `href` attribute could be verified within a Pact contract test, as shown in listing 12.8.

Listing 12.8 Contract Pact search result test

```
test('it should return suggested repositories', async () => {
      provider
        .uponReceiving('search suggested repositories')
        .withRequest({
          method: 'GET',
          path: '/search/suggestions',
        })
        .willRespondWith({
          headers: { 'Content-Type': 'application/json' },
          status: 200,
          body: like([{href: "pact-foundation/pact_broker"}]),
        });

      await provider.executeTest(async mockProvider => {
        const suggestions = await fetchSearchSuggestions(mockProvider.url);
        expect(suggestions).toHaveProperty('href');
      });
    });
```

The method shown in listings 12.7 and 12.8 of dividing E2E test coverage between E2E scenarios and contract tests is possible using the provider-driven contract testing (PDCT) approach demonstrated in chapter 11 as well.

Summary

- Integration tests are still important for testing that build configurations are deployed successfully.
- Contract tests can be implemented as early as from when the OpenAPI documentation is created.
- Integration tests are suitable for migration when they verify the structure of the API response.
- Legacy integration tests can be refactored to contract tests to improve stability and reduce maintenance.
- Contract tests focus on a range of API scenarios, including error conditions, where integration tests overlap in terms of retrieval of data and happy path scenarios.
- Integration tests that verify status codes, headers, and data types—instead of specific values—are good candidates to convert to contract tests.
- Teams save time debugging and reduce cost on integration environments by converting to contract tests.
- E2E tests can be split into two sets of tests: where E2E tests use mocks, and contract tests verify the mocks.

appendix A Tool comparisons

This appendix contains content that supports the decisions made within this book, for example, other contract testing tools. The following sections provide insight into Lewis and Marie's tool review process, which every individual should do before starting to implement contract testing.

A.1 Contract-based tools

In this section, we describe the different tools associated with contract testing from Pact to Postman.

A.1.1 Pact

According to GitHub, the Spring cloud contract was released in 2016 (https://mng.bz/WVQ1) versus pact-ruby, which was released in March 2014 (https://mng.bz/86qw), making the Pact the original contract testing framework. The fact that Pact supports so many languages and has more than 1,000 stars on pact-ruby, pact-js, and pact-jvm shows its popularity and the main reason why we've chosen Pact as our tool for the book. Pact's ecosystem, as partially mentioned within the contract testing life cycle, includes the Ruby core library that all the language implementations are built on, Pact Broker, can-i-deploy command-line interface (CLI) tool, Docker images, and much more supported by the amazing Pact community. The core Ruby implementation of the Pact framework has developed the integral components for contract testing to run as smoothly as possible, including fundamentals such as configuring the consumer mock server to intercept the consumer request, type matching of fields, provider states for data setup, and contract generation.

Pact offers the ability for consumers and providers to use the framework in most of the supported languages. In most circumstances, the consumer and provider tests are authored in different languages, but with serverless cloud computing, this may not be the case for much longer. Throughout the implementation chapters of the book, we'll focus on pact-js, pact-jvm, the SaaS Pact Broker provided by PactFlow, and the can-i-deploy tool.

A.1.2 Pact Broker

Pact offers an open source broker that can be hosted within your current infrastructure as it comes bundled, as Terraform or inside a Docker container. Alternatively, the software as a service (SaaS) version can be set up and supported by PactFlow (acquired by SmartBear). Setting up the Pact Broker will be discussed further in chapter 7. The broker is the first step to sharing contracts between consumer and provider. The core functionalities supported by the open source broker includes versioning, tagging, and webhooks. The broker also contains the API key and user management for interacting with the broker by users and via continuous integration.

A.1.3 PactFlow

PactFlow offers the SaaS implementation of the Pact Broker on a subscription basis. As well as this it also provides additional features such as single sign-on (SSO) and Bi-directional contract testing support (PDCT). Throughout the book we'll be using PactFlow alongside the code examples to enable readers to get setup quickly. If you're working in a small development team or trialing contract testing I would suggest using the PactFlow to get off the ground. It provides a free five contracts account for exactly this reason.

A.1.4 Pact CLI

Pact CLI is a key part of the Pact ecosystem, integral for publishing contracts and also used to interact with the Pact Broker for contract status. Built into the CLI is the can-i-deploy command which the consumer relies on for status updates on the verification of their contract. This Pact Broker client provides all the commands needed within continuous integration (CI) such as tagging version, environments, and releases.

A.1.5 Pact Plugins

Recently, Pact created the infrastructure for plugins, which integrates with their tools. For example, different protocols such as gRPC are supported via a plugin. This approach aims to extend support for many more use cases using the Pact shared core.

A.1.6 Swagger Mock Validator

A notable mention, which has come out of the Pact community, is the swagger-mock-validator created by Atlassian. This CLI tool, similar to the can-i-deploy Pact tool, compares mocks with OpenAPI specs. Mocks are supported in Pact and WireMock formats. Specifications supported in Swagger 2 and OpenAPI 3 formats. This means the mocks are always up-to-date with the API specification as it evolves.

Benefits of Pact

- Large set of different languages supported
- Large active community involved in supporting through code contributions and forums
- Backing from testing giant SmartBear (as they have a vested interest in the success of PactFlow that they acquired in 2022)
- Extensive number of blogs and tutorials exist online (some supplied by the authors of this book)

Downsides of Pact

- Doesn't support all protocols natively, for example, protocol buffers
- Doesn't support all transports natively, for example, gRPC

A.1.7 Spring Cloud Contract

Spring enables consumer-driven contract (CDC) development of JVM-based applications (https://mng.bz/NBq1). Spring supports HTTP and messaging routes. With this framework, the consumer can create the contracts and share them in multiple different ways (check https://mng.bz/EOqO for the examples). Using the framework stub runner, the provider implementation generates the stubs that can be used with the contracts to verify that both work together. Some of the great features from this framework include automatically generating boilerplate test code and enabling stubs to be used by other projects.

Spring Cloud also provides a way to write contracts with YAML allowing applications in other programming languages to use the Spring Cloud JVM implementation. You don't need to understand Java to use this framework, but you do need to be able to work with YAML, which can be tricky at times too with indentation problems.

Benefits of Spring Cloud Contract

- Native support within JVM projects
- Multilanguage support with YAML files

Downside of Spring Cloud Contract

- Contracts packaged in the provider repository

A.1.8 Postman

Postman providers can produce an OpenAPI blueprint, and consumers can build their requests and share the collection with the provider (https://mng.bz/Dpqw). This is a great way to use a tool you may be familiar with and gain some of the benefits of contract testing. As discussed previously, one of the main benefits of consumer-driven contract testing (CDCT) is enabling communication between distributed teams. In addition, the opportunity for consumers to supply the provider team with test scenarios removes any assumptions and unknowns around how the API is being used. Provider-driven contract testing (PDCT) is also a way to use tools such as

Postman, allowing you to use your existing collections to verify against the OpenAPI specification.

Benefits of Postman

- Popular tool for integration testing reduces the need for testers or developers to learn a new tool for contract testing
- Built-in capabilities for sharing contracts between projects with collections and blueprints.

Downside of Postman

- Contracts don't live alongside the code.

A.2 Schema-based tool

In this section, we describe the JSON Schema tool associated with schema-based testing.

A.2.1 JSON Schema

JSON Schema is a vocabulary that allows you to annotate and validate JSON documents (https://json-schema.org). With Assertible, which facilitates verifying an API response with a JSON Schema, you can perform a form of schema testing (https://mng.bz/lrl8). Schema testing is a way to verify that a JSON response conforms with the defined schema. This provides a quick way for teams to validate that the implementation matches with the defined schema. If both teams verify against the defined schema, then they can have assurances that the integration will marry up. This can be run at the static analysis phase. However, with this approach, the HTTP codes aren't specifically covered within the schema itself. In addition, by sharing the full schema definition as the provider, you have to assume that the fields are being used by all consumers, making changes difficult. Let's look at some of the pros and cons of schema-based testing and contract testing.

Pros for schema testing

- Easy to set up
- Integrates with other tools such as OpenAPI Spec V3
- No dependency on environments

Pros for contract testing

- Helps visualize how consumers are using the service
- Generates contracts alongside application code
- Allows evolution of time

Cons for schema testing

- HTTP details such as status codes and methods aren't defined in a set way with schemas.
- Specific requirements of a consumer can't be tracked with a schema, for example, one consumer uses all the fields within the response, whereas another

consumer only uses a subset. However, the whole schema is often used by consumers as the object is converted in code.

CONS FOR CONTRACT TESTING

- Multiple steps are required to determine whether code change can be deployed, and multiple CI pipelines need to sync in order to determine the result.
- Infrastructure required to run contract testing end-to-end includes setting up broker and language-specific implementations, for example, PactNet middleware for state setup.

A.3 Pact Broker hosting options

Table A.1 lists the pros (denoted by +) and cons (denoted by –) of Pact Broker options.

Table A.1 Pros and cons for each form of Pact Broker

SaaS (PactFlow)	Own Storage Solution	Open Source
– Higher running costs; PactFlow provides a yearly subscription depending on the number of users, integrations, and features (though compared to cross-browser tools it's very cheap).	+ Low running costs; storage solutions such as AWS S3 or GitHub Enterprise are relatively cheap.	+ Low running costs; open source Pact Broker can be run in a container, which offers a cheap option. For example, with Amazon Elastic Container Service (Amazon ECS), you only pay for what you use.
+ Easy setup and free account; features such as user management and five free integrations means getting started is simple.	+ No barrier to getting started; adopting existing infrastructure reduces the barrier to getting sign-off for new tooling or provisioning new infrastructure.	– Infrastructure needs to be provisioned and configured; often new tools and infrastructure will need to go through an approval process that can cause delays.
+ Security authentication; an API token provides a secure way to interact with the Pact Broker and Single Sign-On (SSO) options such as GitHub or Google.	+ Slots into existing secure infrastructure; it has the ability to run within an existing secure network.	– Only username and password authentication method is available.
+ Additional features, including OpenAPI spec support; this means teams can use their existing contracts and adopt contract testing quickly.	– Lack of out-of-the-box contract testing features; logic will need to be configured around integrating with CI and also organizing the contracts logically.	+ Simple UI and core consumer contract testing features provide everything needed to adopt contract testing into CI and gain confidence from releasing microservices.

appendix B Setting up project requirements for consumer contract testing (web applications)

This appendix contains a comprehensive step-by-step guide on how to set up the project requirements for consumer-based contract testing, especially for web applications. Sections B.1 and B.2 cover how to install Node and pact-js. On the other hand, section B.3 covers how to fork (using Git and GitHub) or download the example project that we'll be using for the hands-on exercises for this book. If you also need to install a code editor, section B.4 covers how to download Visual Studio Code (VS Code).

B.1 Installing node

To use Pact locally on your machines, you first need to have Node installed. Node is a JavaScript runtime that is known for its nonblocking and event-driven architecture.

> **DEFINITION** Node documentation refers to Node.js as an open source and cross-platform JavaScript runtime environment (https://nodejs.org/en).

Node allows you to write JavaScript code that runs directly in a computer process instead of in a browser. Historically, JavaScript could only be used for web development and client-side scripting. The introduction of Node means that you can now also use JavaScript for server-side scripting. Because Node is asynchronous, you can perform tasks concurrently and more efficiently. Instead of waiting for a task to complete before moving on, the program can continue executing other tasks while waiting for the asynchronous task to finish.

To install Node, head over to their Download page, and select the appropriate installer for your operating system (https://nodejs.org/en/download), as shown in figure B.1.

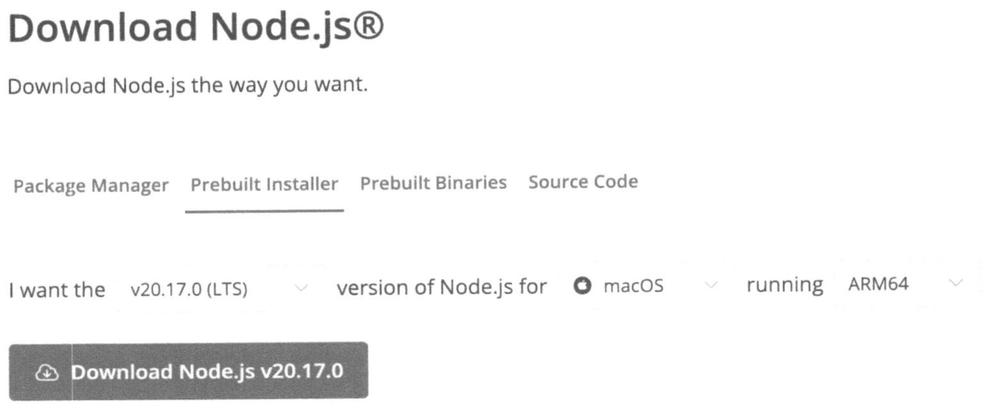

Download Node.js®

Download Node.js the way you want.

Package Manager Prebuilt Installer Prebuilt Binaries Source Code

I want the v20.17.0 (LTS) version of Node.js for macOS running ARM64

Download Node.js v20.17.0

Figure B.1 Download page for Node.js

Once you've successfully downloaded Node, you can verify that the installation was successful by opening your terminal of choice and typing in the following command:

```
node -v
```

This should return the version that you've downloaded, which—as of writing this book—is 18.18.0. Later versions of Node should be backward compatible, but to be sure, check out the up-to-date requirements of pact-js, which you can find at https://mng.bz/DpOw.

B.2 Installing pact-js

When you install Node, it also comes with npm, which is a tool that is commonly used to manage and share JavaScript packages or libraries. You can think of npm similar to a big supermarket that contains different products for your needs. Each package in npm is like a product on the supermarket shelf, which has a unique name and barcode. When you find a package, you can add it to your shopping cart and check out. This is equivalent to the following command:

```
npm install "PACKAGE_NAME"
```

In a supermarket, you need to have a trolley (in the US, a shopping cart) to put your items in, especially if you need to get a lot of products. It's similar to JavaScript projects that you want to start locally; you need a folder to put the packages in that you're going to get. Before we install pact-js, we need to initialize our project directory, especially if you haven't created any existing projects. To do this, go to your terminal of choice, and type in the following commands:

```
mkdir pact-js-project
cd pact-js-project
```

This creates a brand-new folder called pact-js-project. In the same folder, let's also initialize npm by typing in the following command:

```
npm init -y
```

You should see a file, package.json, which contains a similar output to the following:

```
{
  "name": "pact-js-project",
  "version": "1.0.0",
  "description": "",
  "main": "index.js",
  "scripts": {
    "test": "echo \"Error: no test specified\" && exit 1"
  },
  "keywords": [],
  "author": "",
  "license": "ISC"
}
```

Now that you've initialized an npm project, the next step is to add pact-js to your project. In the same folder and terminal, let's add pact-js by typing in the following command:

```
npm install --save-dev @pact-foundation/pact@12.1.0
```

This will install pact-js version 12.1.0 into your npm project's development dependencies. We've provided a version number here so that the code demonstration we'll use won't break, just in case Pact introduces breaking changes in future versions. Your package.json file will be updated and will have the following additional information:

```
"devDependencies": {
   "@pact-foundation/pact": "^12.1.0"
}
```

If you want to install the latest version, you can run the following command instead:

```
npm install --save-dev @pact-foundation/pact@latest
```

That's it when setting up Pact locally on your machines. The preceding steps show in detail how to set up an npm project from scratch. However, most of the time, there's already an existing project to start with. In this case, you only need to install pact-js and not initialize an npm project. Let's look at how we can set this project up locally in one of two ways:

- Forking the project (recommended)
- Downloading the project

B.3 Forking the project

To clone the GitHub project locally, you need to have Git installed on your machines. If you don't have Git installed, head to their Downloads page at https://git-scm.com/downloads, and select the correct installer for your operating system. Once installed, type the following command into your terminal to verify the Git version:

```
git -v
```

In addition, you also need to have a GitHub account. If you don't have an account, head to https://github.com/signup, and follow the sign-up instructions. Once you have an account, you're ready to fork the project. To do that, visit https://github.com/mdcruz/pact-js-example, and click Fork, as shown in figure B.2.

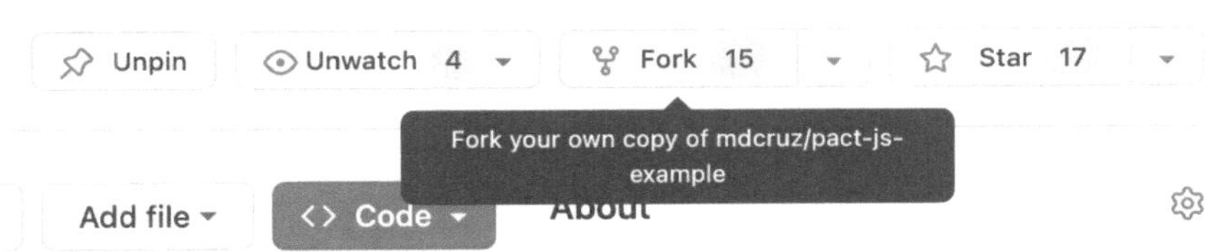

Figure B.2 Forking the example GitHub project

Clicking Fork will lead you to a different page, as shown in figure B.3. For simplicity, keep all the fields as is. The Owner field should be populated with your GitHub account name.

Click Create Fork. Once complete, you should have your copy of the GitHub project. The next step is for you to clone the forked project to your local machines. To do that, click the Code button. Under Clone, you'll see multiple ways to do it, as

Create a new fork

A *fork* is a copy of a repository. Forking a repository allows you to freely experiment with changes without affecting the original project. View existing forks.

Required fields are marked with an asterisk (*).

Owner * **Repository name ***

Choose an owner / pact-js-example

By default, forks are named the same as their upstream repository. You can customize the name to distinguish it further.

Description (optional)

An example framework for using PactJS to do contract testing

☑ **Copy the** `main` **branch only**

Contribute back to mdcruz/pact-js-example by adding your own branch. Learn more.

Create fork

Figure B.3 Creating a new fork page

shown in chapter 4, figure 4.8. You can either clone the GitHub project via HTTPS or Secure Shell (SSH). For cloning the project using HTTPS, make sure you're in the HTTPS tab and click the Copy icon highlighted with the rectangle in figure B.4 to copy the GitHub project URL. If you want to clone the project via SSH, you can follow the step-by-step instructions as listed in the GitHub documentation (https://mng.bz/lrN8).

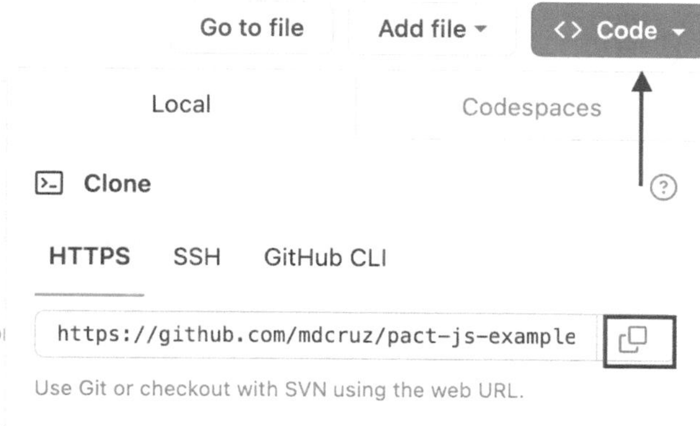

Figure B.4 Cloning the example GitHub project

On your terminal, go to a folder where you want to clone the GitHub project by using the `cd` command. Once you're in your preferred folder, type `git clone`, and paste the GitHub project URL. The GitHub name will be your GitHub name:

```
git clone https://github.com/mdcruz/pact-js-example.git
```

After you run the command, you should now see the contents of the GitHub project on your local machines. The GitHub project contains all the dependencies that you require for contract testing. To install the project dependencies that came with the project, run the following command in your terminal where the project is located:

```
npm install
```

B.4 Downloading the project

While downloading the project manually provides the easiest way, downloading the GitHub project will mean losing access to source control, and your changes won't be tracked. We recommend that you fork the GitHub project to create a copy of the project and clone it locally. If you still want to download the project manually, visit https://github.com/mdcruz/pact-js-example/, and switch to the Setup-Contract-Tests-Consumer branch by clicking the Branches list, as shown in figure B.5.

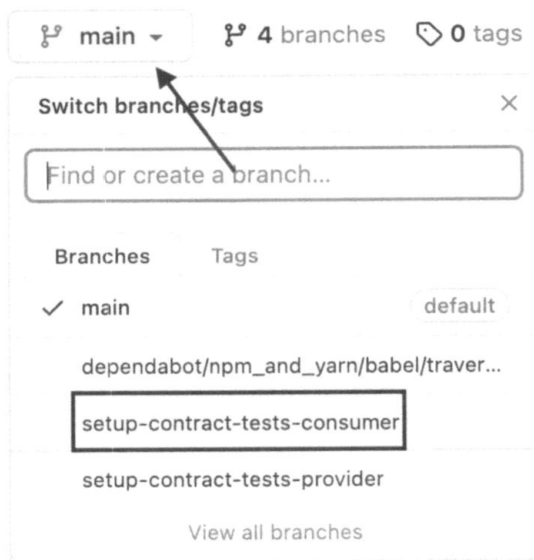

Figure B.5 Switching to the Setup-Contract-Tests-Consumer branch

This branch contains the application code we'll be working with, which we'll use to set up contract tests. Therefore, it's vital that you switch to the correct branch because other branches, especially the main branch, will contain the complete contract testing setup. Next, click the Code button followed by clicking Download ZIP, as shown in figure B.6.

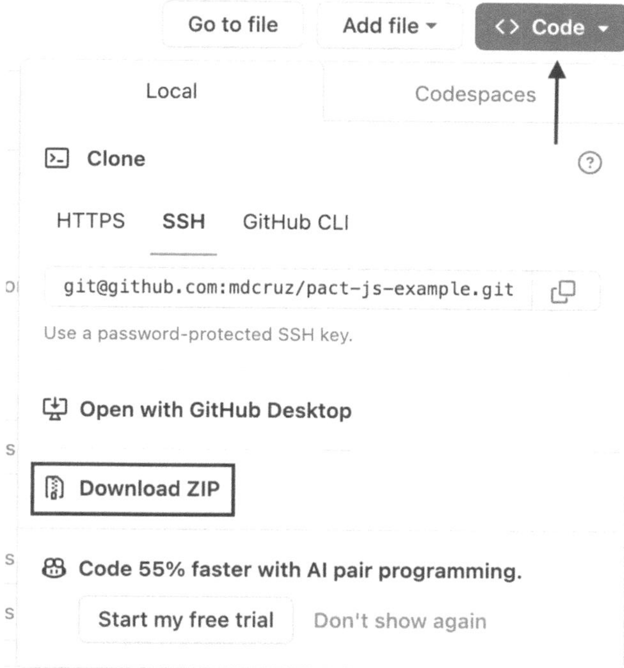

Figure B.6 Downloading the GitHub project manually

This will save the zip file to your local downloads. Unzip the file, and save it to your preferred folder of choice. To install the project dependencies that came with the project, also run the following command in your terminal where the project is located:

```
npm install
```

B.5 Installing Visual Studio Code

If you haven't got a visual text editor in your machines, you can download VS Code (https://code.visualstudio.com/) for free and follow the instructions depending on your operating system, as shown in figure B.7. VS Code is Microsoft's free coding editor. You're free to use other code editors such as Sublime Text or Atom. The important thing is that you use a code editor that you're comfortable with.

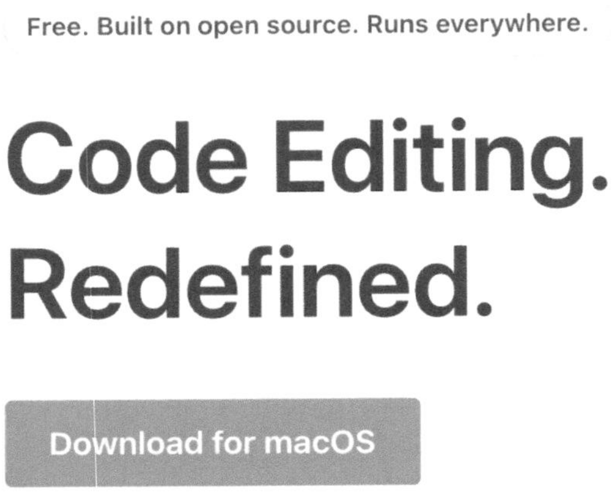

Free. Built on open source. Runs everywhere.
Code Editing.
Redefined.
Download for macOS

Figure B.7 Download page for VS Code

appendix C Answers to chapter exercises

This appendix contains the answers to the different chapter exercises found in the book.

C.1 Answers to the chapter 5 exercise

The code can be added to the consumer-mobile/app/src/test/java/com/example/movie/MoviesApiPactTest.kt test file:

```
@Pact(provider = "MoviesAPI", consumer = "MoviesAndroidApp")
fun addMoviePact(builder: PactDslWithProvider): V4Pact {
    val requestBody: DslPart = PactDslJsonBody()
      .stringType("name")
      .integerType("year", 2004)
 val responseBody: DslPart = PactDslJsonBody()
      .integerType("id", 100)
      .stringType("name", "Shaun of the Dead")
      .integerType("year", 2004)
 return builder
      .given("movie doesn't exist")
      .uponReceiving("a request to add a movie")
      .path("/movies")
      .method("POST")
      .headers(mapOf("Content-type" to "application/json"))
      .body(requestBody)
      .willRespondWith()
      .status(200)
      .headers(mapOf("Content-type" to "application/json"))
      .body(responseBody)
      .toPact(V4Pact::class.java)
}
```

```
@Test
@PactTestFor(providerName="MoviesAPI",
pactMethod = "addMoviePact",
providerType = ProviderType.SYNCH)
fun `should add movie`(mockServer: MockServer) {
     var client = MovieClient(mockServer.getUrl())
  val add = Add("Shaun of the Dead", 2004)
  val response = runBlocking { client.addMovie(add)}
  assertEquals(response.name, "Shaun of the Dead")
}
```

C.2 Answers to chapter 6 exercises

The code marked as bold is the additional code you must add to consumer-web/consumer-contract.spec.js:

```
const path = require('path');
const { addNewMovie,
        deleteMovie,
        fetchMovies,
        fetchSingleMovie } = require('./consumer');
const { PactV3, MatchersV3 } = require('@pact-foundation/pact');

const {
  eachLike,
  integer,
  string,
} = MatchersV3;

const provider = new PactV3({
  dir: path.resolve(process.cwd(), 'pacts'),
  consumer: 'WebConsumer',
  provider: 'MoviesAPI',
});

const EXPECTED_BODY = { id: 1, name: "My movie", year: 1999 };

describe('Movies Service', () => {
  describe('When a GET request is made to /movies', () => {
    test('it should return all movies', async () => {
      provider
        .uponReceiving('a request to all movies')
        .withRequest({
          method: 'GET',
          path: '/movies',
        })
        .willRespondWith({
          status: 200,
          body: eachLike(EXPECTED_BODY),
        });

      await provider.executeTest(async mockProvider => {
        const movies = await fetchMovies(mockProvider.url);
        expect(movies[0]).toEqual(EXPECTED_BODY);
```

```
      });
    });
  });

  describe('When a GET request is made to a specific movie ID', () => {
    test('it should return a specific movie', async () => {
      const testId = 100;
      EXPECTED_BODY.id = testId;

      provider
        .given('Has a movie with specific ID', { id: testId })
        .uponReceiving('a request to a specific movie')
        .withRequest({
          method: 'GET',
          path: `/movie/${testId}`,
        })
        .willRespondWith({
          status: 200,
          body: {
            id: integer(testId),
            name: string(EXPECTED_BODY.name),
            year: integer(EXPECTED_BODY.year),
          }
        });

      await provider.executeTest(async mockProvider => {
        const movies = await fetchSingleMovie(mockProvider.url, testId);
        expect(movies).toEqual(EXPECTED_BODY);
      });
    });
  });

  describe('When a POST request is made to /movies', () => {
    test('it should add a new movie', async () => {

      const name = 'Harry Potter and the Philosopher\'s Stone';
      const year = 2001;

      EXPECTED_BODY.name = name;
      EXPECTED_BODY.year = year;

      provider
        .uponReceiving('a request to add a new movie')
        .withRequest({
          method: 'POST',
          body: {
            name,
            year,
          },
          path: '/movies',
        })
        .willRespondWith({
          status: 200,
          body: {
            id: integer(EXPECTED_BODY.id),
```

```
          name,
          year,
        }
      });

    await provider.executeTest(async mockProvider => {
      const movies = await addNewMovie(mockProvider.url, name, year);
      expect(movies).toEqual(EXPECTED_BODY);
    });
  });

  test('it should not add a movie that exists already', async () => {

    const name = 'Harry Potter and the Philosopher\'s Stone';
    const year = 2001;

    EXPECTED_BODY.name = name;
    EXPECTED_BODY.year = year;

    provider
      .given('an existing movie exists', { EXPECTED_BODY })
      .uponReceiving('a request to add an existing movie')
      .withRequest({
        method: 'POST',
        body: {
          name,
          year,
        },
        path: '/movies',
      })
      .willRespondWith({
        status: 409,
        body: {
          error: string(`Movie ${name} already exists`)
        }
      });

    await provider.executeTest(async mockProvider => {
      const movies = await addNewMovie(mockProvider.url, name, year);
      expect(movies.error).toEqual(`Movie ${name} already exists`);
    });
  });
});

describe('When a DELETE request is made to /movies', () => {
  test('it should throw an error if movie to delete does not exist', async
   () => {
    const testId = 643256;

    provider
      .uponReceiving('a request to delete a movie that does not exists')
      .withRequest({
        method: 'DELETE',
        path: `/movie/${testId}`,
      })
```

```
        .willRespondWith({
          status: 404,
          body: {
            error: string(`Movie ${testId} not found`)
          }
        });

      await provider.executeTest(async mockProvider => {
        const movies = await deleteMovie(mockProvider.url, testId);
        expect(movies.error).toEqual(`Movie ${testId} not found`);
      });
    });

    test('it should delete an existing movie successfully', async () => {
      const testId = 100;
      EXPECTED_BODY.id = testId;

      provider
        .given('there is a movie with specific ID', { id: testId })
        .uponReceiving('a request to delete a movie that exists')
        .withRequest({
          method: 'DELETE',
          path: `/movie/${testId}`,
        })
        .willRespondWith({
          status: 200,
          body: {
            message: string(`Movie ${testId} has been deleted`)
          }
        });

      await provider.executeTest(async mockProvider => {
        const movies = await deleteMovie(mockProvider.url, testId);
        expect(movies.message).toEqual(`Movie ${testId} has been deleted`);
      });
    });
  });
});
```

The code marked as bold is the additional code you must add to provider/provider-contract.spec.js:

```
const { Verifier } = require('@pact-foundation/pact');
const { importData, movies, server } = require('./provider')

const port = '3001';
const app = server.listen(port, () =>
console.log(`Listening on port ${port}...`));

importData();

const options = {
  provider: 'MoviesAPI',
  providerBaseUrl: `http://localhost:${port}`,
```

```
  pactBrokerUrl: process.env.PACT_BROKER_BASE_URL,
  pactBrokerToken: process.env.PACT_BROKER_TOKEN,
  providerVersion: '1.0.0',
  publishVerificationResult: true,
  consumerVersionTags: ['main'],
  stateHandlers: {
    'Has a movie with specific ID': (parameters) => {
      movies.getFirstMovie().id = parameters.id;
      return Promise.resolve({
        description: `Movie with ID ${parameters.id} added!`
      });
    },
    'an existing movie exists': (parameters) => {
      movies.insertMovie(parameters);
      return Promise.resolve({
        description: `Movie with ID ${parameters.id} added!`
              });
    },
  }
};

const verifier = new Verifier(options);

describe('Pact Verification', () => {
  test('should validate the expectations of movie-consumer', () => {
    return verifier
      .verifyProvider()
      .then(output => {
        console.log('Pact Verification Complete!');
        console.log('Result:', output);
        app.close();
      })
  });
});
```

C.3 Answers to the chapter 7 exercise

The code marked as bold is the additional code you must add to the graphql/consumer/graphql-client-contract.spec.js file:

```
const path = require('path');
const { getMovies, getMovieById } = require('./graphql-client.js')
const { Pact,
        GraphQLInteraction,
        Matchers } = require('@pact-foundation/pact');

const {
  eachLike,
  integer,
  string,
} = Matchers;

const provider = new Pact({
  port: 4000,
```

```
  dir: path.resolve(process.cwd(), 'pacts'),
  consumer: 'GraphQLConsumer',
  provider: 'GraphQLProvider',
});

const EXPECTED_BODY = { id: 1, name: "My GraphQL movie", year: 1999 };

describe('GraphQL example', () => {
  // Set up the provider
  beforeAll(() => provider.setup());

  // Generate contract when all tests done
  afterAll(() => provider.finalize());

  // Verify the consumer expectations
  afterEach(() => provider.verify());

  describe('When a query to list all movies on /graphql is made', () => {
    beforeAll(() => {
      const graphqlQuery = new GraphQLInteraction()
        .uponReceiving('a movies request')
        .withQuery(
          `
          query MoviesQuery {
            movies {
              id
              name
              year
            }
          }
        `
        )
        .withOperation('MoviesQuery')
        .withVariables({})
        .withRequest({
          method: 'POST',
          path: '/graphql',
        })
        .willRespondWith({
          status: 200,
          headers: {
            'Content-Type': 'application/json; charset=utf-8',
          },
          body: {
            data: {
              movies: eachLike(EXPECTED_BODY),
            },
          },
        });
      return provider.addInteraction(graphqlQuery);
    })

    test('returns the correct response', async () => {
      const response = await getMovies();
      expect(response.movies[0]).toEqual(EXPECTED_BODY);
```

```
    });
  });

  describe('When a query to list a single movie on /graphql is made', () => {
    beforeAll(() => {
      const graphqlQuery = new GraphQLInteraction()
        .uponReceiving('a single movie request')
        .withQuery(
          `
          query MovieQuery($movieId: Int!) {
            movie(movieId: $movieId) {
              id
              name
              year
            }
          }
        `
        )
        .withOperation('MovieQuery')
        .withVariables({ movieId: 1 })
        .withRequest({
          method: 'POST',
          path: '/graphql',
        })
        .willRespondWith({
          status: 200,
          headers: {
            'Content-Type': 'application/json; charset=utf-8',
          },
          body: {
            data: {
              movie: {
                id: integer(EXPECTED_BODY.id),
                name: string(EXPECTED_BODY.name),
                year: integer(EXPECTED_BODY.year)
              },
            },
          },
        });
      return provider.addInteraction(graphqlQuery);
    })

    test('returns the correct response', async () => {
      const response = await getMovieById(1);
      expect(response.movie).toEqual(EXPECTED_BODY);
    });
  });
});
```

C.4 Answers to chapter 10 exercises

The code marked as bold is the additional code you must add to the .github/workflows/contract-test-sample.yml file:

```
name: Run contract tests

on: push

env:
  PACT_BROKER_BASE_URL: ${{ secrets.PACT_BROKER_BASE_URL }}
  PACT_BROKER_TOKEN: ${{ secrets.PACT_BROKER_TOKEN }}
  GITHUB_SHA: ${{ github.sha }}
  GITHUB_BRANCH: ${{ github.ref_name }}

jobs:
  contract-test:
    runs-on: ubuntu-latest
    steps:
      - uses: actions/checkout@v4
      - uses: actions/setup-node@v4
        with:
          node-version: 18
      - name: Install dependencies
        run: npm i
      - name: Run web consumer contract tests
        run: npm run test:web:consumer
      - name: Run graphql consumer contract tests
        run: npm run test:graphql:consumer
      - name: Publish contract to Pactflow
        run: npm run publish:pact
      - name: Run provider contract tests
        run: npm run test:provider
      - name: Run graphql provider contract tests
        run: npm run test:graphql:provider
      - name: Can I deploy provider?
        run: npm run can:i:deploy:provider
      - name: Can I deploy GraphQL provider?
        run: npm run can:i:deploy:graphql:provider
      - name: Record provider deployment
        run: npm run record:provider:deployment
      - name: Record GraphQL provider deployment
        run: npm run record:graphql:provider:deployment
      - name: Can I deploy web consumer?
        run: npm run can:i:deploy:consumer
      - name: Can I deploy GraphQL consumer?
        run: npm run can:i:deploy:graphql:consumer
      - name: Record web consumer deployment
        run: npm run record:web:consumer:deployment
      - name: Record GraphQL consumer deployment
        run: npm run record:graphql:consumer:deployment
```

The code marked as bold is the additional code you must add to the graphql/provider/graphql-server-contract.spec.js file:

```
const { Verifier } = require('@pact-foundation/pact');

const options = {
  provider: 'GraphQLProvider',
```

```
  providerBaseUrl: `http://localhost:4000/graphql`,
  pactBrokerUrl: process.env.PACT_BROKER_BASE_URL,
  pactBrokerToken: process.env.PACT_BROKER_TOKEN,
  providerVersion: process.env.GITHUB_SHA,
  publishVerificationResult: true,
  providerVersionBranch: process.env.GITHUB_BRANCH,
  consumerVersionSelectors: [
    { mainBranch: true },
    { matchingBranch: true },
    { deployedOrReleased: true }
  ],
};

const verifier = new Verifier(options);

describe('Pact Verification', () => {
  test('should validate the expectations of GraphQLConsumer', () => {
    return verifier
      .verifyProvider()
      .then(output => {
        console.log('Pact Verification Complete!');
        console.log('Result:', output);
      });
  });
});
```

The code marked as bold is the additional code you must add to the package.json file:

```
...

"scripts": {
    "test:web:consumer": "jest consumer-web/consumer-contract.spec.js",
    "can:i:deploy:consumer": "pact-broker can-i-deploy -pacticipant
    WebConsumer --version=$GITHUB_SHA --to-environment production",
    "record:web:consumer:deployment": "pact-broker record-deployment
    --pacticipant WebConsumer --version $GITHUB_SHA
    --environment production",
    "publish:pact": "pact-broker publish ./pacts
    --consumer-app-version=$GITHUB_SHA --branch=$GITHUB_BRANCH
    --broker-base-url=$PACT_BROKER_BASE_URL
    --broker-token=$PACT_BROKER_TOKEN",
    "start:provider": "cross-env PORT=3001 node
    provider/provider-service.js",
    "test:provider": "jest provider/provider-contract.spec.js
    --testTimeout=20000 --forceExit",
    "can:i:deploy:provider": "pact-broker can-i-deploy
    --pacticipant MoviesAPI --version=$GITHUB_SHA
    --to-environment production",
    "record:provider:deployment": "pact-broker record-deployment
    --pacticipant MoviesAPI --version $GITHUB_SHA
    --environment production",
    "start:graphql:server": "npm run start:provider
    & node graphql/provider/graphql-server.js",
    "test:graphql:consumer": "jest
    graphql/consumer/graphql-client-contract.spec.js",
```

```
    "can:i:deploy:graphql:consumer": "pact-broker can-i-deploy
    --pacticipant GraphQLConsumer --version=$GITHUB_SHA
    --to-environment production",
    "record:graphql:consumer:deployment": "pact-broker
    record-deployment --pacticipant GraphQLConsumer --version $GITHUB_SHA
    --environment production",
    "test:graphql:provider": "npm run start:graphql:server
    & jest graphql/provider/graphql-server-contract.spec.js
    --testTimeout=20000",
    "can:i:deploy:graphql:provider": "pact-broker can-i-deploy
    --pacticipant GraphQLProvider --version=$GITHUB_SHA
    --to-environment production",
    "record:graphql:provider:deployment": "pact-broker record-deployment
    --pacticipant GraphQLProvider --version $GITHUB_SHA
    --environment production",
    "start:kafka": "docker compose -f ./events/kafka-cluster.yml up -d",
    "produce:kafka:message": "node events/event-producer/index.js",
    "consume:kafka:message": "node events/consumer-event/server.js",
    "test:event:consumer": "jest
    ./events/consumer-event/src/movies/movie.handler.pact.test.js",
    "test:event:producer": "jest --testTimeout 30000
    ./events/event-producer/src/movie.event.pact.test.js"
  },

...
```

index

F

G

H

I

J

K

M

Y